INTERPRETING
THE HISTORICAL
BOOKS

HANDBOOKS FOR OLD TESTAMENT EXEGESIS
David M. Howard Jr., series editor

INTERPRETING THE HISTORICAL BOOKS

An Exegetical Handbook

Robert B. Chisholm Jr.

David M. Howard Jr.
SERIES EDITOR

Kregel
Academic

Interpreting the Historical Books: An Exegetical Handbook

© 2006 by Robert B. Chisholm Jr.

Published by Kregel Academic, an imprint of Kregel Publications, 2450 Oak Industrial Dr. NE, Grand Rapids, MI 49505.

Library of Congress Cataloging-in-Publication Data
Chisholm, Robert B.
   Interpreting the historical books: an exegetical
handbook / by Robert B. Chisholm Jr.
       p. cm. (Handbooks for Old Testament exegesis; 2)
       Includes bibliographical references.
       1. Bible—O.T. Historical Books—Criticism, interpretation, etc. I. Title.
BS1205.52.C45   2006
222'.06—dc22   2006028902

ISBN 978-0-8254-2764-0

Printed in the United States of America

6 7 8 9 10 / 25 24 23 22 21 20 19 18

To my brother,
Douglas Chisholm,
with whom I have had many spirited
and stimulating discussions
about biblical and
theological issues.

NORTHERN KINGDOM—ISRAEL

Samaria falls under attack from Shalmaneser V and Sargon II (722/721)

Jeroboam II revives Israel

Jehu falls to Assyrian rule under Shalmaneser III (841)

Jehu wipes out Ahab's line and part of Judah's line (841)

Israel vs. Assyria at Qarqar under Shalmaneser III (853)

Samaria made capital of Israel (880)

Kingdom Splits (931)

Jeroboam II (793–753)

Jehu (841–814)

Ahab (874–853)

Omri (885–874)

Solomon Reigns (971–931)

David Reigns (1011–971)

Saul Reigns (1051–1011)

SOUTHERN KINGDOM—JUDAH

Uzziah (792–740)

Uzziah reestablishes Judah

ELIJAH

ELISHA

ISAIAH
MICAH
HOSEA

JONAH
AMOS

SECOND HALF OF 8TH CENTURY B.C.

FIRST HALF OF 8TH CENTURY B.C.

9TH CENTURY B.C.

10TH CENTURY B.C.

11TH CENTURY B.C.

JUDGES

KINGSHIP ESTABLISHED

(2166 B.C.– 1806 B.C.)

Patriarchs
- Abraham
- Isaac
- Jacob
- Joseph

Jacob goes to Egypt (1876)

Exodus (1446)

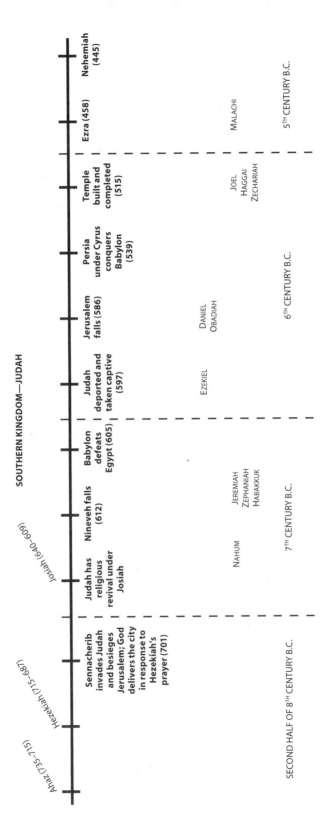

SOUTHERN KINGDOM—JUDAH

Ahaz (735–715)

Hezekiah (715–687)

Josiah (640–609)

Sennacherib invades Judah and besieges Jerusalem; God delivers the city in response to Hezekiah's prayer (701)

Judah has religious revival under Josiah

Nineveh falls (612)

Babylon defeats Egypt (605)

Judah deported and taken captive (597)

Jerusalem falls (586)

Persia under Cyrus conquers Babylon (539)

Temple built and completed (515)

Ezra (458)

Nehemiah (445)

NAHUM

JEREMIAH
ZEPHANIAH
HABAKKUK

EZEKIEL

DANIEL
OBADIAH

JOEL
HAGGAI
ZECHARIAH

MALACHI

SECOND HALF OF 8TH CENTURY B.C.

7TH CENTURY B.C.

6TH CENTURY B.C.

5TH CENTURY B.C.

Chart creator and designer: Rev. Errol G. Coner; revised by Robert B. Chisholm Jr.

CONTENTS IN BRIEF

CONTENTS

SERIES PREFACE

AN APPRECIATION FOR THE RICH diversity of literary genres in Scripture is one of the positive features of evangelical scholarship in recent decades. No longer are the same principles or methods of interpretation applied across the board to every text without regard for differences in genre. Such an approach can, however, lead to confusion, misunderstanding, and even wrong interpretations or applications. Careful attention to differences in genre is, then, a critical component of a correct understanding of God's Word.

The Handbooks for Old Testament Exegesis series (HOTE) offers students basic skills for exegeting and proclaiming the different genres of the Old Testament. Because there is no one-size-fits-all approach to interpreting Scripture, this series features six volumes covering the major genres in the Old Testament: narrative, law, poetry, wisdom, prophecy, and apocalyptic. The volumes are written by seasoned scholar-teachers who possess extensive knowledge of their disciplines, lucid writing abilities, and the conviction that the church and the world today desperately need to hear the message of the Old Testament. These handbooks are designed to serve a twofold purpose: to present the reader with a better understanding (principles) of the different Old Testament genres, and provide strategies (methods) for preaching and teaching these genres.

These volumes are primarily intended to serve as textbooks for graduate-level exegesis courses that assume a basic knowledge of Hebrew. There is no substitute for encountering God's Word in its original languages, even as we acknowledge the limitations of language in plumbing the depths of who God is. However, the series is also accessible to those without a working knowledge of Hebrew, in that an English translation is always given whenever Hebrew is used. Thus, seminary-trained pastors for whom Hebrew is a distant memory, upper-level college students, and even well-motivated laypeople should all find this series useful.

Each volume is built around the same six-chapter structure as follows:

1. The Nature of the Genres
2. Viewing the Whole
3. Preparing for Interpretation
4. Interpreting the Text
5. Proclaiming the Text
6. Putting It All Together

Authors are given freedom in how they title these six chapters and in how best to approach the material in each. But the familiar pattern in every volume will serve students well, allowing them to move easily from one volume to another to locate specific information. The first chapter in each handbook introduces the genre(s) covered in the volume. The second chapter covers the purpose, message, and primary themes in the individual books and canonical sections under consideration. The third chapter includes such diverse matters as historical and cultural backgrounds, critical questions, textual matters, and a brief annotated bibliography of helpful works. The fourth chapter sets forth guidelines for interpreting texts of the genre(s) under consideration. The fifth chapter details strategies for proclaiming such texts. The final chapter gives one or two hands-on examples of how to move through different stages of the interpretive process, in order to demonstrate how the principles discussed previously work out in practice. Each volume also includes a glossary of specialized terms.

The Scriptures themselves remind us in many ways about the importance of proper interpretation of God's words. Paul encouraged Timothy to "do your best to present yourself to God as one approved by him, a worker who has no need to be ashamed, rightly explaining the word of truth" (2 Tim. 2:15 NRSV). In an earlier day, Ezra the scribe, along with the Levites, taught God's Word to the postexilic community: "So they read from the book, from the law of God, with interpretation. They gave the sense, so that the people understood the reading" (Neh. 8:8 NRSV). It is my prayer, and that of the authors and publisher, that these handbooks will help a new generation of God's people to do the same.

Soli Deo Gloria.

—DAVID M. HOWARD JR.
Series Editor

PREFACE

When people hear the word "history," they usually think of dates, names, places, and events. History writing is not usually a popular genre of literature, for people typically think of it as a dry record of bare facts about what happened in the past. For this reason some might shy away from reading the historical books of the Old Testament. However, a closer look at the literature reveals that it contains many exciting and fascinating stories, and most people, especially in our contemporary postmodern context, love a good story. Because of this literary dimension, the historical books read more like a historical novel complete with plot structure and character development. God himself even appears as a character in the unfolding drama. When one considers that these stories are true, they take on special relevance. In fact, of all the stories that have been written in human history, the biblical stories are the most relevant, for they alone are inspired Scripture. To be sure, some of those seemingly dry facts that we normally associate with history—lists, genealogies, and dates—are present, but even these details take on significance when we see them as contributing to the larger story in which they are embedded. These larger stories are sometimes called narratives. To get the most out of reading the Old Testament historical books, one needs to know something about how the narrative genre "works." To that end, chapter 1 seeks to answer the question, "What Is Narrative Literature?" The chapter concludes with a list of interpretive principles that one should keep in mind as one reads narrative literature, whether it be in the historical books or elsewhere in the Old Testament.

The historical books of the Old Testament include Joshua, Judges, Ruth, 1–2 Samuel, 1–2 Kings, 1–2 Chronicles, Ezra, Nehemiah, and Esther. Following the arrangement of the ancient Greek version of the Old Testament (the Septuagint), these twelve books are grouped together in the English Bible and follow a rough chronological sequence. They tell the story of Israel from the conquest of Canaan in Joshua's day to the return from the Exile centuries later, though there is some overlap between Samuel, Kings, and Chronicles. The Hebrew Bible, which consists of the Law, Prophets, and Writings, arranges the books differently. Joshua, Judges, 1–2 Samuel, and 1–2 Kings appear in the Prophets. Collectively they are known as the Former Prophets.[1] The remaining six historical books appear in the Writings. Within this third section of the Hebrew canon, Ruth and Esther are two of the five Megilloth, or Scrolls (the others are Song of Songs, Ecclesiastes, and Lamentations), while Ezra–Nehemiah and 1–2 Chronicles are at the tail end of the Hebrew Bible.[2]

Technical words are defined in the glossary at the back of the book and are identified in the text by boldface print as they appear in new sections.

---

1. Within the second part of the Hebrew Bible, the Latter Prophets include Isaiah, Jeremiah, Ezekiel, and the Twelve (i.e., the so-called Minor Prophets).
2. For a concise discussion of the canonization of the Old Testament see Paul D. Wegner, *The Journey from Texts to Translations: The Origin and Development of the Bible* (Grand Rapids: Baker, 1999), 101–18. For a more thorough analysis of the subject, consult Roger Beckwith, *The Old Testament Canon of the New Testament Church and Its Background in Early Judaism* (Grand Rapids: Eerdmans, 1985).

ABBREVIATIONS

AB   Anchor Bible

ANEP   Pritchard, James, ed. *The Ancient Near East in Pictures Relating to the Old Testament.* Princeton, 1954.

ANET   Pritchard, James, ed. *Ancient Near Eastern Texts Relating to the Old Testament.* 3d ed. Princeton, 1969.

AUSS   *Andrews University Seminary Studies*

BDB   Brown, F., S. R. Driver, and C. A. Briggs. *A Hebrew and English Lexicon of the Old Testament.* Oxford, 1907.

BHS   *Biblia Hebraica Stuttgartensia*

BSac   *Bibliotheca sacra*

CBQ   *Catholic Biblical Quarterly*

COS   Hallo, W. W., ed. *The Context of Scripture.* Leiden, 2003.

DSS   Dead Sea Scrolls

HALOT   Koehler, L., W. Baumgartner, and J. J. Stamm. *The Hebrew and Aramaic Lexicon of the Old Testament.* Translated and edited under the supervision of M. E. J. Richardson. Study Edition. 2 vols. Leiden, 2001. (The publisher has also made available an electronic version, as well as a more expensive five-volume print edition, which is identical in content to the Study Edition but has larger print.)

IBHS	Waltke, Bruce K., and M. O'Connor. *An Introduction to Biblical Hebrew Syntax.* Winona Lake, Indiana: Eisenbrauns, 1990.
JANESCU	*Journal of the Ancient Near Eastern Society of Columbia University*
JAOS	*Journal of the American Oriental Society*
JBL	*Journal of Biblical Literature*
JNSL	*Journal of Northwest Semitic Languages*
JSOTSup	Journal for the Study of the Old Testament: Supplement Series
LXX	Septuagint
NAC	New American Commentary
NET	New English Translation
NICOT	New International Commentary on the Old Testament
NIV	New International Version
NIVAC	NIV Application Commentary
OTL	Old Testament Library
PRU	*Le palais royal d'Ugarit*
SBLDS	Society of Biblical Literature Dissertation Series
SJOT	*Scandinavian Journal of the Old Testament*
VT	*Vetus Testamentum*
WBC	Word Biblical Commentary
WTJ	*Westminster Theological Journal*

1

WHAT IS NARRATIVE LITERATURE?

THE HISTORICAL BOOKS ARE OFTEN classified as narrative literature because they give an account of Israel's history in story-like fashion. Old Testament narrative, as it appears in the historical books, encompasses several literary types, including stories, reports, genealogies, and lists. Stories have a **plot structure** and usually exhibit character development. They vary in length. The story of Ehud, for example, covers a mere nineteen verses (Judg. 3:12–30), while the story of David occupies half of 1 Samuel and all of 2 Samuel. A report lacks plot structure and character development; it typically provides a brief summary of an event or a king's reign. Reports are interspersed throughout 2 Kings (e.g., 2 Kings 15). Genealogies consist of tribal and subtribal family trees (e.g., 1 Chron. 1–9). Various types of lists appear, including, among others, defeated kings (Josh. 12:7–24), boundaries and cities (interspersed throughout Josh. 13–21), warriors (2 Sam. 23:8–39), and returning exiles (Ezra 2). Other literary genres are embedded within narrative literature, including victory songs (e.g., Judg. 5) and prayers (e.g., 1 Sam. 2:1–10). The interpreter's task is to explain the story line of the literature and to show how the variety of material contributes to the whole.

THE LITERARY DIMENSION IN NARRATIVE

Evangelicals affirm that Old Testament narratives, including the stories, are historically accurate, yet they also recognize that narratives, especially the stories, have a literary dimension. Old Testament narratives do not simply inform the reader what happened. The literature has an aesthetic, literary dimension that contributes to its overall theological purpose. In other words, Old Testament narratives tell Israel's story in an engaging, dramatic fashion that highlights God's relationship with his people. By the time the story is finished, it has painted a picture of God that contributes to the Bible's overall divine portrait. The story's literary dimension is often the means whereby the raw facts of history are given a theological dimension.

Basic Elements of a Story

The stories of the Old Testament, like all stories, have three basic elements: setting (where and when the story takes place), characterization (how the participants in the story are presented and developed), and plot (how the story line unfolds and engages our minds and hearts).[1]

Setting

Setting has physical, temporal, and cultural dimensions.[2] A story's physical setting can be geographical and/or topographical. For example, Samson's confrontation with the lion takes place near the vineyards of Timnah (Judg. 14:5), while Elijah's confrontation with Ahaziah's military captains occurs at an unidentified hill (2 Kings 1:9). Usually references to physical setting simply help the audience visualize the scene; the elements of the physical setting are the props on the stage, as it were. But physical setting can occasionally have a more significant function. As a Nazirite, Samson is prohibited from drinking the fruit of the vine (Num. 6:4; cf. Judg. 13:4). When Samson approaches the vineyards of Timnah, the story takes on an ominous mood and we realize that threats

---

1. See Leland Ryken, *How to Read the Bible as Literature* (Grand Rapids: Zondervan, 1984), 35.
2. Ibid.

to Samson's Nazirite status are present in his environment. The same is true later in the story when Samson falls in love with a woman who lives in the Valley of Sorek (literally, "grape valley").[3] Her home territory has an ominous name and she proves to be Samson's downfall by successfully tempting him to compromise his Nazirite status in exchange for her charms. In 2 Kings 1 Elijah is sitting on a hill when the captains approach him and demand that he come down. The attitude of the first two captains shows that they regard the prophet as subject to the king's orders, but Elijah, as the Lord's prophet, actually has authority over the king and his messengers, as symbolized by his physical position above them.

The temporal setting of a story can be significant. For example, the book of Ruth opens with the words, "During the time of the judges." This simple temporal clause informs the reader when the story occurred, but it takes on greater significance as the story unfolds. The time of the judges was a period of moral chaos when people followed their own moral code, not God's (Judg. 17:6; 21:25). But the story of Ruth shines brightly against this dark background as it depicts characters that demonstrate the virtues of compassion and loyal love, qualities that were for the most part absent in the period of the judges.

An awareness of a story's cultural background is especially important to interpretation. For example, one cannot appreciate fully the significance of Elijah's actions in 1 Kings 17 without some understanding of West Semitic mythology. Elijah's journey to Phoenicia takes place during the reign of Ahab, who married a Phoenician wife and made Baal worship a state religion in Israel (1 Kings 16:30–34). Baal was the Canaanite storm god, responsible for making the crops grow. How appropriate and ironic that the Lord brings a drought upon the land as a punishment for Ahab's apostasy (1 Kings 17:1)!

According to West Semitic myth, the arrival of a drought signaled that Baal had been defeated, at least temporarily, by his archenemy Mot, the god of death and the underworld. During times of drought, Baal was a captive of Mot and unable to carry out his responsibilities as king, which included caring for the needy and ensuring fertility.

Against this background Elijah's actions in 1 Kings 17 take on great significance. Through Ahab, the god Baal, as it were, invades Israelite

---

3. See *HALOT,* 1362; and Stanislav Segert, "Paronomasia in the Samson Narrative in Judges xiii–xvi," *VT* 34 (1984): 458.

territory. But now, while Baal is incapacitated and unable to reward his worshipers for their loyalty, the Lord's prophet invades Baal's home turf. Through his prophet Elijah, the Lord cares for a needy widow by miraculously supplying the staples of life (flour and oil). While Baal languishes in the underworld as death's prisoner, the Lord demonstrates his power over death by resuscitating the widow's son. The events recorded in 1 Kings 17 set the stage for the conflict between Elijah and Baal's prophets at Carmel (1 Kings 18). Baal's prophets cut and slash themselves in an effort to resurrect their god from the underworld. West Semitic myth indicates that this self-mutilation was a mourning rite designed to facilitate Baal's return. But the Lord reveals that he is sovereign over the elements of the storm as he consumes the sacrifice with lightning and then sends a torrential downpour.

An awareness of West Semitic myth also helps one better understand the significance of Gideon's tests with the fleece (Judg. 6:36–40). At the Lord's command, Gideon destroys his father's Baal altar. When the townspeople threaten to kill Gideon, his father challenges Baal to defend his own honor. He gives Gideon a new name, Jerubbaal, meaning or at least suggesting by **soundplay**, "Let Baal fight." Gideon's choice of signs is not arbitrary or random. The tests are designed to demonstrate the Lord's control of the dew. According to West Semitic myth, Baal controlled the rain and the dew. In one legend Baal's weakness results in the disappearance of rain and dew.[4] One of Baal's daughters is even named "Dew" ("Tallaya").[5] Gideon had destroyed Baal's altar, depriving him of sacrifices. His new name, Jerubbaal, made him a target for one of Baal's lightning bolts. By seeing a demonstration of God's sovereignty over the dew, an area supposedly under the control of Baal, Gideon can be assured that he is insulated from Baal's vengeance.[6]

Characterization

Characters are one of the necessary ingredients of any story. Without them, all we have is an empty stage or a still life devoid of plot. Since

---

4. For the text see J. C. L. Gibson, *Canaanite Myths and Legends,* 2d ed. (Edinburgh: T & T Clark, 1978), 115.

5. See ibid., 46, 48.

6. See Fred E. Woods, *Water and Storm Polemics Against Baalism in the Deuteronomic History* (New York: Peter Lang, 1994), 68–69.

characters play such an essential role, it is vital to analyze how an author depicts them and how characters function. One must seek to answer the following questions: How does the author present the character? How, if at all, does the character develop in the course of the story? In what way(s), if any, is the character an example to follow or avoid? What does the character's experience teach us about how God relates to people?

One must pay special attention to how a narrator evaluates each character, including any comments about a character's inner thoughts or motivation. For example, the various characters in Judges 17–21 can be evaluated in a negative manner in light of the summary statement that appears near the beginning and at the end of the section (cf. 17:6; 21:25). The main participants in the stories illustrate the observation that "each man did what he considered to be right," regardless of what God's law demanded. We are even given insight into Micah's greedy motive for hiring the wandering Levite (Judg. 17:13).

Unfortunately, narrators usually offer few, if any, direct **evaluative** comments of this type. They prefer simply to describe a character's appearance and actions, leaving it to the reader to form an evaluation based on the overall presentation of the character throughout the story. This makes the interpretive task challenging and somewhat subjective. For example, the first half of the story of David seeks to convince the reader that David is indeed God's chosen king, in contrast to Saul, whom the Lord rejected. Generally speaking, the narrator presents David in a positive light, at least in comparison to Saul, but this does not mean that everything David does must be given a positive spin. David's story ends up a tragedy in many respects as his family and kingdom disintegrate around him. As the story unfolds, several disturbing facts foreshadow David's moral fall. For example, despite his successes, which were the result of God's protective presence and blessing (2 Sam. 5:10, 12), David has a harem, in violation of the Deuteronomic law (Deut. 17:17; 2 Sam. 3:2–5; 5:13–16). While these wives, who seem to be "local girls," do not turn his heart to other gods (the primary concern of Deut. 17:17), his expanding harem does suggest that David has a fascination with the royal trappings of his society. His action sets a bad precedent that eventually causes conflict within his royal court and leads to Solomon's blatant disobedience of God's law (cf. 1 Kings 11). David also fails to discipline his sons Amnon (2 Sam. 13:21 [LXX,

DSS; cf. NRSV, ESV text notes]) and Adonijah (1 Kings 1:6). He proves to be a very human, complicated character. He displays great faith, but also the worst of human flaws.

There are various ways one may evaluate characters. They may be categorized by their role in the story. Major characters are those upon whom the narrator focuses his attention, while minor characters usually fulfill a single function. A story can have more than one major character, but there is usually only one central character, or **protagonist**. Central characters can be presented positively or negatively. Some are heroes (e.g., Ehud); others are failures (e.g., Saul). Many are a very human-looking mixture that falls between these two poles (e.g., David). Since Israel's story is, for the most part, one of human failure, characters often have a tragic dimension (e.g., Jephthah, Samson, Saul, David).

Characters may also be categorized according to the extent of their development. They can be round or flat. Round characters look very human and display a wide range of emotions and character traits. Their weaknesses and failures, as well as their strengths and successes, are recorded (e.g., Abraham, Jacob, Gideon, Samson, Samuel, Saul, David, Elijah). Flat characters are one-dimensional, usually displaying only a limited number of character traits (e.g., Ehud, Abimelech the son of Gideon, Boaz).

When evaluating characters, one should consider both of these categories. To visualize this we can make extent of character development a vertical axis with "round" at the top pole and "flat" at the bottom. We can then make character role an intersecting horizontal axis with "major" at the left end and "minor" at the right end.

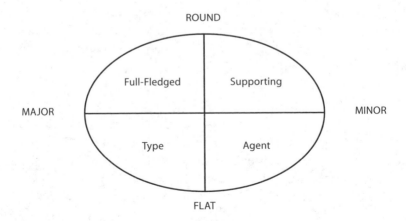

Characters who appear in the upper left quadrant created by the intersecting axes are major and round. Such characters may be labeled full-fledged. Most of the major characters in the longer stories of the Bible are full-fledged (e.g., Saul and David).

Characters in the upper right quadrant are round, but minor. We may call them supporting actors or actresses. There are relatively few characters of this type in the Old Testament. Jonathan is a prime example (1 Sam. 13–14; 18–20; 23; 31). His character is developed to some degree, though not to the extent of Saul or David. As a minor character, he serves primarily as a **foil** to Saul. Where Saul falters, Jonathan demonstrates faith and courage. Whereas Saul falsely accuses David and seeks to kill him, Jonathan recognizes David as God's chosen king and swears allegiance to him. He is also a tragic example of how Saul's failure negatively impacts so many of those who are close to him.

Characters in the lower left quadrant are major, but flat. We may label them types. Types usually provide an example of one character trait that is to be emulated or shunned. For example, Ehud is a type of the courageous leader whose faith becomes a channel through which God delivers his people from oppression (Judg. 3:12–30). Apart from Ehud's faith, which is revealed in bold and decisive action in a single episode of his life, we know almost nothing else about the man.

Finally characters in the lower right quadrant are minor and flat; they usually function as mere **agents** in the story. They have a limited role to fulfill and normally are not intended as models for behavior. Occasionally an agent serves as a foil for a major character. For example, Orpah is a foil for Ruth (Ruth 1:4–19). When Naomi urges the girls to return to Moab, Orpah does what one expects—she says good-bye and goes home. But Ruth's love for Naomi causes her to stay with her mother-in-law, even when such devotion seems illogical and downright foolish. Orpah is not a bad person; on the contrary she is a good daughter-in-law who had treated Naomi well. She deserves and receives Naomi's blessing (Ruth 1:8). But Ruth is beyond good—her love for Naomi transcends the norm. So the comparison between the two girls is not expressed in terms of bad versus good, but good versus great. The narrator's purpose in mentioning and describing Orpah is to highlight Ruth.

One of the striking features of biblical stories is that God often appears as a character. The interpreter is in an awkward position, for it may seem sacrilegious to view God as a character in a story and to analyze him like one would the hero of a novel. However, we must resist the urge to shy away from such analysis. After all, by entering into human history and inscripturating stories in which he plays a prominent role, God invites us to learn something about himself from these literary presentations of his self-revelation in space and time. In analyzing how God is characterized, we must remember that these stories reflect God's self-revelation in a form that is culturally **contextualized** and conditioned. When we open Scripture, we discover that the very first book contains stories, not a systematic theology. These stories are not so much concerned with making philosophical pronouncements about the divine character as they are with revealing a personal, dynamic God who longs to relate to his people and move them toward the goal he has for them.

If one looks only for **ontological** truth about God in biblical narrative, one is likely to become frustrated with the diversity that is evident in the characterization of God. But if one approaches the text as it is and seeks to discover what it says about how God relates to human beings, one will come away invigorated and encouraged by the portrait of an omnipotent, sovereign creator who enters into his world in an intimate, personal manner. In Genesis he pays Abraham a personal visit (Gen. 18) and even stoops to wrestle with one particularly recalcitrant character (Gen. 32:22–32)!

We also detect God working behind the scene, through and in spite of human actions and choices, as he providentially transforms the sinful, mean-spirited actions of a hate-filled band of brothers into the redemption of a family, in fulfillment of his promise to an obedient servant who once passed a difficult test of faith (Gen. 37–50; cf. Gen. 22).[7] In the end these elements complement one another—the poles of **transcendence** and **immanence**, as well as the intermediate dimension of **providence**, reflect God's relationship to his world.

Plot

The third basic element in a story is its plot, or sequence of events. At the heart of a plot is a conflict that involves the central character. Such

---

7. For a study of the characterization of God in Genesis see W. Lee Humphreys, *The Character of God in the Book of Genesis: A Narrative Appraisal* (Louisville: Westminster John Knox, 2001).

conflicts usually involve a test or challenge. The conflict can be external to the protagonist, pitting him against an **antagonist**. Examples would be David's battle with Goliath (1 Sam. 17), Saul's ongoing attempt to kill David (1 Sam. 18–27), or Elijah's confrontation with Baal's prophets and their sponsor, the evil queen Jezebel (1 Kings 18). Conflicts can also be internal to the protagonist, as in the story of Elijah (1 Kings 19). These external and internal dimensions can both be present in a story. For example, within the framework of Elijah's external conflict with Jezebel, a deeper, more profound conflict takes place within the prophet's soul. Despite his success on Mount Carmel, he wavers in the face of Jezebel's threat against his life and flees to distant Mount Sinai, all but abandoning his prophetic call. The Lord confronts him there, tries to encourage him, and gives him a renewed commission. The Lord commands him to anoint, in order, Hazael (as the new king of Syria), Jehu (as the new king of Israel), and Elisha (as his prophetic successor) (vv. 15–18). But Elijah loses the internal struggle. He goes directly to Elisha and anoints him (v. 19), as if to say to God, "I quit—let Elisha take over." Eventually Elisha, not Elijah, announces Hazael's rise to the throne of Syria (2 Kings 8:13) and anoints Jehu as king over Israel (2 Kings 9:6).

As an interpreter seeks to appreciate how a story's plot contributes to the significance of the story, it is helpful to have some categories with which to work. The final goal of exegesis is not to label a story's plot type or fit the story into a taxonomy of forms, but thinking about the plot type and structure of a story can help one get a handle on the story's dramatic features and its function within its larger narrative context.

Biblical stories display a variety of plot types. On one side of the spectrum we find tragedies, punitive stories, and negative example stories. In a tragedy the protagonist, who has the potential or at least the opportunity to succeed and achieve greatness, fails and falls, often because of a very human, but fatal flaw. Biblical examples abound—Samson, Saul, and David being some of the better-known tragic figures.

Punitive stories highlight the theme of God's justice. An evildoer violates God's moral standards and then reaps the consequences of his behavior, often by a combination of direct divine intervention and providential manipulation of events, as in the case of the murderous tyrant Abimelech and the Shechemites (Judg. 9). Abimelech murders his half-brothers and becomes ruler of Shechem. In response to Jotham's curse, the Lord sends a spirit to stir up hostility between Abimelech and the Shechemites. Through a series of reports delivered in a timely manner, Abimelech attacks and destroys Shechem, but is then killed by a woman armed with a millstone.

Negative example stories present a character in a negative light as an example to avoid. The story of Jephthah, while it has a tragic dimension, is best viewed as a negative example story (Judg. 10–12). Jephthah has a just cause and is energized for battle by God's Spirit, but his faith wavers and he bargains with God, promising a human sacrifice in exchange for a victory over the Ammonites. Having painted himself into a corner, he is forced to offer his daughter as a burnt offering to fulfill a vow that arose out of fear and reflected the influence of paganism upon his thinking. His weak faith and lack of foresight make him the antithesis of what Israel needs in a leader.

One can distinguish these plot types by the emotional response they produce in the reader. Tragedies bring tears of sorrow to our eyes, punitive stories bring a sense of satisfaction when the evildoer gets what he or she deserves, and negative example stories make us frown and shake our heads in disapproval at the disturbing behavior of the central character.

On the positive side of the spectrum, one finds comic plots, reward stories, and admiration stories. In a comic plot the protagonist faces challenges and obstacles but overcomes them through faith and divine intervention. For example, the book of Ruth is a comic plot type. The story's central character, Naomi, is reduced to poverty by the death of her husband and two sons. She returns home a bitter woman who feels that God is her enemy. But as the Lord providentially intervenes in her circumstances through the devotion of her daughter-in-law Ruth and the kindness of her relative Boaz, her attitude is transformed. In the story's final **scene** her friends, who heard her spew out her bitter resentment upon her arrival in Bethlehem, remind her that the Lord has blessed her with a grandchild who will protect her in her old age.

Reward stories, like punitive stories, illustrate God's justice. But in reward stories God rewards a character for being faithful and obedient. The story of the Shunammite woman (2 Kings 4:8–17) is a good example. She makes it a practice to provide for Elisha's comfort when he passes through Shunem. As a reward for her kindness, Elisha, apparently in his capacity as a prophet, announces she will finally have a son.

Admiration stories, in contrast to negative example stories, present a character in a positive light as an example to follow. The story of Esther illustrates this plot type. Esther finds herself in a strategic, though precarious, position in the king's harem. When Mordecai challenges her to step forward and intercede on behalf of her people, she answers the call and risks her life to save her people.

These positive plot types can also be distinguished by the emotional response they produce in the reader. Comic plots bring tears of joy to our eyes, reward stories prompt a hearty cheer when the faithful character gets what he or she deserves, and admiration stories make us smile and nod our heads in approval at the commendable behavior of the central character.

Plot types are often combined in a single story. While one plot type may be dominant or primary, other elements are sometimes present. For example, 1 Samuel 25 is essentially an admiration story. David is tempted to seek vengeance against Nabal, a fool who shows no respect for the future king of Israel. But David listens to the voice of wisdom embodied in Abigail, refrains from violence, and allows the Lord to punish Nabal. At the same time, the antagonist Nabal is a negative example of one who opposes God's chosen king; his death also gives the story a punitive element. The story of Esther is an admiration story, but it also has elements of a punitive plot type in that the antagonist, Haman, is justly punished for his sin and ends up hanging from the gallows he erected for Mordecai. When one focuses on Naomi, the central character in the book of Ruth, the story is a comic plot, but in Ruth's shining example one also detects the elements of both reward and admiration stories.

Plot structure can vary, depending on the story's length, complexity, and plot type(s). The structure of negative example and admiration stories can be quite simple. Following some reference to the story's setting, the protagonist typically faces a challenge or test that he or she fails (e.g., the story of Cain in Gen. 4:1–16) or passes (e.g., the story of Abraham's offering of his son Isaac in Gen. 22:1–19). Elements of the punitive or reward stories sometimes appear as the story concludes.

Tragic and comic plots are usually more complex. Once the setting has been established a conflict arises, creating a complication in the plot that begs to be resolved. As the story unfolds, this tension is eventually resolved one way or the other, but usually not without plot twists and additional tension. For example, the reward story in 2 Kings 4:8–17 is immediately followed by a comic plot in which the Shunammite woman faces a terrible challenge to her faith. While working in the field (v. 18 = setting), her son suddenly complains of a severe headache (v. 19 = complication). The tension mounts as the boy dies on his mother's lap (v. 20). This unexpected twist in the overall plot of the chapter threatens to undermine the preceding reward story. The tension continues as the woman lays her son on the prophet's bed and travels to Mount Carmel (vv. 21–26). One gets the impression she is quite stoical about what has happened, but one suspects that this cannot possibly be the case. Her true feelings explode from within her when she meets Elisha and suggests that he may have played a cruel trick on her (vv. 27–28). Yet one detects her faith in her posture (v. 27, she grabs hold of Elisha's feet) and her words (v. 30, she insists on staying with Elisha). The tension is relieved to some degree when Elisha instructs Gehazi to run ahead and try to revive the boy (vv. 29–30), but it reaches an unbearable level when he returns and reports that the child did not respond (v. 31). The plot reaches its peak in verse 34 as the prophet stretches out on the boy and the boy's skin grows warm. As the boy begins breathing again, the reader breathes a sigh of relief, for the plot's complication has been resolved and its tension diffused. As the woman takes the boy in her arms, the reader is convinced of the integrity of the Lord's prophet and of the One who sent him.

Structural Features

Discourse Structure

In addition to **plot structure**, Old Testament stories also exhibit **discourse structure**.[8] Examining and outlining the discourse structure helps one see the basic contours of the story at the surface level

---

8. For studies of Hebrew narratival structure see Roy L. Heller, *Narrative Structure and Discourse Constellations: An Analysis of Clause Function in Biblical Hebrew,* Harvard Semitic Studies 55 (Winona Lake, IN: Eisenbrauns, 2004); Robert D. Bergen, ed., *Biblical Hebrew and Discourse Linguistics* (Winona Lake, IN: Eisenbrauns, 1994); and David Allan Dawson, *Text-Linguistics and Biblical Hebrew,* JSOTSup 177 (Sheffield: Sheffield Academic, 1994).

and contributes to analysis of **dramatic structure** and other literary features (see below). A story's discourse structure is comprised of three main elements: the main line of the narrative, offline constructions, and quotations.

The main line is essentially the story line—the sequence of actions that forms the backbone of the story. Stories can begin in a variety of ways, but the story line proper is typically initiated and then carried along by clauses introduced by *wayyiqtol* (or past tense) verbal forms (often called *waw* consecutive with the imperfect). Most *wayyiqtol* clauses are sequential or consequential, but they can also have a variety of less common functions.[9] The following list, though not exhaustive, identifies the primary functions of *wayyiqtol* clauses:

1. Initiatory: The *wayyiqtol* clause sets the story proper in motion.
2. Sequential: The clause describes an action that follows the preceding action.
3. Consequential: The clause describes an action that follows the preceding action both logically and temporally.
4. Introductory: Often a *wayyiqtol* clause (especially one consisting of וַיְהִי, lit. "and it was," and a temporal word or phrase) introduces an **episode** or **scene** by providing background for the story to follow.
5. Flashback: Sometimes the narrator interrupts the sequence of events and uses a *wayyiqtol* clause to refer to a prior action that now becomes relevant. The flashback can initiate an episode or scene, refer back to an action that preceded the episode or scene chronologically, or, more often than not, recall an event that occurred within the time frame of the story being related.
6. Focusing: A *wayyiqtol* clause often has a focusing or specifying function. It can focus on a particular individual involved in the event just described, give a more detailed account of the event or

---

9. For more detailed analysis of the use of *wayyiqtol* forms in narrative discourse with illustrations of proposed categories, see Robert B. Chisholm Jr., *From Exegesis to Exposition: A Practical Guide to Using Biblical Hebrew* (Grand Rapids: Baker, 1998), 119–23; Bill T. Arnold and John H. Choi, *A Guide to Biblical Hebrew Syntax* (New York: Cambridge University Press, 2003), 84–87; Christo H. J. van der Merwe, Jackie A. Naudé, and Jan H. Kroeze, *A Biblical Hebrew Reference Grammar* (Sheffield: Sheffield Academic, 1999), 165–68; and Bruce K. Waltke and M. O'Connor, *An Introduction to Biblical Hebrew Syntax* (Winona Lake, IN: Eisenbrauns, 1990), 547–54.

an aspect of the event, or provide a specific example of a preceding statement.

7. Resumptive: A *wayyiqtol* clause can serve a resumptive function. When used in this manner it follows a supplementary, focusing, or flashback statement; such examples can be labeled resumptive-(con)sequential. On a few occasions the resumptive *wayyiqtol* repeats a statement made prior to the embedded comment or scene that interrupted the narrative; these clauses can be labeled resumptive-reiterative.

8. Complementary: A *wayyiqtol* clause sometimes complements the preceding statement by giving the other side of the same coin or by describing an action that naturally or typically accompanies what precedes.

9. Summarizing or concluding: A *wayyiqtol* clause occasionally makes a summarizing statement, often in relation to the preceding narrative, and/or can be used to conclude a narrative or scene, sometimes with a formulaic comment.

Offline clauses deviate from the *wayyiqtol* pattern. Most often the conjunction is immediately followed by a non-verb, usually the subject of the clause (sometimes called a disjunctive clause). The predicate then follows, whether stated (typically a perfect verbal form or a participle) or implied (in equative sentences where a subject is connected to its predicate by an implied "to be" verb; e.g., וְהָאִשָּׁה טוֹבַת מַרְאֶה מְאֹד, "the woman [was] very beautiful," 2 Sam. 11:2). Offline constructions often are descriptive and do not further the action of the story. In such cases they tend to provide background or supplemental information. Sometimes, however, they do contribute to the story line by describing a contrastive or oppositional action. In other cases they shift the dramatic focus from one character or participant to another. The following list, though not exhaustive, identifies the primary functions of offline clauses:

1. Introductory or backgrounding: Offline clauses sometimes formally mark the beginning of a new scene or episode; in this case they typically provide background information for the story that follows.

2. Supplemental: Offline clauses very frequently give supplemental (or parenthetical) information that is embedded within a story.
3. Circumstantial: Offline clauses sometimes describe the circumstances attending to an action, such as time or manner.
4. Contrastive: Sometimes an offline clause describes an action that contrasts with what precedes or qualifies it in some way.
5. Dramatic: An offline clause, especially when introduced by וְהִנֵּה, "and look!" can have a dramatic function, inviting the audience to enter into the story as a participant or eyewitness. This device can also signal a shift in focus from one character or participant to another, sometimes involving a flashback.
6. Concluding: Offline clauses can be used to signal **closure** formally for an episode or scene.

Quotations (including dialogues), the third main element in a story's discourse structure, are very common in Old Testament narrative. Quoted speech displays various **discourse types** and functions (see discussion below). The syntactical structure of quotations can vary, depending on the discourse type.

Since a picture is often better than a thousand words, we offer a sample outline of the discourse structure of a passage (Judg. 4). *Wayyiqtol* clauses that form the main line of the story are translated in regular font, while offline constructions are in bold. Quotations are italicized. Our proposed classification of each *wayyiqtol* and offline clause appears in the third column of the chart. Comments on the discourse structure are included after each paragraph. The translation is a slight adaptation of the author's translation prepared for the NET Bible.

Judges 4 has three main literary units—a prologue (vv. 1–3), the story proper (vv. 4–22), and an epilogue (vv. 23–24).

1–3	Prologue	Type of Clause
1a	The Israelites again did evil in the LORD's sight	initiatory and sequential
1b	**after Ehud's death.**	circumstantial
2a	The LORD turned them over to King Jabin of Canaan, who ruled in Hazor.	consequential
2b	**The general of his army was Sisera;**	supplemental
2c	**who lived in Harosheth Haggoyim.**	supplemental
3	The Israelites cried out for help to the LORD, for Sisera had nine hundred chariots with iron-rimmed wheels and he cruelly oppressed the Israelites for twenty years.[10]	resumptive-consequential

Comments on the Prologue

1. This next major episode in Judges begins with the formulaic report, "The Israelites again did evil in the LORD's sight" (see 3:7, 12). The *wayyiqtol* form initiates the action, but it is also sequential in relation to the preceding literary unit (3:12–31). It introduces a historical account that postdates the story of Ehud recorded in the previous chapter.

2. The offline clause in verse 1b is circumstantial/temporal, informing us that the rebellion described earlier in the verse took place after Ehud's death.

3. The supplemental offline clause in verse 2b introduces us to Sisera, who plays an important role in the following story. The accompanying offline clause in verse 2c provides further information about this character's place of residence.

---

10. The final clause of verse 3 begins with a disjunctive structure (*waw* + subject + verb), but it seems to be an extension of the preceding causal clause (cf. Gen. 2:5).

4–22	Story Proper	Type of Clause
4	**Now Deborah, a prophetess, wife of Lappidoth, was leading Israel at that time.**	introductory-backgrounding
5a	**She would sit under the Date Palm Tree of Deborah between Ramah and Bethel in the Ephraimite hill country.**	introductory-backgrounding/specifying
5b	The Israelites would come up to her to have their disputes settled.	complementary
6a	Deborah sent messengers	initiatory
6b	and summoned Barak son of Abinoam from Kedesh in Naphtali.	sequential
6c	She said to him:	sequential or specifying
6d	*"Is it not true that the LORD God of Israel is commanding you? 'Go, march to Mount Tabor! Take with you ten thousand men from Naphtali and Zebulun!*	
7	*I will bring Sisera, the general of Jabin's army, to you at the Kishon River, along with his chariots and huge army. I will hand him over to you.'"*	
8a	Barak said to her:	sequential
8b	*"If you go with me, I will go. But if you do not go with me, I will not go."*	
9a	She said:	sequential
9b	*"I will indeed go with you. But you will not gain fame on the expedition you are taking, for the LORD will turn Sisera over to a woman."*	
9c	Deborah got up	sequential
9d	and went with Barak to Kedesh.	sequential
10a	Barak summoned men from Naphtali and Zebulun to Kedesh.	sequential
10b	Ten thousand men followed him.	sequential
10c	Deborah went up with him as well.	reiterative

11a	**(Now Heber the Kenite had moved away from the Kenites, the descendants of Hobab, Moses' father-in-law.**	supplemental
11b	He settled near the tree in Zaanannim near Kedesh.)	resumptive-sequential
12a	When Sisera heard that Barak son of Abinoam had gone up to Mount Tabor,	resumptive-sequential
13a	he ordered all his chariotry—nine hundred chariots with iron-rimmed wheels—and all the troops he had with him to go from Harosheth Haggoyim to the River Kishon.	consequential
14a	Deborah said to Barak:	sequential
14b	*"Spring into action, for this is the day the LORD is handing Sisera over to you! Has the LORD not taken the lead?"*	
14c	Barak quickly went down from Mount Tabor	consequential
14d	**with ten thousand men following him.**	circumstantial
15a	The LORD routed Sisera, all his chariotry, and all his army before Barak with the edge of the sword.	sequential
15b	Sisera jumped out of his chariot	sequential
15c	and ran away on foot.	sequential
16a	**Now Barak chased the chariots and the army all the way to Harosheth Haggoyim.**	dramatic shift in focus
16b	Sisera's whole army died by the edge of the sword;	sequential
16c	**not even one survived.**	complementary-reiterative/ emphatic
17a	**Now Sisera ran away on foot to the tent of Jael, wife of Heber the Kenite, for King Jabin of Hazor and the family of Heber the Kenite had made a peace treaty.**	dramatic shift in focus
18a	Jael came out to welcome Sisera.	sequential
18b	She said to him:	sequential
18c	*"Stop and rest, my lord! Stop and rest with me! Don't be afraid!"*	

18d	So Sisera stopped to rest in her tent	consequential
18e	and she put a blanket over him.	sequential
19a	He said to her:	sequential
19b	*"Give me a little water to drink, for I am thirsty."*	
19c	She opened a goatskin container of milk	sequential
19d	and gave him some milk to drink.	sequential
19e	Then she covered him up again.	sequential
20a	He said to her:	sequential
20b	*"Stand watch at the entrance to the tent. If anyone comes along and asks you, 'Is there a man here?' say, 'No.'"*	
21a	Then Jael wife of Heber took a tent peg in one hand	sequential
21b	and a hammer in the other.	complementary
21c	She crept up on him,	sequential
21d	and drove the tent peg through his temple	sequential
21e	and it went into the ground	sequential
21f	**while he was asleep—**	circumstantial
21g	for he was exhausted—	supplemental/explanatory
21h	and he died.	resumptive-consequential
22a	**Now Barak was chasing Sisera.**	dramatic shift in focus
22b	Jael went out to welcome him.	sequential
22c	She said to him:	sequential
22d	*"Come here and I will show you the man you are searching for."*	
22f	He went with her into the tent	consequential
22g	**and there he saw Sisera sprawled out dead**	dramatic shift in focus
22h	**with the tent peg in his temple.**	circumstantial

Comments on the Story Proper

1. The offline clause in verse 4 introduces a new character who plays an important role in the story proper (vv. 4–22). This clause marks the transition to the story proper (the account of Israel's deliverance from oppression) and provides background information for the narrative.

2. The offline clause in verse 5a gives more specific background information about Deborah's role as judge. The *wayyiqtol* form in verse 5b does not initiate the story; it complements the preceding statement by informing us that the Israelites would come to Deborah to have their legal disputes settled.

3. After the background information of verses 4–5, the *wayyiqtol* form in verse 6a initiates the action of the story proper.

4. Verse 11, introduced by an offline clause ("Now Heber"), provides parenthetical information which, though interrupting the narrative (note that vv. 10 and 12–13 focus on the deployment of forces), promises to be significant in the unfolding story and raises the reader's curiosity.

5. The *wayyiqtol* form in verse 11b introduces a clause that is sequential to the preceding supplemental clause (see v. 5).

6. The offline clause in verse 16a shifts the focus from the fleeing Sisera back to the victorious Barak. Offline clauses perform this same function in verses 17a (shifting the focus back to Sisera), 22a (shifting the focus back to Barak), and 22g (shifting the focus to the dead Sisera). This series of offline clauses also has a structural function in the discourse. The offline clause in verse 16a ("Now Barak") marks the transition from the battle *per se* to its aftermath. In verses 17–21 the fleeing Sisera (cf. v. 15b) becomes the focus as the scene shifts from the general region mentioned in verse 16 to the tent of the aforementioned Heber (cf. v. 11). An offline clause ("Now Sisera") marks this shift in scene. In verse 22a, also introduced by an offline clause (literally, "And look,"), the focus returns to the pursuing Barak (cf. v. 16), who arrives at Heber's tent to find that a woman has already disposed of the enemy general. The final offline clauses (22g and 22h) provide closure for the scene. The description of Sisera's murder is thus

bracketed by references to Barak's pursuing the enemy (cf. vv. 16, 22), highlighting the fact that the glory of killing the Canaanite general escapes him (cf. v. 9), despite his earnest efforts.

7. The switch to the perfect in verse 16c is expected after the negative particle. The clause has no conjunction at the beginning; this is not surprising given its complementary-reiterative (and therefore emphatic) function.

8. The circumstantial clause in verse 21f tells us what we suspect (cf. v. 19), namely, that Jael is able to kill Sisera in this manner because he fell asleep. However, by delaying reference to this, the narrator adds to the drama of the deed.[11] As we read the actions described in verse 21a-d, we may suspect that Sisera is asleep, but we are not completely sure of this. This downplaying of Sisera's vulnerability makes Jael's deed appear even more heroic and courageous.

9. The *wayyiqtol* form in verse 21g introduces a clause that is subordinate to the preceding circumstantial clause and gives the explanation for his falling asleep so readily. For other examples of a *wayyiqtol* clause having an explanatory function, see Numbers 1:48 and Isaiah 39:1.

10. The offline clause in verse 22a dramatically invites the audience to share an observer's perspective (note הִנֵּה, "and look!").

11. The offline clause in verse 22g dramatically invites the audience to share Barak's perspective (note הִנֵּה, "and look!"). With its tone of finality, it also signals closure for the story proper.

23–24	Epilogue	Type of Clause
23	That day God humiliated King Jabin of Canaan, before the Israelites.	summarizing
24	Israel's power continued to overwhelm King Jabin of Canaan, until they did away with King Jabin of Canaan.	consequential

---

11. In this regard see the comments of Adele Berlin, *Poetics and Interpretation of Biblical Narrative* (Winona Lake, IN: Eisenbrauns, 1994), 71.

Comment on the Epilogue

The epilogue (vv. 23–24), though linked to the preceding narrative by a *wayyiqtol* form, is marked by a shift in subject ("God") and the phrase "in that day." The use of the divine name "God" rounds off the narrative of Israel's deliverance. The account is set in motion when Deborah announces the word of the LORD God of Israel (v. 6); it concludes with the statement that this same God won the victory just as he had promised. The threefold reference to King Jabin of *Canaan,* links these concluding verses to the introduction (cf. v. 2, note that Jabin is called "king of *Hazor*" in v. 17) and establishes an **inclusio** for the entire narrative.

Dramatic Structure

In addition to their **discourse structure**, Old Testament stories also exhibit a **dramatic structure** complete with episodes and scenes. One can detect the transition between episodes and scenes in a variety of ways. A change in setting, whether temporal or geographical, often signals a transition. Narrators sometimes use formal transitional signals such as the temporal indicator וַיְהִי or an offline disjunctive clausal structure (conjunction + subject + verb). They may also employ the literary device of **inclusio** to mark out an episode or scene. In this case certain words or phrases appear at both the beginning and conclusion of a literary unit and form a frame or bracket around it.

The lengthy narrative unit in Judges 6:1–10:5 provides a good illustration of this type of dramatic structure. The central section of the book of Judges (3:7–16:31) is divided into six distinct literary units, each of which begins with a reference to the Israelites doing evil in the sight of the Lord (3:7–11; 3:12–31; 4:1–5:31; 6:1–10:5; 10:6–12:15; 13:1–16:31). The reference to Israel's doing evil in 6:1 thus signals a new narrative cycle within the book's central section. The literary structure of this cycle includes a prologue (6:1–10), a main narrative consisting of six episodes (6:11–8:27), an epilogue (8:28–32), and a sequel (8:33–10:5):

	Title	Reference
Prologue:	The Same Old Story	6:1–10
Story proper:	From Coward to King	6:11–8:27
Episode 1:	Getting a skeptic's attention	6:11–24
Scene 1:	Startling encounter	6:11–18
Scene 2:	Up in smoke	6:19–21
Scene 3:	A skeptic worships	6:22–24
Episode 2:	Taking baby steps	6:25–32
Scene 1:	A busy night	6:25–27
Scene 2:	Trouble in town in the morning	6:28–32
Episode 3:	Time for the ultimate test	6:33–7:23
Scene 1:	Facing off with the enemy	6:33–35
Scene 2:	Hesitating again	6:36–40
Scene 3:	Reducing the army to a remnant	7:1–8
Scene 4:	Reassuring the general	7:9–14
Scene 5:	Responding to the challenge	7:15–23
Episode 4:	Enter Ephraim	7:24–8:3
Episode 5:	Tracking down the oppressors	8:4–21
Scene 1:	No support	8:4–9
Scene 2:	Defeating the enemy	8:10–12
Scene 3:	Vengeance, part one	8:13–17
Scene 4:	Vengeance, part two	8:18–21
Episode 6:	Gideon rejects the crown—or does he?	8:22–27
Epilogue:	Trouble Brewing	8:28–32
Sequel:	Civil War	8:33–10:5
Prologue:	Israel returns to Baal worship	8:33–35
Story proper:	The rise and fall of "King" Abimelech	9:1–57
Episode 1:	Abimelech murders his brothers	9:1–6
Episode 2:	Jotham appeals for justice	9:7–21
Episode 3:	A curse cracks a skull	9:22–57
Epilogue:	Stability restored	10:1–5

The prologue (6:1–10) includes a report of oppression (vv. 1–6) and a prophetic message (vv. 7–10). The temporal indicator (וַיְהִי) at the beginning of verse 7 formally separates the two sections, while verbal repetition (note "the Israelites cried out to the LORD" in both v. 6b and v. 7a) links them thematically and formally.

The limits of episode 1 (6:11–24) are marked by an inclusio (note the references to Ophrah and the Abiezrite[s] in both vv. 11 and 24).[12] The episode divides into three scenes: introductory dialogue (vv. 11–18), report of Gideon's sacrifice (vv. 19–21), and concluding dialogue (vv. 22–24). The offline clause at the beginning of verse 19 marks the transition

---

12. See Barry G. Webb, *The Book of the Judges: An Integrated Reading*, JSOTSup 46 (Sheffield: Sheffield Academic Press, 1987), 148–49.

from the initial dialogue to the account of the sacrifice, while the offline clause at the end of verse 21 brings the report to its conclusion.

A temporal indicator and a reference to nighttime introduce the second episode in the narrative (6:25–32). The episode can be divided into two scenes (vv. 25–27, 28–32), corresponding to the references to nighttime (the appearance of לַיְלָה, "night," near the beginning of v. 25 and at the end of v. 27 forms an inclusio for vv. 25–27) and to morning (v. 28a). The verb שָׁכַם, "rise early," and the הִנֵּה ("look!") clause in verse 28 also signal a shift from Gideon's nighttime deed to its aftermath. The repetition of the words בַּעַל ("Baal"), נָתַץ ("pull down"), and מִזְבֵּחַ ("altar") in verses 28 and 32 provides an inclusio for the second scene. (These same terms are clustered in v. 30b, just before the pivotal point where the subject shifts from the townspeople to Gideon's father.)

Episode 3, the account of the battle proper (6:33–7:23), contains five scenes. The first (6:33–35) begins with an offline clause (v. 33) reminding us of the larger problem that was introduced in verses 1–10 and has been lurking in the background. Three more offline clauses (vv. 34–35) lay the foundation for what follows. The stage seems to be set for a battle, but Gideon is not quite ready for that step yet. Instead he seeks confirmation of success. This second scene (6:36–40) displays two panels, each of which reports Gideon's request (vv. 36–37, 39) and God's response (vv. 38, 40).

Shifts in name (note "Jerubbaal") and focus (the author describes the location of the Israelite and Midianite campsites) mark the transition to scene 3 (7:1–8). The offline clauses in the second half of verse 8 signal closure for the scene. The reference to the location of the Midianite camp forms an inclusio with verse 1. Apart from the frame (vv. 1, 8b), the scene consists of four subunits, each of which is introduced by the words, "the LORD said to Gideon" (vv. 2–3, 4–5a, 5b–6, 7–8a).

A temporal indicator and a reference to nighttime (v. 9a; cf. 6:25) introduce scene 4 (7:9–14), which describes how the Lord gives Gideon further confirmation of success. The references to God's giving the enemy into Gideon's hands (vv. 9, 14) form an inclusio for the scene. The central parenthetical offline clause (v. 12) functions as a pivot between the Lord's instructions (vv. 9–11) and Gideon's response (vv. 13–14).

In scene 5 (7:15–23), which is introduced by a temporal indicator, the long-awaited battle finally arrives. The scene consists of Gideon's instructions and preparations (vv. 15–18), and the battle account proper (vv. 19–23), which is introduced by a description of Gideon's army's movements (v. 19a).

The fourth episode (7:24–8:3), introduced by an offline clause, describes the Ephraimites' contribution to the battle and their dispute with Gideon. Verses 24–25 report Gideon's invitation and the Ephraimites' positive response. In 8:1–3 Gideon resolves a conflict with the Ephraimites, who were offended because they had not been summoned to war earlier. The final clause, introduced by אָז, "then," reports the resolution.

In episode 5 (8:4–21) we read of Gideon's attempt to track down the Midianite chieftains Zebah and Zalmunna and the remnants of their army. The episode has two parallel panels (vv. 4–9, 13–17 // vv. 10–12, 18–21) comprised of four distinct scenes (vv. 4–9, 10–12, 13–17, 18–21). In verses 4–9 the men of Succoth and Peniel refuse to support Gideon, for they are not convinced that he will emerge victorious. The offline clause at the beginning of verse 10, which informs us of the Midianite chieftains' location and troop strength, introduces the next scene in the narrative—Gideon's surprise attack and final victory. The offline clause at the end of verse 12 rounds off the scene. Verses 13–17, which describe how Gideon fulfills the threats he made against Succoth and Peniel, correspond to verses 4–9. Verses 18–21, which describe the execution of Zebah and Zalmunna, correspond to and complete verses 10–12.

The sixth and final episode (8:22–27), though closely linked with the preceding (note the introductory *waw* consecutive and the reference to the Midianite jewelry in v. 26 [cf. v. 21]), is marked by a change in subject (the men of Israel now speak) and theme (kingship).

The conclusion (8:28–32) contains an expected formulaic summary about deliverance and peace (v. 28; cf. 3:11, 30; 5:31b), but also provides information concerning Gideon's family, death, and burial (vv. 29–32). The references to Joash, Ophrah, and the Abiezrite(s) form an inclusio for the entire Gideon narrative (cf. 6:11) and contribute to its closure. (Though this cycle of the book's central section begins in 6:1, Gideon, its main character, is not introduced until 6:11.) At the same time, this information lays the foundation for the following section by mentioning Abimelech, his seventy half-brothers, and Shechem.

The story of Abimelech is the sequel to the Gideon narrative. Together with 6:1–8:32, it forms one large literary unit. It contains a prologue (8:33–35), the main narrative (9:1–57), and an epilogue (10:1–5). The sequel is introduced by וַיְהִי (8:33) and a reference to Israel's persistence in Baal worship. The prologue sets the stage for the main narrative by giving the background for Abimelech's rise to power, while the epilogue records how a semblance of stability is restored to the land following his death, but not without negative repercussions.

The main narrative has three episodes. A reference to Abimelech marks the transition from the prologue to the first episode. Verses 1–6 tell how Abimelech forms an alliance with the citizens of Shechem and murders his brothers. References to Abimelech and Shechem appear in verses 1 and 6, as does the verb הָלַךְ, "go," forming an inclusio for the unit. Verses 7–21 record Jotham's fable. References to Jotham's movements bracket the unit. In both the introduction and conclusion (vv. 7b, 20) to his speech he addresses Shechem's nobles (בַּעֲלֵי שְׁכֶם, "leaders of Shechem"). Abimelech again becomes the focus of the narrative in verse 22, which introduces the third episode. This long account begins and ends with statements about the Lord's intervention (vv. 23–24, 56–57). The main portion of the episode (vv. 25–55) tells how the Lord providentially brings about Abimelech's demise and Shechem's destruction. This section is divided into three scenes. The first deals with Gaal's rebellion (vv. 26–41). After Gaal's departure (v. 41), a second scene begins with וַיְהִי (v. 42a) and the dawning of a new day. With Abimelech's movement from Shechem to Thebez (v. 50) a new scene begins, though it is not formally introduced.

Paneled Sequences

One can often detect other literary structures embedded within a story. One such structure is **paneled sequencing**, where repeated elements appear in successive movements.[13] The Gideon story surveyed

---

13. This structure, while repetitive in nature, is an especially effective story-telling technique when a story is heard. Only after the invention of the printing press could literature be made widely available for reading. The stories of the Bible were, for the most part, heard, not read. Many of the structural devices and rhetorical techniques of the biblical stories reflect this oral dimension. See H. Van Dyke Parunak, "Oral Typesetting: Some Uses of Biblical Structure," *Biblica* 62 (1984): 153–68.

above includes at least two examples of such paneling. In 6:36–40 Gideon conducts two tests to verify the Lord's ability to give him victory in the upcoming battle. The accounts of both tests display the same literary structure:

Panel One (6:36–38)

Request for a sign (v. 36)
Description of sign (v. 37)
Fulfillment of sign (v. 38)

Panel Two (6:39–40)

Request for a sign (v. 39a)
Description of sign (v. 39b)
Fulfillment of sign (v. 40)

The fifth scene in the story (8:4–21) oscillates back and forth between Gideon's dealings with Succoth/Penuel and with the fleeing Midianite kings:

Panel One (8:4–12)

Gideon threatens Succoth/Penuel (vv. 4–9).
Gideon captures the kings (vv. 10–12).

Panel Two (8:13–21)

Gideon punishes Succoth/Penuel (vv. 13–17).
Gideon executes the kings (vv. 18–21).

Sometimes introductory panels use repetition of action to build dramatic tension, which is resolved as the story unfolds. Significant changes in the repeated pattern, especially in the final panel, signal plot resolution and closure. For example, the scene of the boy Samuel's first prophetic encounter with God (1 Sam. 3:4–14), embedded within the larger episode, displays four panels:

Panel One (3:4–5)

The Lord calls Samuel (v. 4a).
Samuel replies (v. 4b).
Samuel runs to Eli (v. 5a).
Eli tells Samuel to go back to sleep (v. 5b).
Samuel goes back to sleep (v. 5c).

Panel Two (3:6–7)

The Lord calls Samuel (v. 6a).
Samuel goes to Eli (v. 6b).
Eli tells Samuel to go back to sleep (v. 6c).
The narrator comments (v. 7).

Panel Three (3:8–9)

The Lord calls Samuel (v. 8a).
Samuel goes to Eli (v. 8b).
Eli understands the Lord is calling the boy
   (v. 8c).
Eli tells Samuel to go back to sleep (v. 9a).
Eli instructs Samuel how to respond (v. 9b).
Samuel goes back to sleep (v. 9c).

Panel Four (3:10–14)

The Lord approaches Samuel (v. 10a).
The Lord calls Samuel (v. 10b).
Samuel responds as instructed (v. 10c).
The Lord reveals his message to Samuel (vv.
   11–14).

Other examples of paneled sequences include Delilah's seduction of Samson (Judg. 16:6–21), the account of the civil war with Benjamin (Judg. 20:18–36a), and Elijah's encounter with the king's captains (2 Kings 1:9–15).[14]

Chiasmus

Chiasmus (named for the Greek letter *chi,* which is shaped like an X) is a symmetric literary structure in which the second half of a literary unit mirrors the first half. The most basic form of a chiasmus is a simple AB // B'A' structure:

    A
        B
        B'
   A'

Sometimes there is a pivotal element C that has no corresponding member: AB/C/B'A':

    A
        B
             C
      B'
   A'

Some scholars seem particularly eager to find chiastic structures throughout biblical literature, but one often gets the impression that the proposals are more a testimony to the scholar's creativity than a design intended by the biblical author. Generally speaking, chiasmus is more common in smaller literary units, such as a poetic verse or strophe. The larger the unit, the more contrived and artificial the proposal usually appears to be.

---

14. For an analysis of the paneled structures of Judges 16:6–21 and 2 Kings 1:9–15, see Robert B. Chisholm Jr., *From Exegesis to Exposition: A Practical Guide to Using Biblical Hebrew* (Grand Rapids: Baker, 1998), 162–63.

Nevertheless, one can occasionally detect chiastic structures in stories. For example, God's dealings with Gideon in Judges 7:1–14 mirror Gideon's earlier actions (as recorded in Judg. 6). Using the word אִם, "if," Gideon initially requests a miraculous sign from God (6:17). Having received his sign and having mustered a large army, he then asks for further confirmation through two tests involving a fleece (6:36–40). Once more he prefaces his remarks with the word "if" (v. 36). But then the Lord takes away the army, doing so through a two-part plan involving testing and observation (7:1–8; cf. 6:36–40). Then, using Gideon's favorite word, "if," the Lord grants him a final confirmatory sign (7:9–14). The structure is thus chiastic:

A   Gideon asks for and receives a sign (6:17–24).
   B   Gideon gathers an army and seeks confirmation of God's promise through two tests (6:33–40).
   B'   God dismantles the army through two tests (7:1–8).
A'   God offers Gideon a confirmatory sign (7:9–14).

Note that the initial sign occurs in broad daylight, while the final sign occurs at night. Gideon's tests occur at night; God's tests take place during the day.

Though a chiastic structure is present, it is important to note that it is not the dominant literary structure for the story. Several verses (6:25–32) do not seem to fit into the chiastic arrangement. If we look at the larger structure that extends through 7:23, we detect the following outline:

A   Gideon asks for and receives a sign (6:17–24).
   B   Gideon accepts a challenge to destroy the Baal altar (6:25–32).
      C   Gideon gathers an army and seeks confirmation of God's promise through two tests (6:33–40).
      C'   God dismantles the army through two tests (7:1–8).
A'   God offers Gideon a confirmatory sign (7:9–14).
   B'   Gideon accepts the original challenge to deliver Israel from Midian (7:15–23).

There is a chiastic structure embedded within the larger structure (AC // C'A'), but the B/B' elements are located in different positions due to the demands of the **plot structure**.

It is relatively rare to find a chiastic structure encompassing an entire story, but the book of Esther appears to be arranged symmetrically according to the following outline:[15]

A   Prologue: Persian festival and ascension of Esther (1:1–2:23)
  B   Complication: The Jews endangered by their archenemy (3:1–15)
    C   Response: Mordecai's strategic appeal (4:1–17)
      D   Development: Esther's first banquet (5:1–8)
        E   Centerpiece: The fall of Haman and the rise of Mordecai (5:9–6:14)
      D'   Consequence: Esther's second banquet (7:1–10)
    C'   Resolution: Mordecai's strategic appeal (8:1–17)
  B'   Dénouement: The Jews victorious over their enemies (9:1–19)
A'   Epilogue: Jewish festival and ascension of Mordecai (9:20–10:3)

Overlapping Accounts and Flashbacks

Old Testament narratives do not always proceed in a chronologically linear "A-to-Z" fashion. A narrator may juxtapose two complementary accounts of an event, adding details in the process, or he may interweave events thematically, rather than chronologically.[16] In either

---

15. The following outline is that of Gordon H. Johnston, "A Funny Thing Happened on the Way to the Gallows! Irony, Humor, and Other Literary Features of the Book of Esther," in *Giving the Sense: Understanding and Using Old Testament Historical Texts,* ed. David M. Howard Jr. and Michael A. Grisanti (Grand Rapids: Kregel, 2003), 384. Johnston extends the outline to include episodes and proposes an elaborate symmetric structure in which the book's episodes correspond.

16. Brichto calls the first of these techniques the synoptic/resumptive technique. He explains: "Essentially it is the treatment of one event two times. The first narration of the event . . . is usually *briefer* (hence *synoptic*) than the second" and "is an independent, freestanding literary unit." He adds: "The second treatment or episode, usually longer than the first,

case, there is some degree of **temporal overlay** involving chronological flashbacks.

Judges 20:26–48 includes two complementary accounts of the culminating battle in the civil war between Benjamin and the other Israelite tribes (vv. 31–36a, 36b–46) sandwiched between a prologue (vv. 26–30) and an epilogue (vv. 47–48). In the prologue Israel seeks divine guidance (vv. 26–28) and deploys for battle (vv. 29–30). The epilogue describes the aftermath of the battle. We may outline verses 26–48 as follows:

Prologue: Preparation for battle (vv. 26–30)
    Condensed version of battle (vv. 31–36a)
    Expanded version of battle (vv. 36b–46)
Epilogue: Aftermath of battle (vv. 47–48)

The first battle account begins with Benjamin's attack (v. 31). Israel retreats and the Benjaminites cut down thirty Israelite soldiers. However, this is simply a ploy to lure the Benjaminites away from Gibeah (v. 32). Verses 33–36 tell how the Israelite forces, which had divided into two groups, counterattack and defeat the Benjaminites, killing 25,000 soldiers.

Verses 36b–46 are parallel to and complement verses 31–36a. This second account provides a more detailed description of the Israelite strategy and the events that transpired during the battle. It skips the preliminaries to the battle (cf. vv. 26–30) and picks up the story with the Benjaminite attack. The main Israelite force retreats and draws the Benjaminite army away from Gibeah (v. 36b; cf. vv. 31–32). Then 10,000 crack troops, who had been hiding in ambush (cf. vv. 29, 33b), charge into Gibeah, wipe out the residents, and set the town on fire (vv. 37–38; cf. v. 34). When the main force sees the smoke going up from the city, they turn on the Benjaminites (vv. 38–39a). Returning to the point of the initial Benjaminite attack, verse 39b recalls how Benjamin

---

may or may not be able to stand by itself." According to Brichto, one may also use the labels "conclusive" and "expansive" for the respective treatments. He explains that the second treatment provides "a more detailed account (hence *resumptive-expansive*) of how the bottom line of the first episode (hence *conclusive*) was arrived at." See Herbert Chanan Brichto, *Toward a Grammar of Biblical Poetics: Tales of the Prophets* (New York: Oxford University, 1992), 13–14.

confidently pursued the retreating Israelites (cf. vv. 31–32a). Verse 40 then returns to the events described in verses 38–39a, but it reflects the Benjaminite perspective. When the smoke goes up from the city and the Israelites counterattack, the Benjaminites, seeing the rising smoke, recognize too late that they have been tricked (v. 41). Verses 42–46 then give a more detailed report of exactly how and where the fleeing Benjaminite forces are struck down.

Sometimes a narrator presents events in a thematic, rather than strictly chronological, order. For example, Judges 11:29–40 tells how Jephthah defeats the Ammonites, but then, in fulfillment of his rash and foolish vow, is forced to offer up his daughter as a burnt sacrifice. When his daughter learns of her fate, she asks for and receives permission to wander over the hills for two months lamenting the fact that she will never enjoy being a wife and mother (vv. 38–39). The episode concludes with the sobering statement that Jephthah "did to her as he had vowed" (v. 39). Judges 12 records an episode that occurs in the aftermath of Jephthah's victory over the Ammonites. The Ephraimites ask why they were not summoned to the battle. Jephthah explains that he did summon them, but that they did not answer the call. A civil war breaks out in which Jephthah's army annihilates the Ephraimites. It seems likely that this episode occurs shortly after the battle, sometime during Jephthah's daughter's two months of mourning. If so, then 12:1 must be understood as a chronological flashback. In this case the narrator develops and brings closure to one subplot (Jephthah's vow and its horrible consequences) before introducing another (the Ephraimite conflict).

Another example of the interweaving of themes appears in 1 Samuel 27–2 Samuel 1.[17] First Samuel 26:25b describes how David and Saul go their separate ways for the very last time. Over the next six chapters the narrator's attention oscillates between David and Saul. While there is chronological progression in the story as a whole, the material is not in strict chronological sequence. First Samuel 27 tells how a desperate David flees to Philistine territory and becomes a mercenary of Achish, king of Gath. As the Philistines prepare for war with Israel, Achish summons David and his men to join the Philistine army (1 Sam. 28:1–

---

17. For a chart showing the probable chronological order of events in these chapters, see Robert D. Bergen, *1, 2 Samuel*, NAC (Nashville: Broadman & Holman, 1996), 285.

2). The focus then shifts to Saul, who, on the eve of the battle with the Philistines, consults a medium and is told by the spirit of the late prophet Samuel that he will die in battle the next day (1 Sam. 28:3–25). First Samuel 29 switches back to David and his men, who have joined the Philistine army. According to 29:1, the Philistines assemble at Aphek. This event must have been prior to their deploying at Shunem on the eve of the battle (cf. 28:4). Consequently, the events recorded in chapter 29 occur before Saul's visit to the medium, recounted in chapter 28. The suspicious Philistine leaders send David and his men back to Ziklag. When they arrive there after a three-day journey (cf. 1 Sam. 30:1), they discover that the Amalekites have kidnapped their wives and children. They chase down the Amalekites and rescue their families (1 Sam. 30). The focus returns to Saul in 1 Samuel 31, which tells how he is struck down in battle. When the Philistines discover his corpse, they hang it on the city wall of Beth Shan. However, the men of Jabesh Gilead retrieve it, give the bones a proper burial, and then mourn for seven days. Second Samuel 1 returns us to Ziklag and takes us back in time at least five days, because verse 1 informs us that this episode took place on the third day after Saul's death. The oscillating style of these chapters is similar to the film version of Tolkien's *The Lord of the Rings: Return of the King,* where the focus shifts back and forth from Gondor, where Gandalf and company are engaged in battle, to Mordor, where Frodo and Sam continue their journey to Mount Doom. The story moves ahead, but not without chronological flashbacks accompanying the shifts in focus.

Quotation and Dialogue

Old Testament narrative is filled with quotations and dialogues that can contribute to characterization and plot. For example, the seemingly mundane dialogue between Saul and his servant recorded in 1 Samuel 9:5–10 contributes to the narrator's characterization of Saul. Saul appears hesitant and passive, character traits that will spell trouble for him as the story unfolds. He tends to impede action, rather than move it along.[18]

---

18. See V. Philips Long, *The Reign and Rejection of King Saul: A Case for Literary and Theological Coherence,* SBLDS 18 (Atlanta: Scholars, 1989), 202.

As noted earlier, David emerges as a very human character, displaying strengths as well as weaknesses. This ambiguity is apparent in quotations from David strategically positioned at the beginning and end of his story. The first time he speaks in the story (1 Sam. 17:26), he displays a measure of self-interest and greed ("What will be done for the man who strikes down this Philistine?"), as well as a healthy concern for God's honor ("Who is this uncircumcised Philistine, that he defies the armies of the living God?"). On his deathbed he urges Solomon to obey the Lord's law, but then tells his son to bloody his hands by getting revenge against Joab and Shimei (1 Kings 2:1–10).

Samson's first and last words epitomize his life, which was consumed by unbridled sexual passion and an obsession with getting revenge against the Philistines. This explosive combination eventually brought about his demise. The first time he speaks, he says to his parents: "A Philistine girl in Timnah has caught my eye; now get her for my wife" (Judg. 14:2). His final words are a prayer in which he asks to get swift revenge against the Philistines, "Let me die with the Philistines!" (Judg. 16:28, 30).

Quotations and dialogues can also play a significant role in plot development and often appear at strategic points in the story. For example, God urges hesitant Gideon to attack the Midianites, but he also tells him that he should eavesdrop on the Midianite guards if he needs further assurance of success (Judg. 7:9–11). Gideon decides to take God up on his offer. When he overhears the guard's dream report and his colleague's interpretation (vv. 13–14), Gideon is transformed into a mighty warrior (v. 15). Words, strategically placed in Gideon's experience, prove to be the turning point in the story.

Discourse Types

Within quotations one finds a variety of **discourse types**. A single speech may include more than one of these. The main discourse types found in speeches include the following:

1. **Predictive discourse**: The speaker describes what will happen; prophets often speak in this fashion. For example, in 1 Samuel 10:2–6 the prophet Samuel describes to Saul a series of events

that will transpire once Saul departs from him.[19] More sophisticated forms of predictive discourse can include an **evaluative** element. In a prophetic judgment speech, an accusation can introduce an announcement of impending judgment (see 2 Sam. 12:7–12; 2 Kings 1:16–17). Or, on a more positive note, a statement of commendation may precede a promise of blessing (see Gen. 22:15–18).

2. Narrative discourse: Sometimes a speaker rehearses what has happened. In this case the story within the quotation is embedded in the larger story related by the narrator. For example, in Judges 7:13 a Midianite guard relates the details of a symbolic dream to his colleague. In 2 Samuel 11:23–24 Joab's messenger relates the details of a battle to King David.

3. **Hortatory discourse**: Here the speaker urges, commands, or exhorts the listener(s) to perform or refrain from an action. Imperatives and other volitional forms are typically used along with motivational arguments (expository discourse, see no. 4 below). For example, in Judges 4:6–7 Deborah urges Barak to charge into battle and assures him of the Lord's protective presence.

4. Expository discourse: The speaker either explains or argues a case. For example, in her fourth attempt to get Samson to divulge the secret of his strength, Delilah questions the sincerity of Samson's love (Judg. 16:15).[20] As noted above, expository discourse often accompanies hortatory discourse. For example, Naomi urges her daughters-in-law to return to Moab, arguing that she is too old to provide them with new husbands and that they should not have to endure her pain (Ruth 1:11–13).

5. Procedural (or instructional) discourse: The speaker explains *how* to do something. For example, in 2 Samuel 5:23–24 the Lord lays out a step-by-step battle strategy for David to follow. Procedural discourse is closely related to hortatory discourse (see no. 3 above). Though the distinction is slight, hortatory discourse

---

19. See Robert E. Longacre, "*Weqatal* Forms in Biblical Hebrew Prose: A Discourse-modular Approach," in *Biblical Hebrew and Discourse Linguistics,* ed. R. Bergen (Winona Lake, IN: Eisenbrauns, 1994), 51–52. As Longacre points out, the main line verbal form in this type of discourse is *weqatal* (the perfect with *waw* consecutive).

20. Bryan M. Rocine, *Learning Biblical Hebrew: A New Approach Using Discourse Analysis* (Macon, GA: Smyth & Helwys, 2000), 318.

emphasizes *what* should or should not be done, while procedural discourse focuses on *how* a task is to be accomplished. Often a speech will contain both hortatory and procedural elements. For example, in Judges 6:25–26 the Lord urges Gideon to pull down the Baal altar and erect an altar to the Lord in its place (hortatory discourse). Yet he also includes instructions concerning the sacrifice that Gideon is to offer (procedural discourse).

Speech Function

In addition to analyzing the discourse types found in speeches, one can evaluate **speech function**. Discourse type pertains to a speech's form and surface function, while speech function, as defined here, concerns a speech's deeper or underlying purpose(s). At one time speech was viewed as being either cognitive (concerned with objective reality) or emotive (concerned with feelings).[21] Subsequent research has revealed that the situation is far more complex than this. There is actually a wide assortment of speech functions. Many statements are multifunctional because they include more than one or even several of these. Major speech functions include the following:[22]

1. **Informative**: Informative speech is like the evening weather report—a simple, "just the facts" presentation designed to inform the listener(s). Messengers' reports are usually informative (e.g., 1 Sam. 26:1).

2. **Persuasive-dynamic**: According to Macky, dynamic speech is "intended to change hearers personally." As Macky observes, it can be affective ("aimed at arousing emotions"), pedagogical ("intended to illuminate darkness"), or transforming ("intended to change hearers' attitudes, values and commitments, often by first arousing emotion and illuminating the darkness").[23] It often

---

21. See Peter W. Macky, *The Centrality of Metaphor to Biblical Thought* (Lewiston, NY: Edwin Mellen, 1990), 15.

22. This list is adapted from Macky, *Centrality of Metaphor to Biblical Thought,* 16–17; and G. B. Caird, *The Language and Imagery of the Bible* (Philadelphia: Westminster, 1980), 7–36. I have omitted Macky's category "exploratory" because it is more common in modern speech than in the quotations recorded in the Bible.

23. Macky, *Centrality of Metaphor to Biblical Thought,* 16.

presents a case or argument designed to convince the listener(s) of the truth of a statement. For example, in 1 Samuel 22:14–15 Ahimelech the priest defends himself against Saul's accusation. Other examples of persuasive-dynamic speech appear in 1 Samuel 24:9–15 (David's first defense before Saul), 25:24–31 (Abigail's plea to David), and 26:18–20 (David's second defense before Saul).

3. Expressive: Here the speaker verbalizes "feelings without any concern to affect others."[24] Laments, where the speaker expresses grief for the dead, are examples of this type of speech function (e.g., 1 Kings 13:30). As Macky points out, "Very often such expressive speech is integrated with other kinds when we know others hear us."[25] For example, David's response to Nathan's story (2 Sam. 12:5) expresses his sense of outrage, but it is also evaluative (see no. 4 below) and, being in the form of an oath, has a **performative** function (no. 5 below).

4. Evaluative: Here "the speaker expresses his judgment on the quality of something."[26] Samuel's denunciation of Saul (1 Sam. 15:18–19) is evaluative.

5. Performative: Performative language is a speech act in which the statement "performs some non-linguistic act, such as a judge decreeing, 'The defendant is acquitted.'"[27] Samuel's decree in 1 Samuel 15:29–30, solemnized by the statement that God would not "change his mind," is an example of such language for it seals Saul's demise.

6. Relational: Here the speaker seeks "to enhance personal relationships."[28] Jonathan's appeal to David in 1 Samuel 20:14–15 provides an example.

---

24. Ibid.
25. Ibid.
26. Ibid.
27. Ibid. Macky lists imperatives as an example of "performative" language. Certainly imperatives are intended by the speaker to accomplish an action, but the desired action, rather than actually being produced by the command, remains contingent on the listener's willingness to respond favorably. For this reason imperatives are often supported by persuasive and dynamic language that has a motivational or assuring function.
28. Ibid., 17.

When analyzing speech function, it is important to consider the intended response and/or result. For example, Jael's invitation to Sisera (Judg. 4:18) is relational and dynamic on the surface, but her real goal is to lull Sisera into a false sense of security so she can kill him. On the surface Nathan's account of the rich man and poor man (2 Sam. 12:1–4) is informative, but the prophet intends to entrap David. The ruse worked, for Nathan's account prompts David to respond with a statement (vv. 5–6) that is expressive of his outrage, evaluative (he denounces the rich man), and performative (he vows that the rich man must pay the prescribed penalty, thus sealing his own punishment).

When interpreting how quotations contribute to a story, it is helpful to identify both the discourse type and its speech function(s). For example, Samuel's description of the policies of Israel's future king (1 Sam. 8:11–18) is predictive discourse. The language is persuasive and dynamic, not merely informative; it is designed to convince Israel that kingship is ultimately oppressive and to dissuade Israel from demanding a king. Likewise, the predictive discourse in 1 Samuel 10:2–6 is dynamic, not simply informative. The predicted events serve as a sign that God has indeed chosen Saul (v. 1); the sign in turn should motivate him to action (v. 7).

Being sensitive to **language function** can sometimes help the interpreter resolve difficult theological issues. One such example that raises questions regarding God's omniscience is the discourse between God and Abraham concerning the pending destruction of Sodom and Gomorrah. In Genesis 18:20–21 the Lord announces: "The outcry against Sodom and Gomorrah is so great and their sin so blatant that I must go down and see if they are as wicked as the outcry suggests. If not, I want to know." The Lord's words indicate that he intends to discover information. The verb רָאָה, "see," is collocated with interrogative *he* on seven other occasions, always meaning "see if."[29] In each case the discovery of information is in view. In its use elsewhere,

---

29. Genesis 8:8; Exodus 4:18; Numbers 11:23; Esther 3:4; Psalms 14:2 = 53:3 [Eng. v. 2]; Song 6:11. In Numbers 11:23 the collocation אִם לֹא . . . הֲ . . . רְאָה occurs, meaning "see whether or not." The collocation וְאִם לֹא . . . הֲ (note the conjunction prefixed to אִם) appears only here and in Genesis 4:7, where (unlike 18:21) it follows an interrogative clause. However, in both texts a contrast is in view that may be expressed by the translation "otherwise" in the second clause.

the first person prefixed verbal form (imperfect or cohortative) of יָדַע, "know" (cf. אֵדְעָה), has different shades of meaning, including "know for sure" (Gen. 15:8; 24:14; 42:33–34), "know more fully" (Exod. 33:13), "find out, discover" (Num. 22:19; 1 Sam. 22:3), "experience" (Isa. 47:8), and "be aware of" (Ps. 51:3). Since the Lord already has some awareness of the situation in the twin cities (Gen. 18:20), the nuance "know for sure" works very well in verse 21. But this suggests that full knowledge, such as we would expect an omniscient being to possess, is lacking.

It is startling to hear an omniscient God speak in this manner, especially right after he has revealed his supernatural knowledge by reading the skeptical Sarah's thoughts (cf. Gen. 18:12–15). Theologians have traditionally labeled such statements **anthropomorphic**, but this still raises the question: Why would an omniscient God reveal himself in a way that seems misleading and inaccurate? A typical answer is that he must do this because we are so limited in our understanding.[30] In other words, to accommodate our limitations God must present himself as being like us, at least to a certain degree. But this explanation is hardly satisfying. The theologians who label these texts as anthropomorphic claim they understand the truth of the matter—that God really does know all things. So it does not appear that our thinking is so limited after all. If we really can and do grasp the truth that God is omniscient, then the anthropomorphic language, rather than facilitating understanding, just seems to complicate matters!

We need a better explanation that analyzes more carefully the anatomy of the anthropomorphism. To do this we must examine the **metaphorical framework** in which the Lord speaks and then consider the language function of the statement. The context emphasizes the Lord's role as universal judge. Having heard the Lord speak of his concern about the moral condition of Sodom and Gomorrah, Abraham begins to negotiate on behalf of the cities, undoubtedly because of his concern for Lot and his family. Appealing to God's justice, he asks rhetorically, "Will not the judge of the whole earth do what is right?" (v. 25). Judges must get the facts straight before they finalize their decisions and mete

---

30. See, for example, Paul Helm, *The Providence of God* (Downers Grove, IL: InterVarsity, 1994), 52, who cites Calvin on the subject.

out punishment.[31] It seems clear that the Lord assumes a judicial role here and speaks accordingly.

We must also consider the issue of language function. It is likely that the Lord's statement in verses 20–21 is more than merely informative. The Lord feels obligated to share his intentions with Abraham (v. 17). This suggests the language is dynamic, designed to impact Abraham in some significant way and perhaps to prompt him to act. The Lord may be preparing Abraham emotionally for what he has already determined he will do. The angels inform Lot that the Lord sent them to destroy the city because the outcry against it is so great (19:13). They urge Lot to leave the city and announce that the Lord is ready to destroy it. They give no indication that an evaluation is under way. One might assume they have already decided to destroy the city before they arrive and that their purpose for coming is simply to warn Lot. However, one need not draw the conclusion that the city's destiny is sealed before the angels' arrival. By the time the angels speak in 19:13, Sodom's guilt has become evident and the need for judgment has been verified by the Sodomites' morally atrocious behavior (note how the text emphasizes the participation of "all the men—both young and old, from every part of the city of Sodom," in v. 4). The angels come to assess the situation and, if necessary, destroy the city. Having made their assessment, they can speak in retrospect of their mission as one of judgment without necessarily implying this was a foregone conclusion from the outset. If judgment is not a foregone conclusion prior to the angels' arrival, then it is possible that the Lord's statement in 18:20–21 is designed to prompt or at least invite Abraham to intercede, just as he does.[32] This would be a precursor to the theme of Abraham as prophetic intercessor, a role that becomes more prominent in Genesis 20:7.

At the very least, the Lord's statement in 18:20–21, when viewed within the metaphorical framework of God as judge, should convince Abraham that the Lord is committed to fairness (clearly a concern of

---

31. The language of verse 21 reflects this and is associated elsewhere with adjudicating. Several texts associate seeing (רָאָה) with judging (Exod. 5:21; 1 Sam. 24:16 [Eng. v. 15]; 2 Chron. 19:6; Lam. 3:59), while Exodus 3:9 speaks of the people's "cry" (צְעָקָה) coming before (בּוֹא אֶל) the Lord in conjunction with his seeing (רָאָה) the oppression of his people.

32. See Terence E. Fretheim, *The Suffering of God: An Old Testament Perspective* (Philadelphia: Fortress Press, 1984), 49–50; as well as Samuel E. Balentine, *Prayer in the Hebrew Bible: The Drama of Divine-Human Dialogue* (Minneapolis: Fortress, 1993), 145.

the patriarch, cf. 18:25). But this is not all. The language also makes it clear that the people of the twin cities hold their own destiny in their hands. God will not arbitrarily destroy them. On the contrary, like any fair and just judge, he responds to the complaint, examines the evidence, and metes out what is deserved. The use of anthropomorphic language, even if it does mask the **ontological** truth of God's omniscience, more emphatically conveys these truths than theologically "accurate" language would. In this context, apparently the Lord is less concerned with showing off his omniscience than he is with revealing himself as a fair judge, emphasizing the importance of human responsibility, and inviting Abraham to participate in the forging of the future.

The Lord's statement in Genesis 22:12 poses a similar problem. God tests Abraham's loyalty (cf. v. 1) and then pronounces through his angel: "Now I know that you fear God" (v. 12). The temporal adverb (עַתָּה, "now") gives the distinct impression God discovers information he did not previously know. The narrator begins the chapter with a summary statement of what follows: "Some time after these things God tested Abraham." In light of the angel's declaration in verse 12, the verb נִסָּה, "tested," means here "tested with a view to verifying (Abraham's loyalty)."[33] As verse 12 makes clear, the test is designed primarily for God's benefit, not Abraham's.[34]

---

33. The noun clause after יָדַעְתִּי, "I know," reads literally, "that a fearer of God (are) you." The expression יְרֵא אֱלֹהִים, "fearer of God," is descriptive; it is composed of a substantival participle in construct with the qualifying proper name, which functions as an objective and specifying genitive. The expression also appears in Exodus 18:21; Job 1:1, 8; 2:3; Psalm 66:16; Ecclesiastes 7:18; 8:12. In each case it describes the character and/or lifestyle of honest persons who shun evil. The "fear" in view refers (by metonymy) to a reverence for God that results in respect that reveals itself in obedience. Before confirming his covenantal promise to Abraham, God needs to know that Abraham is such a person. The test is of such a nature that it will bring this character quality, if present within the patriarch, to the forefront.

34. Occasionally the verb נִסָּה, "to test," when used of God testing human beings, refers to a test conducted for the benefit of the one being tested (e.g., Deut. 8:16). However, more often the verb refers to a test conducted for the sake of the one doing the testing. In each case a subordinate clause, usually employing a *Qal* infinitival form of the verb יָדַע, "to know," makes this obvious: Exodus 16:4; Deuteronomy 8:2; 13:4 (Eng. v. 3); Judges 2:22; 3:4; 2 Chronicles 32:31. (In Exodus 16:4 and Judges 2:22, the clause is introduced by *he* interrogative.) No such qualifying clause appears in Genesis 22:1, but the angel's declaration in verse 12 makes it apparent that the purpose of the test is the acquisition of knowledge necessary to verify the truth. When used of human beings conducting a test, the verb has this nuance ("test with a view to acquiring information") as well (see Judg. 6:39; 1 Kings 10:1 [cf. v. 6]; Eccl. 2:1; 7:23; Dan. 1:12, 14).

The declaration in verse 12 (עַתָּה יָדַעְתִּי כִּי, "Now I know that") requires closer examination. It occurs in a handful of other texts. In Exodus 18:11 Jethro, having heard of the Lord's mighty deeds on behalf of Moses and the Israelites, affirms: "Now I know [= am convinced] that the LORD is greater than all the gods." In Judges 17:13 Micah, having hired a Levite to serve in his family shrine, states confidently: "Now I know [for sure] God will make me rich." In 1 Samuel 24:21 (Eng. v. 20) Saul, having been spared once more by David, declares: "[Now] I realize that you will in fact be king." (Note that הִנֵּה, "look," appears after עַתָּה, "now," here.) In 1 Kings 17:24 the Sidonian widow, having witnessed Elijah resuscitate her son, observes: "Now I know [am convinced] that you are a prophet." (Note that זֶה, "this," follows עַתָּה, "now," here.) In Psalm 20:7 (Eng. v. 6) the psalmist, probably in response to an oracle of salvation, says: "Now I am sure that the LORD will deliver his chosen king." In each case the statement comes in response to some type of demonstration of the truth now known and may be translated: "Now I realize," "Now I know for sure," or "Now I'm convinced."[35] In each case an advance in knowledge or a confirmation of what was tentatively or less confidently held to be true is in view.

But why does God need to conduct a test to reveal Abraham's character? After all, in other texts, some of which appear to be stating generalizations, individuals affirm that God knows the inner character and thoughts of human beings (1 Chron. 29:17; Pss. 7:10 [Eng. v. 9]; 44:21–22 [Eng. vv. 20–21]; 94:11; 139:1–4; Jer. 20:12). Furthermore God himself says that he knows people's inner character and thoughts (1 Sam. 16:7; Jer. 17:10; Ezek. 11:5).

As in Genesis 18, it is necessary to consider the context. At the beginning of the story God chooses Abraham to be his covenant partner; the arrangement is comparable to the relationship between a king and his subject that we see in the ancient Near East. By the end of the story Abraham has proven his loyalty (see especially Gen. 22:12, 15–18) by obeying God's commands (cf. Gen. 26:5). God elevates the patriarch

---

35. Because of the presence of הִנֵּה, "look!" 1 Samuel 24:21 [Eng. v. 20] may be an exception. Saul may be saying, "Now [as opposed to before] I realize," but it is possible that the construction lays the logical basis for what follows: "Now look, I really do know that you will be king. . . . So now swear to me . . ." In Deuteronomy 26:10 the construction עַתָּה הִנֵּה, "now look," introduces what logically follows the preceding statement, while in Jeremiah 40:4 it seems to highlight the statement that follows.

to the status of a favored subject who now possesses a royal grant from the great King himself.[36] God **contextualizes** his self-revelation to Abraham (and to the readers of his story) within the relational, metaphorical framework of covenant lord, which is a function of his kingship, perhaps the dominant motif of God's self-revelation in the Old Testament. Consequently we may expect to see him act and hear him speak in ways that reflect the relational role he has assumed within this metaphorical framework.

A closer look at how kings sometimes spoke to their faithful subjects may facilitate our understanding of God's statement in Genesis 22:12. As an example, we may consider the relationship between the Hittite king Suppiluliumas (early fourteenth century B.C.), who had incorporated the city-state of Ugarit into his empire, and his subject Niqmandu, the local ruler of Ugarit. When neighboring kings rebelled against their Hittite overlord and attempted to force Niqmandu to join their uprising, Niqmandu remained loyal. After he defeated the rebels, Suppiluliumas officially acknowledged Niqmandu's loyalty and rewarded him. He said: "Niqmandu is with my enemies an enemy, and with my friends a friend. To the Sun, the Great King, his Lord, he is completely devoted and he will keep the treaty of friendship with Hatti. So the Sun, the Great King, has seen the loyalty of Niqmandu."[37]

In the middle of the seventh century B.C. the Assyrian king Ashurbanipal told Sin-tabni-usur, the prefect of Ur, that enemies of the prefect had tried to turn the king against him, but he acknowledged the prefect's loyalty and assured him that the king's favor would extend to his children as well: "He and Ummanigash have conspired to bring about your death; but since I recognize [lit. "know"] your loyalty, I have granted you (increased) favor. . . . and the favors which I shall bestow on you shall be granted even unto the grandchildren."[38]

Though neither of these texts contains an expression that is identical to what we see in Genesis 22:12, both texts do include official declarations that the king recognizes ("the Great King has seen," "I know")

---

36. On the covenant of grant model, see Moshe Weinfeld, "The Covenant of Grant in the Old Testament and in the Ancient Near East," *JAOS* 90 (1970): 184–203.
37. *PRU*, IV, 51 (17.340:11'b–15') (translation is the author's). For another translation see Klaus Baltzer, *The Covenant Formulary,* trans. David E. Green (Philadelphia: Fortress, 1971), 188.
38. Robert H. Pfeiffer, *State Letters of Assyria* (New Haven, CT: American Oriental Society, 1935), 150 (letter 203).

the loyalty of his subject. Within the covenantal framework of God's relationship with Abraham, it is tempting to see the words "Now I know that you are a God-fearer (i.e., a loyal, obedient subject)" as the divine Lord's official declaration to his subject that he has proven his loyalty in the midst of a crisis and is now worthy to be rewarded with a ratified promise.

We must also consider the language function of the Lord's statement. The statement is not merely informative; it is also evaluative (God expresses a positive judgment on the quality of Abraham's character) and performative. As noted earlier, performative language designates "speech that directly performs some non-linguistic act."[39] While the statement in verse 12 is not technically an oath, it is the prelude to the oath of ratification (cf. vv. 15–18) and, for those familiar with how covenantal relationships work, signals that a monumental divine speech act is imminent in response to Abraham's obedience and God-fearing character.

So, by way of summary, why does God mask his omniscience and present himself as testing (v. 1) his servant and discovering the truth about his servant's character (v. 12)? As we suggested with regard to Genesis 18:21, by revealing himself in this fashion God emphasizes that he is in a dynamic relationship with Abraham in which the patriarch's actions and responses play a formative role in how the future will unfold. In short, Abraham, God's responsible covenantal partner, is granted the dignity of causality. Once God assumes the role of overlord we should not be surprised to see him act and hear him speak accordingly. The evaluative and performative language assured the patriarch that the promise was secure due to his loyalty.

Gaps and Ambiguity

All stories inevitably have gaps where the author omits information that the reader may wish had been provided. Sometimes authors omit material only temporarily and for dramatic effect. The story of Jacob's wrestling match with God provides an example of this (Gen. 32:22–32). Initially Jacob wrestles with "a man" (v. 24). Only later do we discover

---

39. Macky, *Centrality of Metaphor to Biblical Thought,* 16.

that Jacob's opponent is actually God (vv. 28, 30). The author assumes Jacob's **limited point of view** and withholds the identity of Jacob's rival for dramatic purposes. Another example of temporary omission occurs in Judges 14:1–4, where Samson demands that his parents make arrangements for him to marry the Timnite girl. The reader is certainly sympathetic to his parents, who object that it would be improper for Samson to marry a Philistine girl. But then the narrator surprises us by announcing that Samson's parents were not aware that the Lord was actually behind this! By withholding this bit of important information, the narrator highlights the uniqueness of the situation and the surprising dimension of God's **providence** in this instance.

Unfortunately for curious readers, authors do not always provide such information. Sometimes the gaps remain due to the fact that we as readers are so far removed temporally, linguistically, and culturally from the world of the text. Many of the gaps we perceive in a story would not have been present for an ancient Israelite audience, for ancient readers would have intuitively understood nuances of their language and aspects of their culture better than we do. This is one of the reasons why it is important for interpreters to learn as much as possible about the workings of biblical Hebrew and about the culture of the Bible.

Even when we make every effort to fill gaps caused by linguistic and cultural barriers, ambiguity often remains, undoubtedly by authorial design in some cases. After all, ancient Hebrew narrative style tends to be descriptive and relatively terse. This naturally creates ambiguity and invites interpretive speculation. Meir Sternberg, in his extensive analysis of gaps and ambiguity, observes that "gap-filling" is sometimes "performed in a wild or misguided or tendentious fashion" that is "launched and sustained by the reader's subjective concerns . . . rather than by the text's own norms and directives."[40] As an example of "illegitimate gap-filling," Sternberg offers some rabbinical readings of biblical stories: "The hypotheses they frame are often based on assumptions that have no relevance to the world of the Bible (e.g., that Jacob and Esau went to school), receive no support whatever from the textual details, or even fill in what the narrative itself rules out. Where

---

40. Meir Sternberg, *The Poetics of Biblical Narrative* (Bloomington, IN: Indiana University, 1987), 188.

there's a will, the midrash will always find a way."[41] In Christian circles preachers who engage in gap-filling sometimes justify such speculation by calling it "sanctified imagination."

In the face of such excesses, it may be tempting to avoid gap-filling altogether. However, while we should proceed with interpretive caution and not "over-interpret" a text, neither should we overreact and "under-interpret." Sometimes an author gives us enough information to attempt to resolve ambiguity. In such cases it is valid to read the textual clues, connect the dots, as it were, and propose reasonable explanations that are consistent with what the author tells us in the context and with the dictates of common sense.

For example, in 2 Samuel 11:16–17 we read how Joab arranges for Uriah to die in battle. He does not follow David's secret instructions (v. 15), but uses an alternative method. The reader naturally seeks a reason for this discrepancy. Common sense readily allows us to fill the gap in the story. David tells Joab to place Uriah in the front lines and then have his men withdraw suddenly so that Uriah will be isolated and killed. The plan is, of course, ridiculous and betrays David's emotional panic. After all, how would one execute such a preposterous plan— by having each soldier whisper to the next, "Fall back, but don't tell Uriah"? Even if Joab were to conspire against Uriah, what would this do to the soldiers' morale? Furthermore, Uriah would retreat when he saw the others doing so. Surely Joab sees that the king's order makes no sense tactically, but he also makes sure that he accomplishes the king's overall goal—the death of Uriah. He puts Uriah in the front lines and then orders a frontal assault of the enemy position, making it almost certain that Uriah will be killed. Of course, several others must die as well, but apparently this is a small price to pay to accomplish the king's wishes. As Sternberg points out, the narrator never evaluates David's plan; he simply allows Joab's response to do that.[42] Neither does the narrator tell us what was going through Joab's mind. He leaves that to the reader's common sense.

The interpreter faces a more difficult challenge in 2 Kings 9:30–31, which tells of Jezebel's response to Jehu's arrival in Jezreel following his assassination of King Jehoram, Jezebel's son. In preparation for Jehu's

41. Ibid.
42. Ibid., 214.

coming, Jezebel beautifies herself and leans out the window. When he arrives, she asks him an insulting, sarcastic question, comparing him to Zimri, who assassinated Elah forty-four years earlier, but then was killed himself a few days later (cf. 1 Kings 16:9–20). The curious reader naturally wonders why Jezebel acts and speaks in this way. Perhaps she feels her fate is inevitable and, as a queen, wants to die in style. But, given the author's characterization of Jezebel prior to this, it is possible that she is offering herself to Jehu. By beautifying herself she attempts to make herself sexually appealing. By comparing Jehu to Zimri she reminds him that he is in a precarious position. As an assassin needing to consolidate his power, he might find her helpful.[43] In other words, through her appearance she is saying, "You want me." Through her question she is saying, "You need me!" This proposal is consistent with the author's earlier characterization of Jezebel as arrogant, power hungry, and conniving.

This examination of possible motivations for Jezebel's actions illustrates the fact that sometimes we are able to propose legitimate alternatives for filling gaps without being able to pin down a precise explanation with confidence. The account of Jael's assassination of Sisera in Judges 4 provides another illustration of this. We know that Jael's husband, Heber, was an ally of Sisera (v. 17). Consequently we expect her to help, not kill, Sisera. Yet when Sisera arrives on the scene, Jael exploits his trust, lures him into a vulnerable position, and kills him with a tent peg and hammer as he sleeps. The text never reveals Jael's motives.[44] Was she defending her honor?[45] Had her sentiments, in contrast to her husband's, been pro-Israelite all along?[46] Or did she simply realize that common sense and expedience now demanded that her clan transfer its allegiance from defeated Sisera to Israel?[47] We cannot

---

43. Richard G. Smith, "Jehu's Revolt in Deuteronomic Perspective" (Th.M. thesis, Dallas Theological Seminary, 1996), 88–92.

44. For a summary of proposals see Victor P. Hamilton, *Handbook on the Historical Books* (Grand Rapids: Baker, 2001), 122–23.

45. See Victor H. Matthews, "Hospitality and Hostility in Judges 4," *Biblical Theology Bulletin* 21 (1991): 16; as well as his commentary, *Judges and Ruth,* New Cambridge Bible Commentary (Cambridge: Cambridge University, 2004), 68–73.

46. See Robert G. Boling, *Judges,* AB (New York: Doubleday, 1975), 97.

47. D. N. Fewell and D. M. Gunn, "Controlling Perspectives: Women, Men, and Authority of Violence in Judges 4 and 5," *Journal of the American Academy of Religion* 56 (1990): 396.

be certain. Apparently for the author, Jael's actions, not her motives, are what really count.

If the text does not provide enough information to fill its gaps, the safest policy is to respect the text's silence and focus on what it does emphasize. In fact, the narrator's refusal to fill a gap may help the reader focus on what the narrator deems important. For example, the story of David's adulterous encounter with Bathsheba (2 Sam. 11:1–5) never gives us insight into Bathsheba's emotions, thoughts, or motives. The focus is on David's actions. A series of *wayyiqtol* clauses informs us, "he got up, walked around, saw, sent, sent [again], and took (NET, "to set")." Along the way Bathsheba is described by both the narrator (v. 2b, in a noun clause and an offline clause) and by David's messenger (v. 3b), but she is not a participant in the main story line until verse 4, where we are told that she "came" to David after "he took" her.[48] The focus quickly returns to David, however, as we are told that "he had sexual relations with her." Only at this point, in the aftermath of the encounter, does Bathsheba become the focus ("she returned, conceived, sent word, said [NET, "saying"]"). It is obvious that the narrator wants to emphasize David's aggressive pursuit of Bathsheba and his culpability. Bathsheba's role in the drama seems to be passive; one must not attempt to exonerate David, even partially, by casting her in the role of a wily temptress. Furthermore, we cannot be sure if resistance to the king's order was even a genuine option for her.

The Narrator's Authority and Perspective

In Old Testament stories the narrator usually assumes an omniscient, divine perspective that transcends the event *per se* and exceeds what a mere eyewitness would have perceived. He can invade the privacy of a character's mind (1 Sam. 20:26), is aware of events and statements that are outside the scope of the source material ordinarily available to biblical authors (Judg. 3:24–25; 5:28–30), and has theological insight into the significance of events (Judg. 14:4). As such the narrator speaks with divine authority. Yairah Amit observes: "The narrator knows all there is to know about the world of the story—even the secret thoughts and feelings of the characters, including God. Therefore, in a biblical story,

---

48. The LXX disagrees with the Hebrew text here, reading "and he [David] came to her."

God is to be trusted for reasons of faith, and the narrator is to be trusted, in this respect, as above God and as the source of the report about God. Both God and the narrator must be trustworthy and hence are benchmarks of trustworthiness for all other personae. Whatever accords with the narrator's statements or God's must be beyond doubt."[49]

The principle of the narrator's authority is foundational to correct interpretation. In the present postmodern hermeneutical milieu, it is in vogue to deconstruct a text and challenge its presuppositions and theological agenda. However, if the Old Testament narratives are truly Scripture, the interpreter must respect the narrator's authority. For example, some deconstruct the story of David's confrontation with Nabal (1 Sam. 25) in such a way as to make Nabal a sympathetic character subjected to extortion by a man (David) running a Mafia-like "protection" racket. David may well have been engaging in a form of extortion, though it is also possible that he did indeed protect Nabal's herdsmen from bandits. Given his precarious situation, David was forced to scrounge in order to survive. At least he had not become a common bandit who simply robbed and pillaged helpless victims. As outlaws go, he was on the more civilized end of the spectrum. However, this is not the focus of the narrator. Without necessarily endorsing David's activity, the narrator depicts Nabal as a fool (v. 3), an assessment with which both Nabal's servant (v. 17) and his wife (v. 25) agree. Nabal's attitude stands in stark contrast to that of his wise wife (cf. v. 3), who is well aware of David's divine calling and destiny (vv. 28–30). Her words suggest that Nabal should have responded positively to David because of who David was—the Lord's chosen king and the protector of Israel. Instead Nabal treated David as if he were merely an outlaw. Through no fault of his own, David may have been forced to stoop to such an occupation, but Nabal should have viewed the situation in a broader light and shown him compassion out of gratitude for what he had accomplished for Israel in the past. If the narrative is indeed Scripture, the interpreter does not have the right to overturn the narrator's depiction and assessment of David and Nabal.[50]

---

49. Yairah Amit, *Reading Biblical Narratives: Literary Criticism and the Hebrew Bible,* trans. Israel Lotan (Minneapolis: Fortress, 2001), 95.

50. For a helpful discussion of the narrator's point of view in the story, see John Kessler, "Sexuality and Politics: The Motif of the Displaced Husband in the Books of Samuel," *CBQ* 62 (2000): 413.

Of course, a narrator will sometimes speak from a **limited point of view**. Occasionally the narrator will, for rhetorical or dramatic purposes, reflect the point of view of one of the characters or of an observer.[51] Narrators sometimes interrupt the main line of the discourse with a clause beginning with וְהִנֵּה, "and look," signaling a shift from an external to an internal point of view.[52] For example, in Ruth 3:8, as Boaz wakes up, we read: "Look! There was a woman lying at his legs." The statement is correct as far as it goes, but it is also much more vague than we might expect. After all, we know the woman is Ruth, because the narrator has told us (vv. 6–7), but he heightens the dramatic effect by assuming Boaz's perspective and thereby inviting us to experience the event as Boaz did.[53]

Unfortunately biblical narrators do not routinely signal their use of a limited perspective. The interpreter must often rely on broader contextual clues to know when this literary device is being utilized. Failure to detect its use can lead to wrong historical conclusions. For example, according to Judges 1:19, the men of Judah, despite being accompanied and energized by the Lord himself, were unable to defeat the people of the plains, because the latter "had iron chariots" in their arsenal. The statement begs us to ask, "Since when have chariots been able to thwart God's purposes and power?" After all, the Lord destroyed the Egyptian chariots in the Red Sea (Exod. 14:23–28; 15:4). He promised to give the Canaanite chariots into Israel's hands and instructed Joshua to burn them (Josh. 11:4–6, 9). Later Joshua assured the tribe of Joseph that the Canaanite iron chariots would not prevent them from conquering the plains (Josh. 17:16–18). In Judges 4–5 we read how the Lord annihilated the iron chariots of Sisera. But according to Judges 1:19, the army of Judah was unable to overcome iron chariots, even though the Lord was with them! In its larger literary context the passage cannot mean what it appears to say. We soon discover there is more here than meets the eye. A few verses later the author explains that the people's failure was really due to spiritual compromise and idolatry (Judg. 2:1–5). Judges 1:19 must reflect the people's limited and warped perspective,

---

51. See Robert B. Chisholm Jr., "A Rhetorical Use of Point of View in Old Testament Narrative," *BSac* 159 (2002): 404–14.
52. See Berlin, *Poetics and Interpretation of Biblical Narrative,* 91–95.
53. See ibid., 91–92.

not the author's own interpretation.[54] The author is toying with his audience here. With tongue in cheek, as it were, he raises our curiosity by giving us a signal that something is wrong. Expecting us to object, he prepares the way for the real explanation for Israel's partial success.

Sometimes it is difficult to know when the narrator is utilizing a limited perspective. For example, 2 Chronicles 28:23 observes that Ahaz "offered sacrifices to the gods of Damascus, who had defeated him" (lit. translation). Are we to take this statement at face value? The text may simply reflect Ahaz's polytheistic perspective: he thought these gods had defeated him. However, we should not rush to this conclusion. In the worldview of the narrator, these gods may actually exist and possess the capability of defeating God's people. Even if this is the case, the Chronicler qualifies this view by making it clear that these gods were able to defeat Judah only because the Lord gave his rebellious people over to the enemy (see vv. 5, 19)

For rhetorical purposes the authoritative narrator sometimes imposes an **idealized perspective** on his account of events that does not necessarily coincide with the historical reality. For example, the book of Judges views Israel in a unified manner that may not have characterized the nation during the period of the judges. The book's prologue speaks of Israel as a nation. While chapter 1 focuses on the individual efforts of the various tribes, the encounter at Bokim is presented as encompassing the entire nation (2:4). The theological interpretation of the period in 2:6–3:6 consistently takes a national perspective. It is Israel that sins, suffers, cries for help, and experiences the Lord's deliverance. This perspective also marks the Othniel account at the beginning of the book's central section (3:7–11). Othniel's tribal affiliation is not mentioned; he is simply Israel's deliverer. From the book's prologue we know Othniel lived in the south, yet he rescued Israel from a northern invader. The **pan-Israelite** perspective also appears in the framework of the book's central section and in the epilogue, where we see the tribes congregating at Mizpah and Bethel to handle the problems raised by the murder of the Levite's concubine.

---

54. See Webb, *The Book of Judges: An Integrated Reading,* 90. Failing to detect the literary irony and obviously troubled by the apparent implications of the statement, the Targum reads here, "because they sinned, they were not able to drive out." See Robert H. O'Connell, *The Rhetoric of the Book of Judges* (Leiden: Brill, 1996), 447.

This pan-Israelite perspective appears to be contrived when one examines the stories of the central section in detail, for the narrated events were restricted to specific locations.[55] The Canaanite oppression under Jabin and Sisera included only the northern tribes. Zebulun and Naphtali were specifically summoned for battle (4:6, 10; cf. 5:18), though the victory song mentions the involvement, as well as the non-participation, of others (5:14–17). Judah is conspicuous by its absence. Gideon's forces came from the northern and central regions (6:35), not the south, and Abimelech, though called a ruler over Israel (9:22), seems to have operated only in the Shechem area. Jephthah operated primarily in the central and southern regions (10:8–9), while Samson's activities were localized in the south. Despite the statement that he ruled Israel for twenty years, he was opposed, at least initially, by the people of Judah (15:11–13).

The localized traditions of the book's central section may very well have originated independently and functioned initially within tribal or regional circles. But to speculate on their prior oral or literary life is ultimately futile. The reality is that the editor responsible for the book in its final form has integrated these stories with the prologue thematically and given them a pan-Israelite framework. This may look artificial and anachronistic, for the united Israel depicted in Joshua reemerges only after the judges' period and then only for a relatively brief time. But it is best to give the narrator the benefit of the doubt. By viewing regional developments as national in scope, the present structure of the book keeps before its readers the ideal of a unified Israel portrayed in Joshua. It also forces readers to consider the broader, theological ramifications of tribal incidents. For the narrator, when one region suffered invasion, Israel suffered invasion. Divine discipline may have impacted only some of the tribes directly, but it expressed God's displeasure with the entire sinful nation. When peace was restored to one region, Israel was made intact and the whole land experienced rest.[56] Portraying regional judges as having national authority reflects the ideal of national solidarity under a suitable leader (Deut. 17:14–20; cf. Judg. 17:6; 21:25). In

---

55. See, for example, Ernst Sellin and Georg Fohrer, *Introduction to the Old Testament,* trans. David E. Green (Nashville: Abingdon, 1968), 207.

56. For more on the book's pan-Israelite perspective, see John Goldingay, *Old Testament Theology,* vol. 1, *Israel's Gospel* (Downer's Grove, IL: InterVarsity, 2003), 531–33.

short, the editorial frame militantly counters the spirit of national disunity and disintegration portrayed in the stories, keeps alive the ideal presented in Joshua, and paves the way for the realization of the ideal under the monarchy.

Macroplot

Old Testament narratives are not simply anthologies of self-contained, isolated short stories. While they may differ from a modern novel, Old Testament narratives do exhibit a **macroplot**—a larger plot that encompasses but also transcends the individual stories. Each individual story must be viewed within the context of this macroplot. Just as one cannot fully or properly appreciate a scene in a movie apart from viewing the entire film, so one cannot understand the purpose of an individual **scene** or story in a biblical narrative apart from its macroplot.

For example, 2 Samuel 16:1–4 tells how Ziba, the servant of Jonathan's lame son Mephibosheth (2 Sam. 9:1–13), meets David as he is fleeing Jerusalem in the face of Absalom's revolt. Ziba brings David a couple of donkeys and a great deal of food. He informs David that his master, Mephibosheth, has stayed in Jerusalem in hopes that Israel will make him king. Taking Ziba's report at face value, David decrees that Mephibosheth's property be given to loyal Ziba. However, one cannot read this scene in isolation. When David returns to the city after Absalom's death, Mephibosheth greets the king, declares his loyalty, and claims that Ziba has lied (2 Sam. 19:24–30). David is not certain who is telling the truth, so he reverses his earlier decree to Ziba and divides Mephibosheth's property evenly between Ziba and Mephibosheth. Mephibosheth declines the offer, claiming that his only concern is the king's safety. Does the text give us any clues to resolve the dilemma? The narrator tells us that Mephibosheth had been mourning since the day David left the city (v. 24). This would be a peculiar way for him to act if he expected to be made king (cf. 2 Sam. 16:3). In retrospect, the explanation given by Ziba for Mephibosheth's absence seems unlikely. Apparently Ziba had been lying.

The **episode** in Genesis 38 seems to be a self-contained story about Judah that has its own **plot structure**. Though it may have once circulated independently among Judah's descendants, it now has a literary context that informs its meaning and significance. It is part of the so-called Joseph story in Genesis 37–50, which is actually the story of how two brothers, Judah and Joseph, were instrumental in their family's history and in the outworking of God's promise to Abraham and the patriarchs.[57] At the beginning of the macroplot Judah is a **foil** for Joseph—his lack of self-control contrasts sharply with Joseph's moral purity (Gen. 39). As the story unfolds, God's providential intervention transforms the greedy, self-righteous Judah of chapter 38 into the self-sacrificing, compassionate Judah of chapter 45 and paves the way for family harmony, which is essential if the covenant community is to experience the fulfillment of God's promise.

As noted earlier, Old Testament narrative encompasses several genres, in addition to its stories. In developing a book's macroplot, an interpreter has the task of explaining how the arrangement of literary materials in any given book contributes to its overall message and purpose. For example, the book of Ruth is a classic example of a story, but it ends with a brief genealogy. At first, this seems like a lame way for such an enjoyable and profound story to end. Careful reflection reveals the genealogy has an important function as the story's epilogue. In the book's final episode the people of Bethlehem ask God to bless the marriage of Boaz and Ruth with a child who will bring the family fame and continue the line of Perez (Ruth 4:11–12). The genealogy shows that the prayer was fulfilled and that God's blessings sometimes extend beyond the lifetime of the recipients. Through Boaz and Ruth's great-grandson David, God rewarded their faithfulness in a way that brought great fame to the family and to his people Israel.

The boundary lists in Joshua 13–21, while quite boring and seemingly irrelevant to modern readers, had both a practical and theological function in their ancient context. If tribes disputed over territorial claims and limits, arbitrators could go to these lists to settle the disagreement. More importantly, the lengthy lists drive home the point that Israel had established a foothold in the land; God had kept his promise to give the land to his people.

---

57. On the literary and thematic relationship of chapter 38 to what immediately precedes and follows, see Robert Alter, *The Art of Biblical Narrative* (New York: Basic Books, 1981), 3–12.

Intertextuality

Foreshadowing

Recognizing that Old Testament narrative is both story and history enables us to detect **intertextuality**, interrelationships between texts. Literary analysis reveals the presence of foreshadowing, a device that is well known in modern literature and film. In Exodus 2:17–19 Moses rescues Reuel's daughters from some shepherds. This brief and apparently minor episode casts Moses in the role of deliverer and foreshadows how the Lord will use him to deliver oppressed Israel. In Judges 14 Samson, empowered by God's Spirit, kills a roaring lion (vv. 5–6) and later eats some honey from the lion's carcass (vv. 8–9). Both of these events reveal important features of Samson's character and have a foreshadowing function in the story. The killing of the lion shows what Samson is capable of accomplishing in God's strength. Later in the story the Philistines attack Samson like a lion.[58] Their shouts correspond to the lion's roar. God's Spirit descends (צָלַח) upon Samson and he supernaturally defeats the Philistines, just as he supernaturally killed the lion. Samson's eating the honey shows he has difficulty controlling his physical desires and suggests that satisfying his appetites is more important to him than maintaining his status as a Nazirite. It also foreshadows his demise, which stems from his unbridled urge for sexual gratification. The sweet honey foreshadows the charms of Delilah, who uses her psychological hold over Samson to destroy him. Samson can resist and defeat lions, but not honey.[59] He is a lion killer with a sweet tooth!

Parallelism and Narrative Typology

Literary analysis also reveals the presence of parallelism at the level of the **macroplot** and **macrostructure**. On one occasion, during the period when Saul is trying to kill David, David finds Saul sleeping in his camp (1 Sam. 26). David's nephew Abishai volunteers to kill Saul,

---

58. Note Hebrew לִקְרָאתוֹ, "to meet him," in both 14:5 and 15:14.
59. See Chisholm, *From Exegesis to Exposition,* 165.

but David orders him not to do so (vv. 7–12), proving his loyalty to Saul. Later in David's career, as he flees for his life from Absalom, one of Saul's relatives, a Benjaminite named Shimei, confronts him (2 Sam. 16:5–14). Shimei throws stones and dirt at David and denounces him as a murderer. According to Shimei, the Lord is punishing David for his crimes against the house of Saul by taking the kingship from him and giving it to Absalom.[60] As Shimei spews out his verbal poison, Abishai volunteers to silence Shimei with one swift stroke of his sword. But David rebukes him and prohibits him from harming Shimei. This episode parallels the earlier incident when Abishai volunteered to kill Saul. David's refusal to kill this Benjaminite drives home the point that David has never initiated or endorsed any hostile actions against Saul or his royal house.

In Judges–1 Samuel the anonymous mothers of Samson (Judg. 13) and Micah (Judg. 17) serve as **foils** for Hannah (1 Sam. 1). In contrast to Samson's mother, whose miraculously conceived Nazirite son failed to understand his true role as the Lord's deliverer and never rose to the level of an effective leader, Hannah supernaturally gives birth to a Nazirite son through whom the Lord will restore effective leadership to Israel. In contrast to Micah's mother, whose misguided actions and obsession with idols contributed to the Danites' unauthorized **cult**, Hannah's commitment to the Lord becomes the catalyst for the revival of genuine Yahweh worship through the spiritual leadership of her son Samuel.

The three accounts even begin the same way:

1. Judges 13:2   וַיְהִי אִישׁ אֶחָד מִצָּרְעָה . . . וּשְׁמוֹ מָנוֹחַ
                      "Now there was a certain man from Zorah . . .
                      whose name was Manoah"

---

60. It is likely that Shimei and other Benjaminites believed that David was responsible for the deaths of Saul and Jonathan (after all, David was employed by the Philistines at the time of Saul's death), Abner (after all, it was David's nephew and right hand man, Joab, who murdered Abner), and Ishbosheth (after all, Ishbosheth's murderers took their victim's head to David). It is possible that Shimei was also referring, at least in part, to the incident recorded in 2 Samuel 21:1–9, which tells how David, as an act of justice and with the Lord's approval, handed seven descendants of Saul over to the Gibeonites for execution.

2. Judges 17:1   וַיְהִי־אִישׁ מֵהַר־אֶפְרַיִם וּשְׁמוֹ מִיכָיְהוּ
"Now there was a man from the hill country of Ephraim whose name was Micaiah"

3. 1 Samuel 1:1   וַיְהִי אִישׁ אֶחָד מִן־הָרָמָתַיִם . . . וּשְׁמוֹ אֶלְקָנָה
"Now there was a certain man from Ramathaim . . . whose name was Elkanah"

The formula "now there was a (certain) man from (geographical name) . . . whose name was (personal name)" seems to be a stylized way of introducing a new story. However, in the Old Testament this formula appears only in these three passages and in 1 Samuel 9:1, where Saul's family background is introduced. This suggests that the introductory formula is a linking device at the macrostructural level.[61]

Literary parallelism sometimes involves **narrative typology**, where earlier characters supply the pattern for a later character in the story. This in turn enables the reader to discern the narrator's evaluation of the later character's career. For example, 1 Samuel 17 depicts a youthful David as a new giant killer in the mold of Joshua, Caleb, and Othniel. However, later, when he succumbs to lust,[62] he turns into a new Samson. Murder, rape, and civil war dominate the literary landscape of 2 Samuel from this point on. The account of the turmoil that takes over his household and kingdom resembles the judges' period as described in the epilogue to the book of Judges (Judg. 17–21), which ironically follows (literarily, though not chronologically) the story of Samson's demise.

Allusion

Sometimes a narrator consciously alludes to an earlier story in order to draw a thematic and/or theological correlation between events. A classic example of literary allusion occurs in Judges 19, which displays

---

61. See Robert B. Chisholm Jr., "The Role of Women in the Rhetorical Strategy of the Book of Judges," in *Integrity of Heart, Skillfulness of Hands: Biblical and Leadership Studies in Honor of Donald K. Campbell*, ed. Charles H. Dyer and Roy B. Zuck (Grand Rapids: Baker, 1994), 46–49.

62. In the Hebrew Bible the statement "he saw a woman" appears in both Judges 16:1 and 2 Samuel 11:2, but nowhere between these two texts.

unmistakable parallels to Genesis 19.[63] In the earlier story, when the angels arrived in Sodom, Lot invited them to his home. They said they would spend the night in the town square, but Lot, aware of the danger that resided in the town, insisted they stay with him. In the Judges 19 account, when the Levite arrives in Gibeah with his concubine, no one shows him hospitality, except for an old man who is not a native of the town. Like Lot, he insists that the visitors not spend the night in the town square. When the men of Sodom found out about Lot's guests, they demanded that Lot send them out so they could rape them. In the same way, the men of Gibeah insist that the old man hand over the Levite so they can abuse him. Like Lot, the old man follows a warped understanding of the law of hospitality by offering two women to the men outside his door. However, in subtle ways, his offer is more calloused than Lot's. Lot offered his two daughters; the old man offers his daughter and another man's concubine. Furthermore, Lot told the Sodomites: "Do to them whatever you please" (Gen. 19:8; lit. "do to them according to what is good in your eyes"). The old man uses almost identical words (Judg. 19:24, lit. "do to them what is good in your eyes"), but he prefaces this with the words: "I will send them out and you can abuse them." The point of the allusion is clear—Gibeah has become the new Sodom, populated by thugs who are morally blind. From the narrator's perspective, this is what can and did happen when "each man did what he considered to be right" (Judg. 17:6; 21:25; lit. "each man did what was right in his eyes").

Another example of literary allusion occurs in 2 Samuel 13, where there are unmistakable echoes of Judges 19. As noted above, David's moral weakness casts him in the role of a second Samson. Samson is the last leader to appear in Judges. Judges 17–21, which directly follow the Samson story, picture a time of anarchy characterized by murder, civil war and the abuse of women—the very things that dominate David's experience after his sin with Bathsheba. Robert Polzin draws several parallels between Judges 19–21 and 2 Samuel 13, the most striking of which are the following:

---

63. For a chart showing the verbal parallels between Genesis 19 and Judges 19, see Daniel I. Block, *Judges, Ruth,* NAC (Nashville: Broadman & Holman, 1999), 532–34.

1. After raping Tamar, Amnon callously tells her, "Get up and leave!" His words echo the Levite's statement to his concubine when he discovered her the morning after her horrible experience, "Get up, let's leave!" In both cases קוּם and הָלַךְ are used.
2. Both crimes are called a "disgraceful thing" (נְבָלָה; Judg. 19:23–24; 2 Sam. 13:12).
3. Israel's response to the concubine's murder (Judg. 19:30) sounds very much like Tamar's appeal to Amnon (2 Sam. 13:12).
4. Both passages use the *Piel* of עָנָה, "abuse, humiliate," to describe the crime (cf. Judg. 19:24; 20:5 with 2 Sam. 13:12, 14, 22, 32).
5. The Ephraimite's appeal to the men of Gibeah ("No, my brothers! Don't do this wicked thing!" Judg. 19:23) is structurally identical to Tamar's words to Amnon ("No, my brother! Don't humiliate me!" 2 Sam. 13:12). As Polzin indicates, "such an expression (*'al* plus 'brother[s]' plus *'al* plus verb) occurs nowhere else in biblical narrative."[64]

To sum up, it seems that the author is subtitling Amnon's rape of Tamar "Gibeah revisited." David's Samson-like sin brought the kind of chaos typical of the judges' period to the royal house. Soon that chaos spread to the whole nation, as Absalom started a civil war and David's sons fought for the crown.

Echoing

Echoing is a literary device that is a sort of *déjà vu* technique. It has been misunderstood by many **source critics**, who typically label it a "doublet" and usually attribute it to different and competing literary sources. In this case an **episode** within the larger story echoes an earlier episode, inviting the reader to note the similarity, make comparisons and/or contrasts, and draw thematic and even theological correlations between the episodes. This kind of repetition may appear to be contrived, but anyone who has seriously reflected on the old adage

---

64. See Robert Polzin, *David and the Deuteronomist* (Bloomington, IN: Indiana University, 1993), 136–38.

"history repeats itself" knows that history and the real life experiences of people are characterized by such repetition and patterns.[65]

A well-known example of this technique can be found in the two accounts in which Abram/Abraham lies about the identity of his wife (Gen. 12:10–20; 20:1–18). In the second episode we learn that Abraham typically used this ploy during his travels (20:13). Later his son even resorts to the same strategy (Gen. 26:7–10). The narrator includes the second story to show that just prior to Isaac's birth, Abraham's character is still flawed and his faith still incomplete, despite all that transpired during the intervening twenty-four years. This heightens the tension of the story as we continue to wonder if Abraham will prove faithful to God's challenge and receive the covenant in its full form (see 17:1–8). It sets the stage for the ultimate test, which Abraham passes with flying colors (22:1–17).

One of the most sophisticated uses of echoing appears in the Jacob story. By the time Jacob returns to Bethel, he has committed himself wholeheartedly to the Lord. The Lord has fulfilled Jacob's condition (!) (cf. 35:3 with 28:20), and Jacob is more than ready to serve him. God again gives him a new name (cf. 35:10 with 32:28) and once more makes Jacob the recipient of the Abrahamic promise (cf. 35:11–12 with 28:13–15). Jacob once more sanctifies the site and names it Bethel (cf. 35:14–15 with 28:18–19).

The repetition of earlier actions and statements in 35:10–15 might suggest that different sources/traditions have been merged in the narrative, but a more likely explanation is that earlier declarations are formalized (made official) and earlier events reactualized in chapter 35. When Jacob returns to Bethel his spiritual journey is complete. God reiterates the promise, linking it with Jacob's new name as if to remind him that dependence on the God who promises is the key to the divine blessing being realized. On his initial visit to Bethel, Jacob is not ready to accept the God who promises on God's terms. But now, after the wrestling match at Penuel, he is prepared to do so. How appropriate that the renaming at Penuel is reactualized as the promise is reiterated and that Jacob reactualizes his worship, this time without making a bargain with God!

---

65. Alter discusses this literary phenomenon and postulates the concept of type scenes to explain at least some of the examples. See Alter, *Art of Biblical Narrative,* 47–62.

Repetition of Keywords

Another rhetorical use of repetition in narrative involves **keywords**. By repeating certain terms or phrases the narrator can develop themes and highlight irony and contrasts. A fine example of this occurs in 2 Kings 1:9–15. One of King Ahaziah's captains disrespectfully demands that Elijah "come down" (יָרַד) from the hilltop where he is sitting and report to the king (v. 9). Elijah responds by calling fire down (יָרַד) on the captain and his fifty soldiers (v. 10a). The narrator then reports that fire did indeed come down (יָרַד) and consume them (v. 10b). A second captain is sent with the same outcome. (Note the threefold use of יָרַד in vv. 11–12). The repetition of the word highlights the fact that the messengers' disrespect (epitomized by their command "come down") is the reason for their destruction (described by the report "fire came down"). In the story's third panel, a third captain finally shows the prophet the respect he is due as God's servant and the king's superior. The Lord commands Elijah to "go down" (יָרַד, v. 15), indicating that the prophet is subject to the Lord's authority, not the king's. This time Elijah, rather than destructive fire, goes down (יָרַד), proving that respect for God's prophet produces positive results, while disrespect has negative repercussions.

Repetition of the keyword נָחַם (in the *Niphal* verbal stem) facilitates irony in the story of Saul's rejection in 1 Samuel 15. According to verse 11, the Lord "regretted" (נִחַם) that he had made Saul king. Later the narrator repeats this point (v. 35). In verse 29 Samuel solemnly affirms that God does not lie or "change his mind" (נִחַם). Amit wrongly concludes that Samuel erroneously says God does not change his mind, when both God and the narrator (vv. 11, 35) state otherwise.[66] Though the same Hebrew verb is used in all three passages, this need not mean that it has the same shade of meaning or connotation in each case. God's and the narrator's statements pertain to a past action (God's making Saul king) that God subsequently regrets. Samuel's statement pertains to God's future course of action with respect to Saul. By saying that God will not change his mind in this case, Samuel marks his announcement about Saul's demise as an unconditional decree. In short, Amit's

---

66. Amit, *Reading Biblical Narratives,* 100–101.

semantic analysis mixes apples and oranges, as it were.[67] By seeing a contradiction, she misses the irony that drips from the passage. God "changes his mind" (regrets) that he made Saul king and consequently decides that he will not "change his mind" (retract his decree) about removing Saul from kingship.

The story of Jonah contains several examples of keywords. The root רעע, "be evil," is especially prominent in the book. In 1:2 Nineveh is characterized as a city of moral "evil" (רָעָה). Though Jonah is commissioned to expose the Ninevites' evil and warn them of impending judgment, he runs away and becomes, ironically, an agent of רָעָה in the pagan world when he jeopardizes the sailors' lives. In 1:7–8 the Hebrew word רָעָה refers to the storm and has the nuance of "disaster," or perhaps even "judgment." When Jonah finally carries out his commission, the Ninevites repent of their "evil" (רָעָה) ways (3:8, 10), prompting God, in accordance with his merciful character (4:2), to relent from sending the "destruction" or judgment (רָעָה) he threatened (3:10). However, God's gracious treatment of the Ninevites causes Jonah to be greatly "displeased" (רָעַע, 4:1). In an effort to ease Jonah's "discomfort" (רָעָה, 4:6), God causes a plant to grow up over the prophet to provide some shade. However, when the Lord removes this plant the next day, one detects the double meaning in the words of 4:6 (lit. "to deliver Jonah from his רָעָה"). God's ultimate purpose is to deliver Jonah from his morally wrong attitude, not to make him physically comfortable. Ironically, the book began with the pagan Ninevites characterized by רָעָה; by its conclusion the word more aptly describes the prophet!

Another keyword in Jonah is the adjective גָּדוֹל, "great." Because Nineveh is such a great city (1:2; 3:2–3; 4:11), its reclamation warrants God's attention and prompts him to intervene in human affairs in extraordinary ways. To get his reluctant, runaway prophet to journey to this great city, the Lord hurls a great wind into the sea that in turn causes a great storm (1:4, 12; the divine action is mirrored in the human realm when the sailors hurl the ship's cargo and eventually Jonah into the sea, cf. 1:5, 15). Though Jonah sleeps through the storm until awakened by the captain of the ship, the sailors respond appropriately with great fear (1:10, 16), something Jonah claims to possess (cf. 1:9). When the

---

67. See Long, *Reign and Rejection of King Saul,* 163.

sailors throw Jonah into the sea, the Lord sends a great fish to rescue him. After expending all this effort, God finally coerces his prophet to go to Nineveh, where the Ninevites repent in mass, even including the animals in the ceremony. However, this development causes Jonah to be greatly displeased (4:1, the book's first emphatic statement about the prophet). As he pouts under the hot sun, God provides him with extra shade, causing him to rejoice greatly (4:6). Ironically, while God is doing great deeds to reclaim a great city—deeds that generate great fear among the pagans—the word גָּדוֹל only applies in Jonah's case to his displeasure over the Ninevites' salvation and his own expression of self-interest.

CONCLUSION: INTERPRETIVE PRINCIPLES

This chapter has attempted to illustrate the importance of recognizing the literary dimension of Old Testament narrative when interpreting this genre of Scripture. Several interpretive principles emerge from our discussion. Here are some guidelines for interpreting narrative literature:

1. Analyze the basic elements of a story (setting, characterization, plot) and determine how they contribute to its message.
2. Identify a text's **discourse structure**, **dramatic structure**, and other structural features and explain how they contribute to the story's message and impact.
3. Analyze the narrative's quotations and dialogues with respect to their **discourse type** and **speech function**.
4. Avoid excesses when filling gaps, but attempt to resolve ambiguity in a cautious manner that is sensitive to context and utilizes common sense.
5. Respect the authority of the narrator and attempt to identify his assessment of events and characters. However, also be alert for the rhetorical use of a **limited or idealized point of view**.
6. Relate individual stories to their **macroplot** and explain how the various genres within a book contribute to its overall message.
7. Be sensitive to matters of **intertextuality** and how they contribute to the message of the narrative.

Some of these features (particularly quotations and intertextual allusions) may not be present in every text, but most narratives do contain nearly all of these elements, if not all of them. In some cases, certain features may be more prominent than others or only minimally represented.

2

PRIMARY THEMES OF
THE HISTORICAL BOOKS

JOSHUA

The book of Joshua tells how Joshua led Israel into the Promised Land. Israel defeated the Canaanites and settled in the land. Joshua gave each tribe its allotted portion of land and urged the nation to be loyal to the Lord and to take possession of the territory granted to them.

Primary Themes

The dominant theme of the book is the faithfulness of God. After the long list of land allocations, the narrator provides this summary: "So the LORD gave Israel all the land he had solemnly promised to their ancestors, and they conquered it and lived in it. The LORD made them secure, in fulfillment of all he had solemnly promised their ancestors. None of their enemies could resist them. Not one of the LORD's faithful promises to the family of Israel was left unfulfilled; every one was realized" (Josh. 21:43–45; cf. 23:14). The earlier accounts of Israel's military successes and the lengthy list of tribal boundaries provide the evidence for the truth of the narrator's assertion. On an individual level, Caleb, a paradigm of faith, received the land the Lord had promised him for his loyalty in the wilderness (14:6–15), as did Joshua (24:29–30).

A corollary of God's faithfulness is his presence with his people. At the very beginning of the book, the Lord assured Joshua of his presence (1:5, 9, 17). When Israel crossed the Jordan, the ark of the covenant, the tangible reminder of the Lord's presence among his people, was paraded before Israel (chaps. 3–4). At Jericho the priests carried the ark as they marched around the city (chap. 6). Before the campaign against Jericho, the Lord sent the general of his heavenly army to assure Joshua of his presence in the battle (5:13–15). The Lord assured Joshua that he, the Lord, would defeat the city (6:2). Joshua later reminded the people, "the LORD your God fights for you" (23:3).

The power of the Lord is displayed and affirmed throughout the book. Rahab, a Canaanite harlot, told the Israelite spies that the native population of the land was paralyzed with fear when they heard of the Lord's mighty deeds at the Red Sea and of his victories over the Amorite kings on the eastern side of the Jordan (2:10–11). The Lord duplicated the Red Sea crossing when he dried up the waters of the Jordan so the people could cross into the Promised Land on dry ground (4:23). Once again news of the Lord's power paralyzed the Canaanites with fear (5:1). In the aftermath of this event, Joshua revealed to the people the Lord's purpose in demonstrating his strength. He wanted all the nations to recognize his power and he desired that this display of his greatness would motivate his people to fear (obey) him (4:24). In the battle at Gibeon the Lord hurled large hailstones down upon the enemy and supernaturally intervened so that Israel could complete the victory (10:6–14). In the north the Israelites defeated the Canaanite forces, even though the enemy had horses and chariots (11:4–9). As if to affirm that the Lord was more powerful than the horses and chariots on which the enemy relied so heavily, Joshua hamstrung the horses and burned the chariots. Later he assured the tribe of Joseph that the Canaanite horses and chariots posed no real obstacle to victory (17:16–18).

However, success would not be automatic. The Lord would enable the people to complete the conquest and to drive out the remaining nations only if they remained loyal to him. They must obey the Law of Moses, avoid alliances with the nations, and reject the gods of the nations (23:5–8). Joshua reminded the people how the Lord had delivered them from Egypt and brought them into the land (24:2–13). He alone was worthy of their obedience and worship; they must not worship the gods of their ancestors, the gods of Egypt, or the gods of the Amorites (24:14–15). The covenant must be preserved. To this end the people renewed the covenant at Gilgal after they crossed the Jordan. The new generation, which had not been circumcised, submitted to the covenantal rite (5:2–9). Following the victory at Ai, Joshua assembled the people at Ebal and Gerizim and read them the Law, reminding them of the covenantal blessings (promised rewards for obedience) and curses (threatened judgments for disobedience) (8:30–35). Joshua warned the people that assimilation to the Canaanite way of life would bring disaster (23:9–13). The faithfulness of the Lord was a two-edged sword. His promises were faithful (23:14), but his threats were just as reliable. If Israel violated the covenant and worshiped other gods, the Lord would remove them from the land he had given them (23:15–16). In a final covenant renewal ceremony Joshua reminded the people that the Lord is "a jealous God" who would punish them for their rebellion (24:19–28).

Earlier in the book the Lord had given Israel vivid object lessons of the importance of obedience. When Achan stole some of the forbidden items from Jericho, he was executed and covered with a heap of stones (7:25–26). Once Israel had purged the evil from its midst, God blessed them with a resounding victory at Ai, where the Israelites raised another heap of stones over the defeated enemy king (8:29). These two heaps of stones stood as perpetual reminders to Israel of the consequences of disobedience and obedience.

In contrast to disobedient Achan, Caleb and Joshua were paradigms of God's blessing. In the wilderness, when the spies tried to discourage the people, Caleb remained loyal to the Lord. The Lord promised him a portion in the Promised Land. When Israel invaded the land, Caleb, empowered by the Lord, took his allotted portion from the powerful Anakites (14:6–15; 15:13–17). Because of his faith and loyalty, Caleb epitomized all that Israel should be and became a model of one whom God rewarded for his allegiance. Joshua too was a model of obedience. He received the Law from Moses and faithfully kept the Lord's commands (11:15). As a model leader he declared before all the people that he and his family would serve the Lord, not the gods of the land (24:15).

Though the people, in response to Joshua's inspirational leadership, eagerly affirmed their desire to follow the Lord (1:16–18; 24:16–18, 21–24), the book of Joshua reminds us how tenuous the nation's foothold in the land actually was. The Gibeonites were able to dupe the Israelites into making a treaty with them. The ruse would not have worked if Israel had simply sought the Lord's counsel in the matter (9:14). Interspersed throughout the book are reminders that Israel failed to dislodge the Canaanites (15:63; 16:10; 17:12–13; 19:47).

Consistent with its emphasis on Israel's obligations as God's covenant people, the book of Joshua stresses the importance of tribal unity within the nation. (This theme is important in the overall history to which Joshua is a prologue, for the unity of the nation would disappear in the centuries that followed.) In the very first chapter we see the trans-Jordanian tribes willingly supporting their brothers and helping them conquer the land west of the Jordan (1:12–18). Later, when the western tribes mistakenly thought the eastern tribes had abandoned the Lord, the matter was cleared up through a careful investigation (22:10–34). The **episode** demonstrates the nation's zeal for the Lord and their commitment to unity.

The Achan episode also contributes to this theme in a significant way. When Achan sinned, the Lord did not regard it as a strictly individual matter. He was angry at the entire nation (7:1) and declared that Israel had sinned (7:11). Though this may seem unfair to our modern sensibilities, the Lord viewed Israel as a corporate entity. An individual's actions could and did adversely affect the entire community. Israel was contaminated in the Lord's sight (7:13), and Israel as a nation had to purge the evil from their midst (7:24–26). This episode stresses the nation's unity in the sight of God.

Overall Purpose

In short, the book's purpose is twofold:

1. It demonstrates that the Lord fulfilled his promise to give his people the land and that his powerful presence was all that Israel needed to be successful against opposition. In the context of the larger history that Joshua introduces, this theme serves as an

apology for the Lord. Israel's subsequent defeats, culminating in
exile, were not due to any deficiency on the Lord's part.

2. The book also challenges Israel to remain faithful to the Lord
   by reminding them that disobedience brings divine discipline
   and threatens to undermine their position as the Lord's covenant
   community. This theme also contributes to the history's apology
   for the Lord. Israel's subsequent failure was due to its rejection of
   the Lord's authority.

JUDGES

Israel had defeated its enemies and established a foothold in the
Promised Land. But, as Joshua passed off the scene, the challenge of
actually occupying the land remained. The book of Judges tells how
the nation failed in this regard. The covenant community disintegrated
morally and socially as it assimilated Canaanite culture and beliefs. God
both punished and delivered wayward Israel, but the downward spiral
continued. The need for competent leadership became apparent, pav-
ing the way for the rise of kingship.

Primary Themes

The book of Judges exhibits three main literary units: a prologue
(1:1–3:6), a central section containing several accounts of individual
judges (3:7–16:31), and an epilogue (17:1–21:25). The prologue contains two parallel, complementary subunits (1:1–2:5; 2:6–3:6), both
of which recount Israel's failure following Joshua's death. Chapter 1
is primarily descriptive, reflecting for the most part an observer's perspective. The narrator does give a theological perspective at points (vv.
19a, 22), but this seems to be for rhetorical purposes, since he allows
the people's perspective to dominate (v. 19b). The matter-of-fact description of Israel's failure to carry out God's commission prompts the
reader to ask: Why did the people fail? The account of the incident
at Bokim (2:1–5) provides at least a partial answer by making it clear
that Israel's failure was not really due to Canaanite military power and
persistence (the impression given by 1:19, 27, 35), but was the result
of assimilation to Canaanite culture and idolatry. The Lord reminded

Israel of his warning that he would not drive out the nations if the people engaged in idolatry.

The second subunit in the prologue (2:6–3:6) is far more theological and **evaluative**. Picking up on the theme of 2:1–5, the narrator identifies idolatry as Israel's fundamental problem (2:11–13). He gives an overview of the period, which displays a cyclical pattern. During this period Israel would sin, prompting the Lord to hand them over to enemies for disciplinary purposes (vv. 14–15). When the people cried out to the Lord (v. 18b), he would raise up deliverers ("judges") to rescue them (vv. 16, 18a). These judges brought some stability for a time, but the people persisted in their ways (vv. 17, 19), prompting the Lord to announce that he would no longer drive out the nations, but would use them to test Israel's loyalty (2:20–3:4). A summary of the period appears in 3:5–6. Verse five reflects the descriptive style of chapter 1 and reiterates its main theme (Israel lived among the native peoples). Like chapter 2, verse 6 is more theological and evaluative in tone, identifying Israel's underlying problem as its assimilation to Canaanite culture and idolatry.

The central portion of the book (3:7–16:31) illustrates the dominant themes of the prologue—Israel's propensity to sin, the Lord's disciplinary judgment, and the Lord's willingness to deliver his people from their oppressors. In the prologue the Lord announced that the conquest would be put on hold until he had tested Israel's loyalty (2:20–3:4). The book's central section gives specific evidence for why this decision was necessary, as it depicts persistent or recurring idolatry and an increasing alienation between God and his people.

The stories also clarify the prologue's simple pattern of prayer followed by divine response. The stories show that God cannot be manipulated like some good-luck charm and that he often operates outside the expected norms. In the Gideon story he confronts his people with their sin before commissioning a deliverer; in the Jephthah story he wearies of intervening, even when they persist in crying out to him and seemingly repent of their idolatry. But in the Samson story he decides to deliver even though no one asks for his help. The prologue depicts God delivering his people through his chosen instruments; the stories show that deliverance often came in unexpected ways, even through flawed instruments.

While the stories illustrate the prologue's thematic concerns, they are not restricted to this literary role. At least two major themes surface in the stories that do not appear in the prologue:

1. The prologue describes the judges in fairly positive terms as instruments of God who attempted to give the people moral guidance (see 2:17). The stories depict them as victorious warriors energized by God, but portray their flaws as well. In fact, one can trace a pattern of declining quality in the judges, culminating in Samson.[1] The prologue indirectly contributes to this thematic development by providing paradigms of competent leadership in Joshua and Caleb, who become **foils** for the failed leaders presented in the stories. But the prologue does not speak of the judges in negative terms. This theme of failed leadership, rather than emerging from the prologue, arises in the stories and paves the way for the epilogue, which specifically laments the moral condition that overtook the land because of the leadership void (see 17:6; 21:25; as well as 18:1 and 19:1).

2. The stories also portray escalating civil conflict, a theme that is not present in the prologue, at least in a direct way. Deborah's victory song criticizes some tribes for not contributing to the common cause (5:15b–17), while Gideon faced opposition from his own countrymen in the aftermath of his victory over the Midianites (7:24–8:17). Gideon's son Abimelech instigated a civil war (chap. 9) and Jephthah massacred the Ephraimites in the aftermath of his victory over the Ammonites (12:1–6). In Samson's story, the men of Judah handed Samson the Danite over to the Philistines. All of this paves the way for the epilogue, where civil conflict is the order of the day.

The epilogue (chaps. 17–21) contains two stories. The first of these (17:1–19:1a) tells of Micah's homemade shrine and how the Danites confiscated his **cultic** equipment and his priest and set up their own

---

1. This pattern of declining leadership runs concurrently with the subtheme of changing female roles. See Robert B. Chisholm Jr., "The Role of Women in the Rhetorical Strategy of the Book of Judges," in *Integrity of Heart, Skillfulness of Hands: Biblical and Leadership Studies in Honor of Donald K. Campbell,* ed. Charles H. Dyer and Roy B. Zuck (Grand Rapids: Baker, 1994), 34–49.

private tribal worship center in the distant north, far from the land they had been allotted. The second story (19:1b–21:25) is a sordid account of rape and murder in Gibeah that precipitated a civil war in Israel. The war nearly wiped out the tribe of Benjamin and resulted in further atrocities against Israelite women. Before going into battle against the Benjaminites, Israel went to Bethel to ask God who should lead the army. The Lord replied that Judah was to take the lead (20:18). This scene is reminiscent of the book's introduction, where the tribes asked the Lord who should lead them against the Canaanites and he picked Judah (1:1–2). The irony is obvious and tragic. At the beginning of the book, Israel was prepared to unite against the common Canaanite foe; at the end of the book, the original ideal had failed to materialize and the tribes were uniting against one of their own brothers.

The theme of the epilogue appears in 17:6 and 21:25 (see as well the abridged version of this in 18:1 and 19:1). The epilogue's two accounts illustrate what happened in Israelite society when there was an absence of competent leadership and show why Israel needed an ideal king (see Deut. 17:14–20).

Overall Purpose

As one reflects on these themes, it becomes apparent that the book has a distinct agenda, which includes at least three major purposes:

1. The thematic emphases of the prologue indicate that Judges, like Joshua, is in part an apology for the Lord, whose reputation was jeopardized by Israel's failure. The prologue explains why Israel failed and makes it clear that the Lord warned the people about this possibility from the very beginning.[2] The rest of the book justifies the Lord's decision to test his people by allowing the enemy to remain in the land. Israel's defeats were punitive, rather than being due to some alleged weakness in the Lord or to the strength of foreigners and their gods.

   Another element in the book's defense of the Lord's honor is the prologue's affirmation of his commitment to his people.

2. See Antti Laato, "Theodicy in the Deuteronomistic History," in *Theodicy in the World of the Bible,* ed. Antti Laato and Johannes C. de Moor (Leiden: E. J. Brill, 2003), 193–96.

Despite their failure and the Lord's harsh divine discipline, he showed compassion and continued to deliver them from oppression. The stories within the book's central section support this affirmation as they tell how the Lord responded to the people's pain and intervened to save them. As Fretheim states: "We are surprised by a God who finds ways of working in, with, and under very compromising situations in which people have placed themselves in order to bring about good. In the midst of unfaithfulness, the faithfulness of God is revealed, a God who never breaks covenant."[3]

A third feature of the book's apology is its polemical dimension. On a very general level, the book demonstrates that Israel's obsession with idols did not bring success. On the contrary, idolatry consistently brought defeat and humiliation. The book is particularly concerned to denounce Israel's devotion to the Canaanite deity Baal (2:13; 6:25–32; 8:33; 10:6). It gives ample reason why Israel should have chosen the Lord over Baal. The Song of Deborah depicts the Lord as the sovereign king who uses elements of the storm to defeat the Canaanite armies (5:4–5). The Gideon account, along with its sequel about Abimelech, also contains a strong anti-Baal polemic. Baal was unable to avenge fully Gideon's (Jerubbaal's) attack on his altar and ended up having his Shechemite temple burned to the ground.[4] The polemical dimension takes a different turn in the Samson story. Samson burned the grain supposedly provided by the Philistine grain god, Dagon (15:4–5).[5] Though Dagon seemed to win the

---

3. Terence Fretheim, *Deuteronomic History* (Nashville: Abingdon, 1983), 98.
4. See Wolfgang Bluedorn, *Yahweh Versus Baal: A Theological Reading of the Gideon-Abimelech Narrative,* JSOTSup 329 (Sheffield: Sheffield Academic Press, 2001).
5. Dagon appears to have been the chief deity of the Philistines (cf. 1 Sam. 5:1–7; 1 Chron. 10:10). Though an older interpretation understood him to be a fish god, it is more likely that he was a weather-fertility deity responsible for crops. In Ugaritic *dgn* refers to "grain," and the storm god Baal is called Dagon's son. For a discussion of the Old Testament and extra-biblical evidence pertaining to this deity, see John Day, *Yahweh and the Gods and Goddesses of Canaan* (Sheffield: Sheffield Academic Press, 2000), 85–90. Day thinks that "grain" is probably a secondary meaning for *dgn* in Ugaritic and that the term is etymologically related to a verbal root "be cloudy, rainy" (87–88). According to Day, "the earliest sources do not particularly connect Dagon with the grain, though they do suggest that Dagon was a storm god, and of course a storm god is implicitly a fertility god, whence the corn would derive" (88). Itamar Singer prefers to see Dagan/Dagon as fundamentally "an

conflict (16:23–24), Samson ended up bringing Dagon's temple to the ground (16:30). The polemic against both of these gods continues in 1 Samuel. Hannah celebrated the Lord's ability to give fertility (1 Sam. 2:1–10), the ark of the Lord humiliated Dagon in the latter's very own temple (1 Sam. 5), and the Lord thundered against and defeated the Philistines following Israel's rejection of Baal worship (1 Sam. 7).

2. The book of Judges also warned Israel of the dangers of assimilation to their environment.[6] As the prologue to the book makes clear, Israel failed to complete the conquest of the land. They intermarried with the Canaanites and embraced Canaanite gods.[7] Their persistent idolatry brought defeat and oppression in its wake. In fact, God decided to put on hold his original plan to give his people the land. The nations would remain to test Israel's loyalty. The stories in the book's central section support this theme. Each account revolves around a divinely enabled deliverer who rescues Israel from oppression brought on by judgment due to idolatry. Though God was sensitive to Israel's self-induced suffering, the vicious cycle continued as long as Israel "did evil in the eyes of the LORD." As Israel became more like the Canaanites, their national identity as God's covenant community began to dissolve. The unified nation of Joshua's time began to disintegrate, making it more vulnerable to invasion, as the stories

earth and vegetation deity." He considers any storm characteristics "as no doubt secondary." See his "Towards the Image of Dagon the God of the Philistines," *Syria* 69 (1992): 437. Singer argues that evidence from the Bible, Amarna, and Canaanite inscriptions indicate that Dagan/Dagon was not a native Canaanite deity. He writes: "The cumulative evidence from various sources leads to the inevitable conclusion that the Philistines and the other Sea Peoples who settled in Palestine did *not* encounter Dagon as one of the gods of the land, and obviously could not have adopted his cult in their new land" (439, emphasis his). Singer asks, "If so, how did Dagon become the main god of the Philistines?" He suggests that they adopted him from the Phoenicians or that they "encountered and adopted the cult of Dagan/Dagon" in Syria before they moved south into Canaan and then "brought Dagon with them" (439–40).

6. Guest demonstrates the importance of this theme in Judges. She probes its social, political, and religious dimensions. See Pauline Deryn Guest, "Dangerous Liaisons in the Book of Judges," *SJOT* 11 (1997): 241–69.

7. Block argues that "the Canaanization of Israel" is "the unifying theme" of Judges. See Daniel I. Block, "Echo Narrative Technique in Hebrew Literature: A Study in Judges 19," *WTJ* 52 (1990): 337–41; as well as idem, *Judges, Ruth*, NAC (Nashville: Broadman & Holman, 1999), 57–59.

illustrate. Tribal conflict threatened the nation's stability; tribal loyalty at the expense of justice eventually precipitated a civil war.

3. The book of Judges also demonstrates Israel's need for competent leadership. The prologue speaks of the judges in positive terms, probably because it is seeking to demonstrate the Lord's provision for his people. When they cried for help, he raised up leaders to deliver them. The stories, in harmony with the prologue, tell how God accomplished great deeds through human leaders. However, the stories also introduce another perspective. They illustrate how lack of faith and wisdom marred Israel's leaders and kept them from realizing their potential. The epilogue looks at Israel's leadership from this more critical perspective. Israel needed a leader who, in accordance with the Deuteronomic ideal (Deut. 17:14–20), would point the nation back to God and his covenant demands and lay the foundation for spiritual renewal. More specifically, Israel needed a king who would ensure social order and cultic purity. Without such a leader, the nation rejected God's authority and each person followed his or her own code of conduct. Only when Israel again acknowledged God as their true King would the original vision, which had seemingly died with Joshua, be realized. The epilogue brings the leadership theme of the stories to its alarming conclusion and paves the way for 1 Samuel, which describes how the Lord restored competent, Joshua/Caleb-like leadership to Israel, at least for a time.

RUTH

At least two main theological themes emerge from the book of Ruth. First, the book demonstrates that God is concerned about needy people. Psalm 146:9 states: "The LORD protects those residing outside their native land; he lifts up the fatherless and the widow." The book of Ruth puts flesh on that theological statement. The book shows how the Lord provided for two needy widows, Naomi and Ruth. Naomi had lost her husband and both of her sons while living in Moab. She returned to Bethlehem a bitter and impoverished woman who had little, if any, hope. But the Lord transformed her situation and lifted her out of the depths. He accomplished this through two people, Ruth and Boaz, who were willing to follow God's principles of loyalty and kindness. So while the book of Ruth shows us that God is concerned about needy people, it also reminds us that he often meets their needs through people who are willing to do what is right and to sacrifice for the good of others.

A second major theme of the book may be stated as follows: God rewards those who are faithful to the God-given relationships to which they have committed themselves. Psalm 18:25 says: "You [addressing the Lord] prove to be loyal to the one who is faithful." The book of Ruth illustrates this truth. Twice in the book the Hebrew word חֶסֶד, "kindness, loyal love, devotion, commitment, faithfulness," is used of Ruth. In 1:8 Naomi says to her daughters-in-law: "May the LORD show you the same kind of devotion you have shown to your deceased husbands and to me." Ruth had already been devoted to Naomi and her family during the days in Moab, even before she took the solemn oath recorded in 1:16–17. Later in 3:10 Boaz says to Ruth: "May you be rewarded by the LORD, my dear. This act of devotion is greater than what you did before." Love is also a word that characterizes Ruth. In 4:15 the women of the town, in response to Obed's birth, say to Naomi: "For your daughter-in-law, who loves you, has given him birth. She is better to you than seven sons." God showed the same kind of commitment and devotion to Ruth that she had shown to others. He gave her a husband, the ability to bear a son, and a famous descendant.

And it did not end there. The concluding genealogy (4:18–22) shows that God's blessings sometimes extend beyond the lifetime of the recipients. Through Ruth's great-grandson David, God rewarded their faithfulness in a way that brought great fame to the family and to his people Israel. Through David and ultimately the Messiah, God's blessings to Ruth were extended to Israel and the whole world. They exceeded her wildest imagination and transcended her lifetime. In the English Bible, the reference to David, coming on the heels of Judges' statement concerning Israel's need for an ideal king, paves the way for David's appearance in 1 Samuel 16.[8]

---

8. In the Hebrew Bible the book of Ruth is not part of the Former Prophets, the portion of the canon that tells the history of Israel. This short book, set in the period of the Judges, appears in the third section of the Hebrew canon, called the Writings. It is one of the five Megilloth

1–2 SAMUEL

The books of Samuel are a single entity in the Hebrew Bible. First and 2 Samuel is the theological heart of the history covered in the Former Prophets, for it records the restoration of the leadership ideal presented in Joshua and anticipated in Judges. The prominence it gives to the Davidic covenant sets the backdrop against which the theology of 1–2 Kings, as well as Israel's history and future, are to be understood.[9]

Primary Theme

First and 2 Samuel continues the story of Israel's history, picking up where Judges leaves off. The books revolve around three major characters—Samuel, Saul, and David—whose stories overlap and intersect. The dominant theme is kingship. Judges anticipates an ideal ruler, like the one described in Deuteronomy 17. The books of Samuel tell how kingship was finally instituted in Israel, but not without a false start and some bumps in the road. By the end of the story, two kings have experienced personal tragedy, seeds of destruction have been sown, and the Deuteronomic royal ideal remains unfulfilled. Yet, as we will see, the canonical shaping of the book keeps alive the royal ideal expressed in the Davidic covenant.

A Prophet Arrives (1 Sam. 1–7)

First Samuel starts with a story of oppression, a theme that appears as well in the epilogue to Judges. Barren Hannah suffered abuse from a rival wife. In her despair she cried out to the Lord for deliverance, asking for a son and promising that she would dedicate him to the Lord. Hannah contrasts with the mothers of Samson and Micah.

(or scrolls), along with Song of Songs, Ecclesiastes, Lamentations, and Esther. In some editions of the Hebrew Bible, Ruth follows Proverbs. This placement is appropriate, for Boaz calls Ruth a "worthy woman" (אֵשֶׁת חַיִל), the same phrase used to describe the "worthy wife" of Proverbs 31:10–31 (see v. 10). Ruth displayed the qualities depicted in Proverbs 31. She was committed to relationships (both to her deceased husband, Mahlon, and her mother-in-law, Naomi) and was industrious.

9. Because of the centrality and theological importance of 1–2 Samuel, this survey devotes more space to it than to the other historical books.

As noted earlier in our discussion of parallelism in narrative, Hannah supernaturally gave birth to a Nazirite son through whom the Lord restored effective leadership to Israel. Samson's mother's miraculously conceived Nazirite son failed to understand his true role as the Lord's deliverer and never rose to the level of an effective leader. In contrast to Micah's mother, whose misguided actions and obsession with idols contributed to the Danites' unauthorized **cult**, Hannah's commitment to the Lord was the catalyst for the revival of genuine Yahweh worship through the spiritual leadership of her son Samuel.

When the Lord delivered Hannah from barrenness and oppression, she praised him. Her song (1 Sam. 2:1–10) expresses important theological principles. According to Hannah, the Lord is the incomparable king and savior who is committed to justice. He brings down the proud and cares for the needy. He is sovereign over life and death, as well as the elements of the storm. In other words, the Lord, not Baal, is the only God worthy of one's worship and the true source of life and fertility. Hannah also anticipated that the Lord would raise up an Israelite king whom he would energize in battle. The militaristic imagery implies that the Lord would deliver Israel from their enemies, just as he had done Hannah. Once more we detect a contrast with Samson's mother, who failed to tell her husband Manoah about her son's destiny as Israel's deliverer (see Judg. 13:5–8).

The sequel to the account of Samuel's birth introduces another important theme from the epilogue to Judges—cultic corruption. Eli's sons had corrupted the Shiloh cult by their godless behavior (1 Sam. 2:12–17, 22–25). The narrator contrasts them with Samuel, who served the Lord (1 Sam. 2:11, 18–21, 26; 3:1a). Through Samuel the Lord confirmed an earlier prophetic judgment oracle against Eli and his priestly house (1 Sam. 2:27–36; 3:1b–18). Because of his lack of respect for the Lord, Eli forfeited a priestly dynasty that the Lord had intended to maintain permanently (1 Sam. 2:30). However, the Lord did not abandon Israel. He would eventually raise up another priestly family to serve him (1 Sam. 2:35). In the meantime, through Samuel's ministry the Lord revitalized the prophetic office and the cult site at Shiloh (1 Sam. 3:19–4:1a).

Important themes emerge in these prophetic oracles that will resurface later in the books of Samuel:

1. The Lord does not tolerate those who treat him with contempt.
2. The Lord's promises are sometimes conditional and can fail to materialize if the recipients of the promises treat him with contempt.
3. The Lord rewards devotion and honors those who honor him.

The ark narrative (1 Sam. 4–7) demonstrates that God's prophetic word is sure. The Philistine army defeated Israel and killed Eli's two sons. When Eli heard the news, he fell over and died. This narrative also shows that the ark, the cultic symbol of God's presence, was not a rabbit's foot that guaranteed success. There was power in the ark, but it could not be manipulated. God chose when and where he would reveal that power. He did not intervene for Israel or prevent the Philistines from taking the ark because his primary concern was to judge Eli. However, just in case the capture of the ark might send the wrong theological message to Israel and its enemies, the Lord demonstrated his power in foreign territory. When the Philistines put the ark in Dagon's temple, Dagon's image fell before it, decapitated as if it were a defeated warrior. Wherever the ark went in Philistine territory, disease followed in its wake. Finally the Philistines sent the ark home, but it did more damage in the border town of Beth Shemesh, where some of the residents failed to treat it with the respect it was due. It remained there until David brought it to Jerusalem.

Eventually the Israelites repented of their idolatry and discarded their Baal idols. Samuel interceded on their behalf and then led Israel into battle against the Philistines. As if to affirm the wisdom of their actions, the Lord thundered from the sky and routed the Philistines, proving that he, not Baal, controlled the storm.

Several themes emerge in this narrative:

1. When God decrees judgment, judgment will fall.
2. God cannot be manipulated into helping his people. When God's people sin, they may experience his opposition, not his deliverance. Repentance is the foundation for renewed divine favor.
3. Even when God appears to be defeated, he remains sovereign and invincible.
4. God expects people to respect his holiness; failure to do so can be dangerous to one's health.

Choosing a King (1 Sam. 8–12)

The issue of kingship comes to the forefront in 1 Samuel 8–12. **Diachronic critics** see multiple sources and competing viewpoints in this section. These chapters supposedly contain two or three traditions of the origin of Israelite kingship:

1. Samuel privately anoints Saul as "leader" (נָגִיד) of Israel (9:1–10:16).
2. Saul is chosen as king (מֶלֶךְ, "king") by lot at Mizpah (10:17–27).
3. Saul is made king in Gilgal following a military victory (11:1–15).

These chapters also allegedly present both positive (9:1–10:16; 11:1–15) and negative (8:1–22; 10:17–27; 12:1–25) perspectives on kingship.

However, a close reading of the text as it stands reveals the faulty nature of this critical consensus, which assumes some serious deficiencies on the part of the editors responsible for the text in its present form. These chapters do not contain multiple and conflicting accounts of the origin of kingship. Samuel anointed Saul privately prior to crowning him king in a public ceremony. This gave Saul some time to come to grips with his commission (the threefold sign shows this was necessary, cf. 1 Sam. 10:1–7) and allowed Samuel to clarify the nature of Saul's kingship prior to the hoopla of the public ceremony (cf. 10:1, 6–7). As the text makes crystal clear (note the appearance of וּנְחַדֵּשׁ, "we will *renew,*" in 11:14), the coronation ceremony after Saul's victory over the Ammonites was a reconfirmation of Saul's kingship, necessitated by the less than enthusiastic response mentioned in 10:27.

In these chapters kingship *per se* is not viewed negatively, but the people's desire for a king like the nations is criticized, for implicit in their request was a rejection of the Lord's authority (8:7). They did not trust the Lord to deliver them from their enemies; like all the other peoples they wanted a visible king who would be their national security blanket and a tangible object of trust.[10] Long before this the Lord anticipated

---

10. For a helpful discussion of how Israel's request for a king was a rejection of the Lord, see Gerald E. Gerbrandt, *Kingship According to the Deuteronomistic History* (Atlanta: Scholars, 1986), 148–49.

Israel would request a king like all of the nations (Deut. 17:14). He was willing to give them a king, but with certain restrictions (Deut. 17:15–20). God's ideal king must not create a large army, make foreign alliances, or accumulate great wealth. He was to be a spiritual leader who promoted God's Law by word and example. (As noted above, this is the kind of king envisioned in Judg. 17:6 and 21:25.) However, in this instance the Lord considered the people's request an affront to his sovereignty, because their request was couched primarily in military terms (8:20), thus "dethroning" the Lord as Israel's warrior. He told Samuel to warn the people about how a typical king would operate and to let the people know that he would not intervene for them when they cried out for deliverance from this king's oppressive rule (1 Sam. 8:9–18). The people disregarded the warning and demanded a king; the Lord was ready to give them what they wanted and be done with it (8:19–22a). But Samuel, in his role as prophetic intercessor, did not carry out the Lord's command right away. Instead he stalled and sent the people home (8:22b).

Shortly after this the Lord instructed Samuel to anoint Saul to be a "leader" (נָגִיד) over Israel. He would deliver them from their enemies and "govern" (עָצַר) them (9:16–17). The absence of the root מלך (mlk, from which the noun "king" and the verb "to rule" are derived) in its nominal and verbal forms is startling in light of its prominence in chapter 8 (see 8:5–7, 9–11, 18–20, 22), and the Lord's fourfold use of the phrase "my people" in 9:16–17 suggests he was not about to relinquish his authority over Israel. (In 8:7 the Lord refers to them simply as "the people.") One's suspicions in this regard are confirmed in chapter 10. At Saul's private anointing Samuel designated him as נָגִיד, "leader," over the *Lord's* inheritance/people (10:1; see LXX). At the public coronation Samuel scolded the people for rejecting the Lord, the God of Israel (vv. 17–19). The people proclaimed Saul "king," but Samuel simply referred to him as "the one whom the LORD has chosen" (v. 24, emphasis added). This contrasts with 8:18, where Samuel referred to the requested king as "your king whom you have chosen for yourselves." Following the coronation, Samuel explained the "regulations of kingship" (מִשְׁפַּט הַמְּלֻכָה) to the people (v. 25). If these regulations were the policies outlined in Deuteronomy 17:14–20, this explains why some responded with such skepticism (v. 27), for the

Deuteronomic regulations clearly place significant limitations upon the Israelite king, and are designed to prevent him from being like the kings of the surrounding nations.[11] According to 12:1–2, Samuel claimed that he had acceded to the people's demand for a king (cf. 8:22), but he went on to emphasize that the Lord remained the theocratic head of the nation to whom both the king and people must remain loyal (vv. 13–15). The Lord, who confirmed the truth of Samuel's words with a miraculous demonstration of his power over the storm, held the destiny of the king and the nation in his hands (vv. 16–25). When the people saw this display of divine power, they confessed their sin and acknowledged that their request for a king was evil.

Several themes appear in chapters 8–12:

1. When God's people demand security apart from him, they act irrationally, for God is the only source of true security (cf. 10:18–19; 12:7–11).
2. Even when God gives his people what they demand, they are still subject to his authority.
3. God promises security in exchange for faithfulness and he even restores security when his sinful people cry out to him.
4. Sometimes a vivid reminder of God's power can bring God's people to their spiritual senses and help them see that rejecting God and his prophetic word is not the path to security.

Kingship Makes a False Start (1 Sam. 13–15)

First Samuel 13–15 describes the demise of Saul, who proved unworthy to lead God's people. Saul was preoccupied with ritual and the formal elements of religion (like Micah and his mother; see Judg. 17). This kept him from attacking the Philistine outpost (cf. 10:7–8 with 10:13–16) after the threefold sign had been fulfilled. Instead of begin-

---

11. Lyle M. Eslinger concludes that the phrase refers to "the 'monarchic constitution' that subordinates the monarchy to the theocracy." He adds: "It is installed before Yahweh as a sign of his continuing political supremacy." See Lyle M. Eslinger, *Kingship of God in Crisis: A Close Reading of 1 Samuel 1–12* (Sheffield: JSOTSup, 1985), 355. Though Eslinger does not seem to equate this constitution with Deuteronomy 17:14–20, Ralph W. Klein thinks it likely that the phrase refers to this passage. See Ralph W. Klein, *1 Samuel,* WBC (Waco, TX: Word, 1983), 100.

ning the deliverance of Israel from the Philistines, Saul went up to the high place, apparently to worship. His obsession with ritual prompted him to offer up sacrifices prematurely, rather than waiting for Samuel to arrive as he had been instructed (13:8–10). His preoccupation with formalism first caused him to delay the attack against the Philistines (14:18–19) and then led to a series of oaths (14:24, 39, 44) that threatened to bring divine judgment down upon his own son (note the obvious parallel to Jephthah and his daughter in Judg. 11), the army, and himself. Saul's obsession with ritual reached its climax when he, contrary to God's specific command, failed to destroy the Amalekite king and the best of the Amalekite livestock because he thought it would be preferable to offer them as a sacrifice to the Lord (15:8–9, 14–15).

The first incident at Gilgal (1 Sam. 13) revealed Saul's flawed thinking. First, his concern about his dwindling forces revealed a belief that the battle would be decided by human armies, not by the Lord. Second, his concern with offering a sacrifice revealed a faulty theology that elevates ritual above obedience (cf. 15:22–23) and tends to think that such ritual can in some way manipulate the Lord. Third, Saul overstepped his bounds. He was the king, but he was under the authority of the prophet, who was the intercessor for the nation (see 7:9; 12:18–19, 23, as well as the girls' statement to Saul in 9:13). This lack of respect for the prophetic office subsequently became a major issue in Israel.

Samuel charged Saul with foolish behavior and accused him of disobeying the Lord's command. Samuel then announced that Saul had forfeited the opportunity to have an enduring dynasty. The Lord would terminate his dynasty and replace him with another whom he had appointed. This new ruler would be a man "after" (lit. "like, according to") the Lord's "own heart." In light of the contextual emphasis on Saul's disobedience, this phrase must mean "like-minded," i.e., "committed to obey the Lord's commands." (Note the use of the phrase "like, according to your heart" in 1 Sam. 14:7, where the NIV translates "heart and soul.")

The second incident at Gilgal (1 Sam. 15) revealed Saul's disrespect for the Lord's absolute authority. Samuel explained that the Lord places higher priority on obedience than ritual (15:22–23; cf. Isa. 1:10–17; Jer. 7:21–23; Hos. 6:6; Amos 5:21–24; Mic. 6:6–8; Mark 12:28–34). In the Lord's sight, rebellion is just as bad as divination and idolatry.

Saul's rebellion violated Samuel's earlier warning (1 Sam. 12:14–15) and the king must pay the consequences. Because Saul rejected the Lord's word, the Lord rejected Saul as king (15:26). Samuel made it clear that this prophetic oracle was an unconditional divine decree, which could not be reversed (15:29).

At least two themes are highlighted in the account of Saul's rejection:

1. The Lord places greater priority on obedience than he does mere ritual.
2. Misplaced priorities and disobedience can bring disaster to the Lord's chosen leaders and destroy their legacy.

The Story of David (1 Sam. 16–2 Sam. 20)

In 1 Samuel 16 David steps onto the stage of Israel's history. At his anointing the Lord made it clear that he would choose the next king on the basis of his own standards, not the people's idea of what a king should look like. Humans look at the outward appearance; the Lord is concerned about inner qualities (1 Sam. 16:7). The Lord's Spirit, the possession of which was essential to rule well, came upon David (16:13). When the Spirit moved from Saul to David, the Lord sent "an evil spirit" to torment Saul and hasten his demise (16:14).

From this point on the story goes out of its way to demonstrate David's superiority to Saul and his innocence in the downfall of Saul's dynasty. Saul was paralyzed with fear before the Philistine champion, but David, like Caleb of old, trusted in the Lord and defeated the giant. The people's affections turned to David, who, despite his absolute loyalty to Saul, became the target of the jealous king's murderous schemes. The Lord providentially protected David and delivered him from Saul's plots and attacks. Saul's son Jonathan, who functions as a literary **foil** to his father, declared his loyalty to David and looked forward to the day when David would rule Israel (20:12–17; 23:16–18). Even Saul was eventually forced to acknowledge that David was innocent of any wrongdoing and would someday be king (24:17–21; 26:21–25). When David was tempted to kill wicked Nabal, Abigail, the embodiment of wisdom, reminded him of his destiny and challenged him to act accordingly (25:28–34). In his jealous rage Saul murdered Ahimelech and the priests of Nob, but David protected the lone survivor (22:11–23). The Lord protected David from harm through special revelation, but he refused to reveal his will to Saul (23:1–14; 28:6). In desperation Saul turned to a diviner, in violation of God's law. She conjured up the spirit of the late Samuel, who pronounced Saul's demise (28:16–19). As in the case of Eli and his sons, Samuel's prophetic word was fulfilled as Saul and his sons died on the battlefield the very next day. While this was happening, the Lord assured David of success through an oracular message (30:7–8) and enabled him to defeat an Amalekite raiding party.

The text exonerates David from any responsibility for Saul's death. The Philistines had dismissed him from their army prior to the battle (1 Sam. 29). When an Amalekite claimed to have killed Saul and gave David the king's crown as apparent proof, David ordered his immediate execution (2 Sam. 1:1–16). David composed a song of lament for Saul and Jonathan, expressing his admiration for and devotion to both of them (2 Sam. 1:17–27). Rather than rushing back to Judah to contend for the throne, he first sought the Lord's will (2 Sam. 2:1). While David accepted the acclaim of Judah, enlisted the support of Saul's loyal subjects, and apparently authorized a war against Ishbosheth's forces, he did not authorize the murders of Ishbosheth or Abner (2 Sam. 2–4). It seems he desired a peaceful transition and intended to welcome Saul's descendants as his subjects. In fulfillment of his promise to Jonathan, he even made Jonathan's lame son Mephibosheth a ward of the state (2 Sam. 9).

David was successful militarily: he took Jerusalem from the Jebusites, defeated the Philistines, and conquered the nations to the east (2 Sam. 5, 8). He also centralized the **cult** in Jerusalem by bringing the ark to the city, though not without incident (2 Sam. 6). When David announced his intention to build a temple (lit. "house") for the Lord, the Lord postponed the project. Instead the Lord made a covenant with David, promising him an enduring dynasty (lit. "house") (2 Sam. 7). If David's descendants were disobedient, the Lord would punish them, but he would sustain the dynasty.

Despite David's successes, all was not well. By building a harem, David planted the seeds of destruction. While in Hebron he fathered six sons from six different wives (2 Sam. 3:2–5). Prior to this, David had only two wives (Ahinoam and Abigail; 1 Sam. 25:43; 30:5), excluding Michal, whom Saul had given to another man (1 Sam. 25:44). At least one of these marriages was apparently contracted for purposes of so-lidifying a political alliance. Maacah was the daughter of King Talmai of Geshur, which was located east of the Jordan River. This description of David's expanding royal court and influence is disturbing in light of Deuteronomy 17:17, which stipulated that the king of Israel must not multiply wives. As the story continues, tensions develop within this crowded royal court, especially between the half-brothers Amnon and Absalom and then Solomon and Adonijah. After David moved to Jerusalem, he took more wives (2 Sam. 5:13–16). In light of the posi-tive assessment of David in the preceding context (vv. 10, 12), one is tempted to say that this note about an expanding harem is included to impress the reader with David's growing status and to picture him as one who was blessed by God with numerous offspring. But through-out David's story the narrator has included negative aspects of David's career, often without comment. As in 2 Samuel 3:2–5, we must look beyond the surface and not allow the positive aspects of David's career to color our interpretation of every detail. Deuteronomy 17:17 prohib-ited Israel's king from multiplying wives. While David's harem appar-ently did not turn his heart from the Lord, his acquisition of more and more wives suggests he had bought into the thinking of the culture to some degree. Furthermore, he set a bad precedent that proved detri-mental to Solomon.

David's insistence on building a harem culminated in the Bathsheba incident, where David, overcome by lust and greed, violated Uriah's wife and then tried to cover up his sin by ordering Uriah's death. David suffered the painful consequences of his blatant violation of God's law. In his response to Nathan's parable David unwittingly pronounced the penalty for his crime as fourfold payment (2 Sam. 12:6). Sure enough, as the story unfolds four of David's sons die. The Lord struck down the anonymous child born to Bathsheba (2 Sam. 12:15–18). Later Amnon (at the hand of his half-brother Absalom), Absalom (at the hand of his cousin Joab), and Adonijah (at the hand of his half-brother Solomon) died violently in fulfillment of Nathan's prophecy that the sword would not depart from David's house (2 Sam. 12:10). When Amnon raped his half-sister Tamar, David did not punish his son. Absalom avenged his sister and murdered Amnon (2 Sam. 13). Seemingly paralyzed, David did not punish Absalom for his crime, just as he overlooked Joab's murderous deeds on more than occasion. David's failure to execute justice came back to haunt him when Absalom presented himself as the rightful king who was concerned that there be justice in Israel (2 Sam. 15:1–12). Absalom's self-promotion culminated in his attempt to take the throne and his subsequent death, which left David emotionally devastated (2 Sam. 15–18).

But David also experienced God's mercy in the midst of punishment. In response to David's confession of sin, the Lord spared his life (2 Sam. 12:13). Following the death of his infant son, the Lord gave him and Bathsheba another son, whom the Lord named Jedidiah ("loved by the Lord"; 2 Sam. 12:24–25). This child, better known as Solomon, eventually became king. Through the ordeal of Absalom's rebellion, David, realizing he was being punished for his earlier crimes, accepted what his enemies dished out as part of God's discipline (2 Sam. 16:10–11). At the same time, however, David hoped for and experienced God's mercy, which tempered his suffering to some degree (2 Sam. 16:12).

Reflecting on David's Career (2 Sam. 21–24)

The final chapters of 2 Samuel are arranged in a **chiastic** structure, where the elements in the second half of the literary unit thematically correspond to those of the first half, but in reverse order, creating a mirror effect:

A   Saul's sin and its atonement: David as royal judge (21:1–14)
    B   The mighty deeds of David's men (21:15–22)
        C   David's song of thanksgiving (22:1–51)
        C'   David's final words (23:1–7)
    B'   The mighty deeds of David's men (23:8–39)
A'   David's sin and its atonement: David as royal priest (24:1–25)

The A/A' and B/B' units of this final section correspond to the course of David's career as it unfolds in 1–2 Samuel. Section A (21:1–14), with its contrast between David and Saul, supplements 1 Samuel

15–2 Samuel 4, which demonstrates that David, not Saul, was the rightful king of Israel and that David was not responsible for the death of Saul and his descendants. On the contrary, David always sought to honor Saul and his family. Sections B (21:15–22) and B' (23:8–39) correspond to 2 Samuel 5–10, which describes David's military victories. Section A' (24:1–25) is thematically parallel to 2 Samuel 11–20, which describes David's moral failure and punishment. Right in the middle of this thematic review, the poetic texts in sections C (22:1–51) and C' (23:1–7) give a theological commentary on the career of David.

The appendix of chapters 21–24 highlights the major themes of David's career—his divine election and superiority to Saul, his success in battle, and God's willingness to restore him to favor following acts of sin and times of chastisement. The events and poems included here epitomize and provide a microcosm of David's career and character. By placing two poems (1 Sam. 2:1–10; 2 Sam. 22), both of which refer to the king as God's anointed one (1 Sam. 2:10; 2 Sam. 22:51), at the beginning and end of 1–2 Samuel, the narrator keeps alive the royal ideal expressed in the Davidic covenant.

1–2 KINGS

Primary Themes

First and 2 Kings trace Israel's history from the accession of Solomon to the Exile, covering a time span of over four hundred years. The story is mainly a tragic one, as Israel violated the demands of their covenant with the Lord and experienced the consequences of disobedience. David's son and successor, Solomon, planted the seeds of idolatry and forfeited most of the kingdom, seemingly jeopardizing God's covenant with David. The kingdom divided, with David's dynasty ruling over only Judah and Benjamin.

In the north idolatry caught hold as Jeroboam I inaugurated an idolatrous **cult** that rivaled Jerusalem's cult, and Ahab eventually made Baal worship a state-sanctioned religion. When the Lord confronted this evil through his prophets, the kings of the north persecuted them. God finally punished this rejection of his authority by sending the northern kingdom into exile.

In Judah idolatry also threatened the nation's security, but two kings in particular, Hezekiah and Josiah, promoted spiritual revivals that enabled Judah to outlive the northern kingdom. But in the end Judah also went into exile. However, there is a silver lining in the story, for God's promise to the Davidic dynasty never died and continued to foster hope for a revival of the nation's fortunes.

Seeds of Destruction: Solomon's Reign (1 Kings 1–11)

First Kings 1–2 describe Solomon's succession to his father's throne. Adonijah had his eye on the throne and began taking steps to solidify his place as the next king. However, with some prompting from Bathsheba, David decreed that Solomon, not Adonijah, should be the next king. David summoned Solomon to his deathbed. He encouraged Solomon to carry out his royal responsibilities with courage, urged him to obey the Lord's commandments, and reminded him of the Lord's covenantal promise to the dynasty (see 2 Sam. 7). However, David then instructed Solomon to exact revenge upon Joab and Shimei and make sure that both died a violent death. This command illustrates the moral ambiguity that characterized David's life. The first time he speaks in the story (1 Sam. 17:26) he displays a measure of self-interest and greed ("What will be done for the man who kills this Philistine?"), as well as a healthy concern for God's honor ("Who is this uncircumcised Philistine that he should defy the armies of the living God?"). Now on his deathbed he urged Solomon to obey the Lord's law, but then also encouraged him to bloody his hands. David's words also illustrate his moral weakness. He acknowledged that Joab was a murderer, yet he never had the courage to bring him to justice and in the end left that task to Solomon. He promised Shimei he would not punish him, but then he went back on his word and told Solomon to kill him. David had passed on his legacy of bloodshed to his son Solomon, whose name ironically means "peace." Viewing himself as the Lord's instrument of justice, Solomon followed his father's advice (1 Kings 2:28–46; see especially vv. 32, 44).

Solomon's violence was not restricted to eliminating his father's enemies. Encouraged by his father to shed blood and eliminate potential enemies, Solomon eliminated his main rival, his brother Adonijah.

After David's death, Adonijah asked to marry Abishag. Solomon interpreted his request as a pretense for seeking the throne. Since Abishag had slept with David (though the aging David did not have relations with her), she could be viewed as part of his royal harem. By asking for a member of his father's harem, Adonijah opened himself to the charge of trying to usurp his father's place. Solomon exploited Adonijah's indiscretion to the fullest. He accused Adonijah of betrayal and ordered his execution. With Adonijah's death, the punishment for David's crime was paid in full (cf. 2 Sam. 12:6).

The ambiguity surrounding Solomon (the one named "peace" who ordered three individuals to be killed) continues in 1 Kings 3–11. On the positive side, the text commends him for his loyalty to the Lord (3:3a). When given his choice of a gift from God, he chose wisdom so that he might rule over the people effectively (3:9). God commended him for his decision and promised him wealth and honor (3:10–13). Solomon's reputation for wisdom spread (3:28; 4:29–34) and the nation prospered (4:20–28). The Lord fulfilled his promise by making Solomon famous and wealthy (9:11; 10:10, 14–18, 21, 25). Solomon built the temple to honor the Lord (8:18–21). He interceded on behalf of the nation, asking God to forgive their sins in the future (8:22–53), while urging the people to be loyal to the covenant (8:54–61). The Lord reiterated his covenant promise to the Davidic dynasty, but warned that idolatry would prompt him to leave the temple and send the people into exile (9:1–9).

Despite these positive features, Solomon's reign was tainted. At the beginning of his reign he married an Egyptian princess in order to seal an alliance with her father, the pharaoh (3:1; cf. 9:16). Later, in blatant violation of God's law, he added hundreds of wives to his harem and worshiped their gods (11:1–8; cf. Deut. 17:17). He accumulated horses and chariots, contrary to God's will (10:26–29; cf. Deut. 17:16), and offered sacrifices on the high places (3:3b). In response to Solomon's idolatry, the Lord announced he would tear the kingdom away from Solomon's son, leaving him only one tribe (for David's sake, 11:9–13; cf. 11:29–39). From this point on, Solomon faced enemies from outside and within his kingdom (11:14–40). The Lord himself engineered the division of the kingdom, prompting Rehoboam to reject the demands of the northern work force (12:1–24; see especially v. 15).

There is great tension in the story, for the Davidic promise seems to be compromised—Jeroboam is even conditionally promised a dynasty like David's (11:37–38), yet the Lord's words seem to hint at a revival of David's dynasty at some point in the future (11:39).

Disintegration and Tragedy: The Divided Kingdom (1 Kings 12–2 Kings 25)

The remainder of 1–2 Kings tells how both the northern (Israel) and southern (Judah) kingdoms eventually went into exile. The story progresses in chronological order, oscillating between the north and south.

In the north Jeroboam I established a rival **cult** so that his people would not travel to Judah to worship. He built two golden calves, placing one in Bethel near the border of Judah and one in Dan in the distant north. He identified them as "your gods who brought you up from the land of Egypt" (1 Kings 12:28) and appointed priests to attend to the high places in Bethel. Because of this blatant violation of the command against making images (Deut. 5:8–9), Jeroboam forfeited the future of both his dynasty and the nation (1 Kings 13:33–34; 14:8–11, 15–16). Over the next two centuries the kings of Israel persisted in perpetuating this rival cult, which 1–2 Kings makes a point of denouncing time and time again (cf. 1 Kings 15:26, 34; 16:2, 19, 26, 31; 22:52; 2 Kings 3:3; 10:29, 31; 13:2, 6, 11; 14:24; 15:9, 18, 24, 28; 17:22). The worst king of all was Ahab, who had the audacity to make Baal worship a state-sanctioned religion (1 Kings 16:30–33; 21:25–26).

In the midst of this idolatry the Lord demonstrated his sovereign authority and established his right to Israel's exclusive worship. In response to Ahab's Baal worship, the Lord brought a famine upon the land, showing that he, not Baal, had authority over agricultural fertility. At Carmel he proved that he, not Baal, controlled the rain. The kings of the north tried to silence God's prophets, but the prophets asserted their authority over the kings. They announced the downfall of several kings (1 Kings 13:1–3; 14:4–16; 16:1–4; 20:35–42; 21:17–24; 22:15–28; 2 Kings 1:3–4) and demonstrated their God-given power to both bless and destroy (1 Kings 13:4–6; 17:1–18:46; 2 Kings 1:9–15; 2:19–25; 4:1–37; 5:1–27; 6:1–23). The Lord wanted the king and the people to recognize him as Yahweh (1 Kings 20:13, 28), the God who delivered them from Egypt and made a covenant with them. But they rejected him (2 Kings 17:7–23). Ironically, a foreign general, who serves as a literary **foil** for Israel, recognized that Israel's God is unique and worthy of exclusive worship (2 Kings 5:15–17).

In the south the seeds of idolatry planted by Solomon took deep root under his son Rehoboam. The people built high places and worshiped Canaanite gods (1 Kings 14:22–24). Rehoboam's son Abijah followed in his father's footsteps, yet the Lord blessed him with a son to carry on the dynasty, in fulfillment of his promise to faithful David (1 Kings 15:3–5). This son, Asa, obeyed the Lord and purged the land of Canaanite religious practices (1 Kings 15:11–13). Unfortunately, he did not eliminate the high places, yet the narrator commends him for his loyalty to the Lord (1 Kings 15:14).

From this point on, Judah's devotion to the Lord fluctuated. Jehoshaphat, like his father, Asa, was loyal to the Lord, but he allowed worship on the high places to continue (1 Kings 22:43). However, his son Jehoram turned from the Lord and followed the practices of Ahab in the north. He even linked the Davidic dynasty with that of Omri by marrying Ahab's daughter Athaliah (2 Kings 8:18). Despite Jehoram's sin, the Lord again showed mercy to Judah because of his promise to David (2 Kings 8:19). Ahaziah, the son of Jehoram and Athaliah, perpetuated his father's idolatry (2 Kings 8:26–27). When Ahaziah was assassinated by Jehu, Athaliah decided to destroy the Davidic line, apparently thinking this would stabilize her power (2 Kings 11:1). Joash's aunt rescued him and hid him in the temple for six years, after which Jehoiada the priest led a successful uprising against Athaliah and installed Joash as king. Jehoiada renewed the covenant between the Lord and the people, who then purged the land of the Baal cult established by Jehoram and supported by Athaliah (2 Kings 11:2–20). Joash and his successors obeyed the Lord, though they did not remove the high places (2 Kings 12:2–3; 14:3–4; 15:3–4, 34–35). When Ahaz took the throne, however, another crisis developed. He sacrificed on the high places and imported pagan religious practices from the northern kingdom (2 Kings 16:3–4). His son Hezekiah reversed his policies. Hezekiah demonstrated his devotion to the Lord by destroying the pagan cults and by eliminating the high places, something that had not been done prior to this in Judah's long history (2 Kings 18:3–6). The narrator commends Hezekiah for his faith and obedience, remarking, "in this regard there was none like him among the kings of Judah either before or after" (2 Kings 18:5). The Lord was with Hezekiah and granted him success (2 Kings 18:7). When the mighty Assyrians surrounded Jerusalem, the Lord miraculously delivered the city in response to Hezekiah's prayer (2 Kings 18:13–19:37). He also healed Hezekiah from a terminal illness and granted him fifteen additional years to live (2 Kings 20:1–11).

Hezekiah's reign proved to be the calm before the storm. Though Hezekiah was the best of Judah's kings to date, his son Manasseh was the worst. He sanctioned Baal worship, instituted a variety of idolatrous practices, and murdered many innocent people (2 Kings 21:1–9, 16). The Lord regarded Judah as more sinful than the native Amorites who had populated the land prior to Israel's arrival. He announced that Jerusalem would fall and that the people would be taken into exile (2 Kings 21:10–15). The downward spiral continued under Manasseh's son Amon (2 Kings 21:20–22), though it was arrested temporarily by Josiah. Josiah repented, submitted to God's law, and purged the land of idolatry. He eliminated the high places, which had been rebuilt after Hezekiah's earlier purge, and even destroyed the high place at Bethel, in fulfillment of an ancient prophecy (2 Kings 22–23). Yet Josiah's noble efforts were too little, too late. Because of Manasseh's sins, the Lord was bent on Judah's destruction (2 Kings 23:26–27; 24:3–4), which swiftly came to pass following Josiah's death (2 Kings 24–25). The Davidic dynasty came to an end, though a Davidic descendant remained alive in Babylon (2 Kings 25:27–30).

The narrator's survey of Judah's history reveals several themes:

1. Unlike the dynasties of the north, several Davidic kings were loyal to the Lord. Two in particular, Hezekiah and Josiah, were zealous defenders of genuine Yahweh worship and enemies of paganism. When compared with the utter failure of the northern kingdom, it becomes apparent that Israel's future is linked to the success of the Davidic dynasty. (See our discussion below.)

2. Some kings, while commended for their loyalty, failed to remove the high places. Several kings of Judah promoted idolatry,

including the Baal cult that had taken root in the north. Jehoram even linked the Davidic dynasty with the house of Ahab, a decision that prompted a radical response from the Lord.

3. Throughout the history of Judah, the Lord was merciful to the dynasty and preserved it from serious threats, including Athaliah's attack on the royal line and Sennacherib's siege of Jerusalem.

4. In the end the Lord was forced to send the nation into exile because of its refusal to perpetuate the reform measures of Hezekiah, one of Judah's greatest kings.

1–2 CHRONICLES

Primary Theme

Chronicles offers a history of Israel that overlaps with and complements the account offered in Samuel–Kings. However, there are significant differences in scope and purpose. Chronicles focuses on the Davidic dynasty and consequently the kingdom of Judah. Overall, its historical portrait is more optimistic than what we find in Samuel–Kings, which highlight the nation's moral descent and political decline. The Deuteronomistic History (see page 128), when read from the perspective of the Exile, does provide a ray of hope for the future. Chronicles, through its more **idealized** presentation of the past, is much more optimistic as it holds up key figures of the past as paradigms of the ideal leader to come.

National Unity and a Royal Ideal: David and Solomon (1 Chron. 1–2 Chron. 9)

First Chronicles begins with genealogical lists that go all the way back to Adam. Once the list reaches Jacob and his sons (1 Chron. 2:1–2), Judah gets prime position (2:3–4:23), but all of the tribes of Israel are represented (4:24–8:40). The exilic community (9:1–34) was mainly comprised of Levites, Judahites, and Benjaminites, though mention is made in passing that some from Ephraim and Manasseh were among the returnees (9:3). The genealogical lists set before the exilic community (the **implied audience** of 1–2 Chronicles) an ideal of a unified Israel headed up by Judah and the Davidic dynasty in particular (3:1–24).

The history proper begins with an account of Saul's rejection due to his disobedience (see especially 1 Chron. 10:13–14) and emphasizes that God transferred the kingship to David (1 Chron. 10:1–11:3). In contrast to 1 Samuel, the narrative does not cover Saul's career, but records only his death. It is clear that the Chronicler's focus is David; Saul's aborted reign was a mere prologue and Saul was a mere **foil** for David.

The account of David's reign (1 Chron. 11–29) highlights his role as worship leader (15:1–16:43), with special emphasis on preparations for the building of the temple and the organization of the temple **cult** (22:1–26:32; 28:1–29:20). The Chronicler also gives careful attention to David's covenant with the Lord (17:1–27) and to his military leadership (11:4–12:40, 14:8–16; 18:1–20:8; 27:1–24), with emphasis on the fact that his support came from all Israel (12:23–40).

Negative incidents in David's career, such as his sin with Bathsheba and murder of Uriah, are suppressed for the most part. Uzzah's unfortunate death is recorded (13:1–14), but David wisely recognized that cultic violations were the cause and he made the necessary corrections to assure that the ark was treated with due respect as it was transported to Jerusalem (15:1–16:6). The plague incident is recorded (cf. 2 Sam. 24), but David repented and interceded as worship leader for the nation (1 Chron. 21:1–22:1). While 2 Samuel 24:1 attributes David's sinful act of numbering the people (cf. 24:10) directly to the Lord's anger and deception, the Chronicler attributes it to "an adversary" (1 Chron. 21:1).[12] All in all, the account of David's reign is a sanitized version of his career that presents David as a model ruler who foreshadows an ideal king to come.

The same holds true for the account of Solomon's reign (2 Chron. 1–9). Solomon, David's handpicked successor (1 Chron. 29:21–25),

---

12. Some understand this as a proper name referring to Satan, but this seems unlikely. Elsewhere in the Old Testament, Satan is referred to with the title *"the* adversary" (note the definite article; cf. Job 1:6–9, 12; 2:1–4, 6–7; Zech. 3:1–2). When the noun שָׂטָן, "adversary," appears without the article, as in 1 Chronicles 21:1, it always refers to a human or national enemy, with the exception of Numbers 22:22, 32, where it refers to the Lord's angel (cf. 1 Sam. 29:4; 2 Sam. 19:23 [Eng. v. 22]; 1 Kings 5:18; 11:14, 23, 25; Ps. 109:6).

received wisdom and wealth from the Lord (2 Chron. 1). The account presents Solomon as temple builder (2:1–5:1) and as worship leader and intercessor (5:2–7:22) who achieved success and fame (8:1–9:28; cf. especially 9:22–23). No reference is made to his many wives (cf. 1 Kings 11:3–8); in fact the daughter of Pharaoh is mentioned as if she were his only wife (2 Chron. 8:11). The picture is not entirely positive, for the concluding verses of the account of his reign refer to his wealth and accumulation of chariot horses (9:25–29; cf. Deut. 17:16–17) and Ahijah's prophecy of God's punishment is briefly mentioned as well (9:29; cf. 1 Kings 11:29–39). Yet the account is, for the most part, idealized. In this regard Dillard and Longman state: "In Chronicles David and Solomon are portrayed as glorious, obedient, all conquering figures who enjoy not only divine blessing but also the support of all the nation." They observe that this "idealization of the reigns of David and Solomon," rather than being "a kind of glorification of the 'good old days,'" instead "reflects a 'messianic historiography'" in which David and Solomon embody an "**eschatological** hope."[13]

A Paradigm for Godly Leadership: Lessons from the Davidic Dynasty (2 Chron. 10–36)

The remainder of 2 Chronicles focuses on the history of Judah (2 Chron. 10–36). It highlights the positive accomplishments of the Davidic kings, especially their leadership in worship (24:4–14; 29:1–31:21; 34:8–35:19), their support of the Levites (17:7–9; 19:8–11), and their opposition to idolatry, especially the high places and the fertility **cult** of Baal and Asherah (14:2–5; 15:1–18; 17:3–6; 19:3; 34:2–7).

God's commitment to the Davidic dynasty, though not mentioned often, is nonetheless an important underlying theme (13:5; 21:7; 23:3). King Abijah reminded the northern kingdom that God had made a permanent covenant with David and would defend the dynasty on the battlefield (13:5–12). The narrator informs us that the Lord spared Judah from destruction because of his promise to David, even when King Jehoram married Ahab's daughter (21:6–7). When Athaliah

---

13. Raymond B. Dillard and Tremper Longman III, *An Introduction to the Old Testament* (Grand Rapids: Zondervan, 1994), 174–75.

usurped the throne of Judah, many made a pact to make Joash king in accordance with God's promise to David (23:3).

The Chronicler emphasizes that kings can win battles against overwhelming odds if they trust in the Lord (13:2–19; 14:8–15; 20:1–30; 25:7–13; 32:1–23), and he makes the point that obedience brings divine blessings (26:5; 27:6). Though outnumbered by two-to-one (13:3), Abijah won a great victory over Israel because the Lord intervened in the battle in response to Judah's trust in him (13:3–18). Asa, outnumbered by the Cushites, won a resounding victory when he cried out to the Lord (14:8–15). Jehoshaphat actually won a victory over a Moabite-Ammonite coalition without the use of an army, as the Lord supernaturally intervened and caused the enemy to panic and self-destruct (chap. 20). When told to send his Israelite mercenaries home, Amaziah obeyed and the Lord rewarded him with victory (25:1–13). When the Assyrians surrounded Jerusalem, Hezekiah, who was confident of the Lord's ability to protect his city (32:6–8), prayed for divine intervention and the Lord destroyed the Assyrian army, forcing Sennacherib to return home (32:1–23).

According to the Chronicler, disobedience, in the form of idolatry (21:6; 22:3; 24:18; 25:14; 28:2–4, 22–25; 33:2–9, 22), foreign alliances (16:1–10; 19:2; 22:5; 28:16–21), and hostility toward God's prophets (16:10; 24:19–22; 25:16), was immediately punished, sometimes by assassination and often in fulfillment of the prophetic word (16:12–13; 21:8–19; 22:7–9; 24:23–26; 25:20–28; 28:5–8; 33:10–11, 22–25).

As in the Deuteronomistic History, the prophets are God's mouthpieces and must be treated with respect. Shortly after he jailed the prophet Hanani (16:10), Asa developed a foot ailment from which he died (16:12). The text states that he failed to seek the Lord, giving the impression that his life may have been spared if he had done so. His disrespect for Hanani was symptomatic of an underlying problem that eventually contributed to his death. During Joash's reign, prophets confronted the people with their idolatry (24:17–19). The king had the prophet Zechariah executed, but before he died the prophet prayed that the Lord would avenge his death (24:20–22). Shortly after this, a militarily inferior Syrian army defeated Joash (24:23–24). Wounded in the battle, Joash was assassinated by his servants (24:25). According to the narrator, his death was the result of what he had done to Zechariah.

Amaziah ordered one of the Lord's prophets to stop preaching, prompting the prophet to announce the king's demise (25:14–16). Shortly after
this, Amaziah foolishly charged into battle against Israel and met defeat
(25:20–24). The narrator informs us that the Lord caused Amaziah to
do this because he desired to punish him for his idolatry (v. 20). For the
rest of his reign, Amaziah was threatened by assassination plots, one of
which eventually succeeded (25:25–28).

The Chronicler gives special consideration to Hezekiah and Josiah,
who promoted temple worship and sought to reunite the northern
kingdom with the southern in accordance with the ancient ideal of a
united Israel (30:1–12; 34:9). Two kings in particular are presented in
a much more positive light than in 1–2 Kings. According to 1 Kings
15:3, Abijah followed the sinful practices of his father Rehoboam,
but in 2 Chronicles 13 he declares his faith in the Lord on the verge
of battle (see v. 11) and wins a resounding victory. Second Kings 21
denounces Manasseh and attributes Judah's eventual downfall to his
sin, but 2 Chronicles 33 depicts him as a repentant sinner who rejects
idolatry and reinstitutes pure worship (see vv. 12–17).

Second Chronicles ends on a positive note, with the Lord moving
the Persian king Cyrus to decree that the exiles may return to Jerusalem
(36:22–23). The point is clear: the Lord still had plans for his people.
The Chronicler sets before the exilic community an ideal of a united
Israel under a Davidic king who promotes the temple cult in Jerusalem.
He reminds the community that God can give success against overwhelming odds, but obedience is essential to receiving his blessing.

EZRA–NEHEMIAH

Ezra

The books of Ezra–Nehemiah pick up Israel's story where
2 Chronicles leaves off (cf. Ezra 1:1–2 with 2 Chron. 36:22–23). The
author emphasizes the Lord's commitment to the future of the exilic
community. He prompted the Persian ruler Cyrus to issue a decree
that the exiles could return to Jerusalem and to authorize rebuilding of
the temple (1:1–4). He also moved several leaders of the exilic community to respond favorably to the decree (1:5–2:70). By using the phrase

הֵעִיר רוּחַ, "stir up the spirit" (1:1, 5), the narrator highlights God's sovereign intervention in human affairs to accomplish his purposes (see also 1 Chron. 5:26; 2 Chron. 21:16; 36:22; Jer. 51:11; Hag. 1:14), in this case the restoration of the exiles to their homeland. The book of Ezra thus opens on a positive note, signaling that the Exile would not thwart God's plan or covenantal promises.

The author's focus is the rebuilding of the temple and the restoration of temple worship (Ezra 3). This dual theme is especially important in the aftermath of the Exile. Prior to the Babylonian invasion of Jerusalem, Ezekiel saw the Lord leave the temple, leaving it vulnerable to destruction (Ezek. 10). The rebuilding of the temple and reinstitution of the **cult** would signal that the Lord had again taken up residence among his people. The Lord's presence in Jerusalem was, of course, vital to the future success of the community.

The returning exiles encountered opposition for nearly a century (4:1–24), but through the instrumentality of the Lord's prophets (Haggai and Zechariah), three different Persian rulers (Cyrus, Darius, Artaxerxes), and Ezra the priest, the temple was finally rebuilt and temple worship reinstituted (5:1–7:28). Ezra was very much aware that the Lord was responsible for the success of the community (7:27–28). He recognized that the Lord had moved the heart of King Artaxerxes. Once more the theme of the Lord's sovereignty over human rulers emerges. The restoration of the exiles truly was the work of God and for that reason promised to be successful.

Ezra commissioned Levites for service, actively sought God's blessing, and offered sacrifices for all Israel (8:15–36). Though most of the returning exiles were descendants of Levi, Judah, or Benjamin (cf. Neh. 11), the community identified itself with Israel in its ancient form consisting of twelve tribes (8:35).

The author also stresses the importance of the ethnic purity of the covenant community. Ezra, a scribe who was conversant with the Law of Moses (7:6), was committed to keeping the Law and teaching it to the community (7:10). Being aware of its regulations regarding intermarriage with foreigners, Ezra was troubled by the fact that many men, including many priests (10:18–44), had taken foreign wives. Ezra confessed the community's sin of intermarrying with the people of the land, and the people, overcome with guilt, put away their foreign wives

(9:1–10:44). Like ancient Israel, the postexilic community was under the authority of the Law; unlike ancient Israel, the postexilic community purified itself from foreign influence. The book of Ezra thus ends on a positive note, portraying a community that responded properly to God's law. If this commitment could be sustained, the future looked bright.

Nehemiah

The book of Nehemiah is concerned with the security of the covenant community in Jerusalem. Burdened by the news that the walls of Jerusalem had not yet been rebuilt, Nehemiah prayed that he would be able to travel to Jerusalem and rebuild the walls (Neh. 1:1–11). He confessed the nation's sins (vv. 6–7), but also reminded God of his promise to restore the people if they repented and renewed their commitment to his Law (vv. 8–9; cf. Deut. 30:1–10). Nehemiah's prayer blends the themes of divine sovereignty and human responsibility in perfect balance. The success of the community was completely dependent on God's favor, but at the same time the people's renewed willingness to obey was the catalyst for God's intervention. This same sequence is apparent in Deuteronomy 30, where repentance and renewed obedience on the part of the exiles (v. 2) prompts the Lord's favor, which brings restoration to the land (vv. 3–5), supernatural moral transformation (v. 6), and renewed divine blessing (v. 9).[14]

The king gave him permission, but once he arrived in Jerusalem and organized the rebuilding project, he and the community faced opposition from the foreigners living in the land (2:1–4:23; 6:1–19). Nevertheless the people completed the work (6:15) and dedicated the wall (12:27–47).

Nehemiah was very much aware that his success was due to the Lord's intervention. The king's willingness to grant him permission to return was due to the "hand of God" (2:8, 18). When he arrived in Jerusalem, he was conscious of God's guidance (2:12). In the face of opposition, he assured the people that God would prosper their

---

14. One sees this same balance between divine sovereignty and human responsibility in prophetic texts that envision the restoration of the exiles. See Isaiah 55:6–13; Jeremiah 29:11–14 in relation to Jeremiah 31:31–37; and Ezekiel 18:31 in relation to Ezekiel 36:24–27.

efforts to rebuild the wall (2:20). When their enemies hurled threats their way, Nehemiah and the people prayed as they continued their efforts (4:4–5, 9). In response the Lord frustrated the enemies' evil intentions (4:15),[15] prompting Nehemiah to assure the people that God was "fighting" for them (4:20). Opposition continued, but Nehemiah prayed for the Lord's intervention against the enemy (6:14). When the people finished the wall, their enemies were disheartened because they realized that God had enabled his people to accomplish this great task (6:16). The dedication ceremony was a worship service in which the people thanked God for granting them joy (12:43).

Nehemiah, Ezra, and the other leaders sought to establish a strong spiritual foundation for the community. Nehemiah promoted social justice (5:1–19) and ethnic purity (13:1–3, 23–31). He urged the people to fear the Lord, an attitude that he modeled before them (5:9, 15). Nehemiah also eliminated irregularities with regard to the temple (13:4–14) and implemented Sabbath observance (13:15–22). Ezra read the Law to the people (8:1–18), prompting them to confess their sins (9:1–3) and to commit themselves to obedience and pure temple worship (9:38–10:39).

The Levites prayed publicly, recalling God's covenant with Abraham and his kindness to Israel, despite their ingratitude and disobedience (9:4–37). The central theme of their prayer is God's great compassion (9:17, 19–21, 27–28, 31). He showed his people mercy and compassion following the incident with the golden calf (vv. 17–18; cf. Exod. 32), during the forty years when they wandered in the wilderness (vv. 19–21), and on many occasions throughout their sin-plagued history (vv. 27–28, 31). God's compassion is, of course, a corollary of his faithfulness, another important theme of this prayer (vv. 32–33). The exiles realized that they were in bondage because of the sins of their fathers, not because of some deficiency on God's part (vv. 34–37). Yet due to God's compassion and faithfulness, they were ready to commit themselves anew to him and trust him with their future (v. 38).

---

15. The Hebrew expression used here (הֵפִיר עֵצָה) literally means "to break/foil a plan." The expression is also used of God's intervention in 2 Samuel 15:34; 17:14; and Psalm 33:10.

Primary Themes

To summarize, the books of Ezra–Nehemiah tell of a revived covenant community, created by the Lord's providential intervention and sustained by his compassion and good favor. The Lord moved the mighty Persian rulers to support the efforts of the returning exiles and he protected his people from hostile enemies. While Jerusalem's walls had been rebuilt, giving it a measure of physical security, the future success of the postexilic community depended on its willingness to obey God's law in civil and cultic matters. It needed to preserve its ethnic identity and the integrity of its temple worship.

ESTHER

The book of Esther tells the story of a Jewish exile named Mordecai and his beautiful cousin Esther. Through a fascinating set of circumstances they were able to save the Jewish exiles from the murderous plot of Haman, an event that gave rise to the Jewish feast of Purim.

The most curious feature of the book is the absence of God's name. Despite this glaring omission, many contend that the book illustrates God's providential control of events. But if this were the case, one would expect some reference to his involvement in human affairs. Considering the narrator's point of view is helpful at this point.[16] The author of the story may have deliberately suppressed God's presence in order to reflect the perspective of the exiles, who lived in a distant land where God appeared to be absent. By masking God's presence and focusing on the characters' role in the deliverance of the exiles, the author also emphasizes the importance of human responsibility in the outworking of God's purposes. Dillard and Longman observe: "This doctrine of divine sovereignty is fundamental to the book of Esther, but it is not a kind of fatalism. For where God's actions and purposes are not transparent, the importance of human obedience and faithfulness becomes the more apparent."[17]

---

16. See our discussion of the narrator's authority and perspective in chapter 1. The following proposal concerning the point of view of the author of Esther appears in almost identical form in Robert B. Chisholm Jr., "A Rhetorical Use of Point of View in Old Testament Narrative," *BSac* 159 (2002): 413–14.

17. Dillard and Longman, *Introduction to the Old Testament,* 196.

As the book's characters step forward and assume responsibility, apparent coincidences unfold in such a way that the exiles are preserved from destruction. As the story concludes, one asks, "Did these exiles simply live a charmed life, or is there more to the story than mere good fortune?" From the perspective of an observer living in the Exile, God was apparently absent. Yet the unfolding of events, especially Esther's being in the right place at the right time, suggests this perspective is **limited**. Even when God appears to be absent, the structure of events reveals his presence. As noted earlier, the book's main literary units are arranged in a symmetric pattern. Events occurring in the book's first half correspond thematically to events recorded in the second half of the book.[18] The centerpiece of the structure is 5:9–6:14, where the roles of Mordecai and Haman are reversed. Within this **episode**, the pivotal **scene** is in 6:1–11, where the king is unable to sleep and ends up granting Mordecai the honor that Haman intended for himself. This turn of events foreshadows the book's conclusion, which tells of the fate of the Jews (chap. 9). Johnston explains, "the dramatic and unexpected reversal in the status of Haman and Mordecai in 6:1–11 foreshadows the eventual reversal in the fate of the Jews: it moves from their being endangered by their enemies to their emerging triumphant over their enemies."[19] The Jews' victory over their enemies (9:1–19) contrasts with their enemies' plots against them (3:1–15). The literary symmetry and foreshadowing suggest that the events, rather than being coincidental, were part of a larger design that must have been orchestrated by God.

By using a limited literary perspective that reflects the reality of life in exile, the narrator makes his point about God's presence more powerfully than if he had imposed an omniscient perspective on the story. Rather than giving readers a theological interpretation of the events, the narrator forces them to seek an answer for themselves to the question posed by the mysterious coincidences of history. Careful reflection on the latter reveals that there is a pattern to events and that they

---

18. Gordon H. Johnston, "A Funny Thing Happened on the Way to the Gallows! Irony, Humor, and Other Literary Features of the Book of Esther," in *Giving the Sense: Understanding and Using Old Testament Historical Texts,* ed. David M. Howard Jr. and Michael A. Grisanti (Grand Rapids: Kregel, 2003), 383–88.
19. Ibid., 388.

are not so coincidental after all. This in turn leads the eyes of faith to only one reasonable conclusion: despite appearances, God was with his people, even in that distant, remote place. Furthermore, even when circumstances look hopeless and threatening, God in his **providence** can provide an escape, especially when his people courageously rise to the challenge and subordinate their own well-being to that of the covenant community.

THEMATIC SUMMARIES

The Deuteronomistic History: Joshua–2 Kings

In the Hebrew Bible the books of Joshua, Judges, 1–2 Samuel, and 1–2 Kings are called the Former Prophets, so named because prophets play such an important role in the history.[20] Scholars have long recognized that these books comprise a single history in which Deuteronomistic themes are prominent. Yet they disagree concerning the overall purpose and extent of this history. Some, following Martin Noth, understand the history primarily in a negative light as an explanation for why the nation was exiled and as an apology for God's decision to judge it. Others see a silver lining in the history. Gerhard von Rad finds some hope in the history because of the promise to David it records. Hans Wolff sees the history as a call to repentance to the exiles. Frank Cross proposes a double redaction of the history, the first coming from Josiah's time and the second from the period of the Exile. The first redaction was designed to motivate Josiah's reforms, the second to motivate the exiles to renewed commitment.[21]

Our survey suggests that this more balanced view of the history, in contrast to Noth's overly pessimistic interpretation, is preferable. The history is, in many ways, a depressing account of the disintegration and exile of God's covenant community. It documents the nation's violation of the Deuteronomic Law and describes how the judgments threatened in Deuteronomy (the covenantal "curses") came to pass.

---

20. Recall that Ruth is placed in the Writings, the third section of the Hebrew canon.
21. For a concise summary of views on the Deuteronomistic History, see Barry L. Bandstra, *Reading the Old Testament,* 2d ed. (Belmont, CA: Wadsworth, 1999), 206–7. See also David M. Howard Jr., *An Introduction to the Old Testament Historical Books* (Chicago: Moody, 1993), 179–82.

However Deuteronomy anticipated this, yet still held out hope for a bright future beyond exile (Deut. 30:1–10). The history provides support for this optimism, albeit in the form of a silver lining in a dark wall of clouds. The history demonstrates God's commitment to his people. Time and time again he showed them mercy; one suspects that even a judgment as radical as the Exile could not deter God from pursuing his people. God promised David and his descendants his enduring loyal love, suggesting a positive ending for Israel's history (2 Sam. 7:15–16). Perhaps this is why the Lord concluded his judgment oracle against Solomon with a brief, but important qualifying statement that the Davidic dynasty would be humiliated, "but not forever" (1 Kings 11:39). Solomon's dedicatory prayer, which alludes to Deuteronomy 30, anticipates the Exile, but also asks that God would respond favorably when his people repent (1 Kings 8:46–53). According to 2 Kings 13:23, the Lord was merciful to Israel during the reign of Jehoahaz because of the covenant he made with Abraham, Isaac, and Jacob. Though this is the only reference to the Abrahamic covenant in the history, it is apparent that God took seriously this promise, which is mentioned several times in Deuteronomy (1:8; 6:10; 9:5, 27; 29:13; 30:20; 34:4). Finally, the preservation of the Davidic line throughout Judah's history offers hope. Indeed 2 Kings concludes with the observation that a Davidic descendant remained alive in Babylon (25:27–30).

The Postexilic Literature: 1–2 Chronicles, Ezra–Nehemiah, Esther

These books reminded the exiles that God was still with his people, no matter where they happened to be. Though his work might be veiled and providential (Esther), God was intervening in history on their behalf. He was sovereign over the powerful Persian kings and committed to establishing a new covenant community in Jerusalem. He was compassionate to his people and faithful to his ancient covenantal promises to Abraham (Neh. 9:7–8) and David (2 Chron. 13:5; 21:7; 23:3). This new community must obey God's law, maintain their ethnic purity, and worship God in his rebuilt temple. As the history of Judah's kings illustrates, continued obedience would bring divine blessing, culminating in the revival of the Davidic-Solomonic dynastic ideal and the fulfillment of the covenantal ideal of a unified Israel committed to and blessed by God.

Overall Thematic Synthesis of the Historical Books

At least two major themes predominate throughout the historical books. First, God's *covenantal relationship* with his people Israel is at the heart of the story. The covenant is renewed in Joshua 23–24, but Judges–2 Kings tell how the most basic stipulation of the covenant (exclusive worship of Yahweh) was violated time and time again, culminating in the exile of the people. The temple, the symbol of the Lord's presence among his people, was left in ruins, and the Promised Land was abandoned. Many years before, Solomon anticipated this development and prayed that the Lord would ultimately restore his wayward people (1 Kings 8:46–53; 2 Chron. 6:36–42). The books of Ezra–Nehemiah tell how Solomon's vision of a renewed covenant community began to take shape as exiles returned to Jerusalem, rebuilt the temple and city walls, and committed themselves to follow the Law of Moses.

Second, the theme of *kingship* dominates the landscape of the historical books. The book of Joshua makes it clear that the Lord was Israel's king, for he was the one who owned the Promised Land and allotted it to his subjects with the expectation that they would honor and worship him in gratitude for his gift. As Israel disobeyed the Lord and lost its moral and ethical compass, it became apparent that Israel needed a human king to exemplify and promote faithfulness to the Lord (cf. Judg. 17:6; 21:25 with Deut. 17:14–20). When Israel demanded a king, they did so for the wrong reasons (1 Sam. 8; cf. Judg. 8:22–23). The Lord gave them a king, but with the understanding that this human ruler was God's vice-regent, subject to divine authority (1 Sam. 12). When Saul disobeyed, the Lord removed him from office and replaced him with David, with whom God instituted a special covenantal arrangement ensuring David of an enduring dynasty (2 Sam. 7; 1 Chron. 17). Solomon's idolatry brought divine punishment on the dynasty, as God tore all but one tribe from David's house and established a rival dynasty in the north. The ensuing history is a grim account of failure and judgment, though some Davidic descendants proved faithful to the Lord. In the end both the northern and southern kingdoms were carried away into exile, though God preserved a Davidic descendant. When the exiles returned from Babylon, neither Judah's independent status nor the Davidic dynasty was restored. Nevertheless, a Davidic descendant, Zerubbabel, became governor (1 Chron. 3), the priesthood was restored, and through the encouragement of the prophets Haggai and Zechariah, the temple was rebuilt and the worship system reestablished. The Chronicler, writing in this context of renewed hope, provides an **idealized** account of the Davidic-Solomonic era, casting a vision of what lies ahead for the Davidic dynasty.

To summarize, the historical books tell a story that begins with great hope as God's people enter their Promised Land. The story takes a tragic turn for the worst as God's people reject his royal authority and turn to other gods. The story seems to come to an end when God sends his people into exile, leaving the temple in ruins, the Promised Land abandoned, and the Davidic dynasty humiliated and robbed of its throne. But from the ruins of exile, a new community rises. They return to their land, rebuild the temple, and renew their commitment to God, armed with the memory of what they once were and with a vision of what they could become. Though the historical books do not resolve the tension in the Old Testament's **macroplot**, they do hint that the future is bright because Israel's God is committed to overcoming all obstacles, even the moral failures of his people, and to bringing his plan for them to fruition in fulfillment of his ancient promises.

3

PREPARING FOR
INTERPRETATION

IN PREPARING TO INTERPRET A TEXT, one should place the text in its historical context, determine what the text is and what it says, and consult the work of others who have paved the interpretive pathway. In this chapter we discuss each of these preparatory aspects of interpretation.

SETTING THE STAGE FOR THE HISTORICAL BOOKS

As we saw in chapter 1, it is essential for the interpreter to recognize the literary dimension of Old Testament stories, but one must also remember that these scriptural accounts are true stories rooted in history. Consequently it is important to understand the historical setting of the historical books. To that end we provide here a survey of the period encompassed by these books, integrating where possible the biblical record with ancient Near Eastern history. The timeline covered by the historical books begins with Israel's invasion of the Promised Land under Joshua and ends in the postexilic period with Nehemiah's rebuilding of Jerusalem.

Biblical Chronology

In reconstructing biblical chronology, scholars first attempt to determine a fixed date or dates. This is done by correlating biblical and ancient Near Eastern data.[1] According to the Assyrian records, there was a solar eclipse in the year of Bur-Sagile (an Assyrian governor). This can be dated June 15, 763 B.C. Ninety years before this (853 B.C.), in the sixth year of his reign, the Assyrian ruler Shalmaneser III fought against a western coalition at Qarqar; King Ahab of Israel was a member of this coalition. In the eighteenth year of his reign (841 B.C.) Shalmaneser III received tribute from King Jehu of Israel. According to the Old Testament, twelve years separated the reigns of Ahab and Jehu, so Ahab's reign ended in 853, while Jehu's began in 841.

With these years in place, scholars can then use the biblical chronological data to date the reigns of kings before and after this. The division of the kingdom occurred in 931 B.C. Solomon's reign began forty years before this in 971 B.C. According to 1 Kings 6:1, Solomon began building the temple in his fourth full year (966 B.C.), 480 years after the Exodus from Egypt. If one takes this figure literally, then the Exodus occurred in 1446 B.C.[2] In this case, Joshua's invasion of the land took place in 1406 B.C.

However, not all scholars are convinced that this dating scheme for the Exodus is correct. On the basis of archaeological and biblical evidence, some place the Exodus in the thirteenth century. They regard the figure of 480 years as stylized, representing twelve generations, which would have actually encompassed approximately 300 years. It is beyond the scope of our discussion to attempt to resolve this debate. In order to accommodate both positions, the following survey will begin around 1400 B.C.

The survey divides Israel's history into four major time periods:[3]

---

1. See Edwin Thiele, *The Mysterious Numbers of the Hebrew Kings,* 3d ed. (Grand Rapids: Zondervan, 1983), 67–78.
2. For a defense of this relatively early date for the Exodus, see Eugene H. Merrill, *Kingdom of Priests: A History of Old Testament Israel* (Grand Rapids: Baker, 1987), 66–75.
3. What follows is a concise survey, designed to give the student an overview of significant events that had a bearing on Israel's history as recorded in the canonical historical books. For more detailed treatments of Israel's history, the reader should consult the standard texts on the subject: V. Philips Long, David W. Baker, and Gordon J. Wenham, eds., *Windows into Old Testament History: Evidence, Argument, and Crisis of "Biblical Israel"* (Grand Rapids:

1. The Conquest, Judges, and United Monarchy (1400–931 B.C.):
   The bulk of the material in the historical books covers this period, including Joshua, Judges, Ruth, 1–2 Samuel, 1 Kings 1–11,
   and 1 Chronicles 10–2 Chronicles 9.
2. The Divided Monarchy (931–722 B.C.): 1 Kings 12–2 Kings 17
   and 2 Chronicles 10–28 cover this period.
3. The Kingdom of Judah (722–586 B.C.): 2 Kings 18–25 and
   2 Chronicles 29:1–36:21 record the key events of this period.
4. The Exile and Return (586–433 B.C.): The final verses of
   2 Chronicles (36:22–23) tell of Cyrus's decree to allow the exiles to return to Jerusalem. The books of Ezra, Nehemiah, and
   Esther also originate in this period.

The Conquest, Judges, and United Monarchy (1400–931 B.C.)

1400–1200 B.C.

In the fourteenth century B.C. Canaan was organized in city-states
that were nominal subjects of the Egyptian Pharaoh. However, the
Amarna correspondence between the kings of the Canaanite city-states
and the Egyptian rulers Amenhotep III (1417–1379) and Ikhnaton
(1379–1362) testify to an unsettled situation in Canaan.[4] A group
known as the *Habiru* is mentioned in the letters as a disruptive influence in the land. Because of the similarity in spelling to "Hebrew,"
some suggest that these *Habiru* were actually the invading Israelites.

However, this proposal is problematic for a variety of reasons.
References to the *Habiru* are not limited to the Amarna letters. Ancient
Near Eastern texts dating from various times and places mention them.
The references appear as early as the Ur III period (late third millen-

Eerdmans, 2002); John Bright, *A History of Israel,* 4th ed. (Louisville: Westminster John
Knox, 2000); Walter C. Kaiser, *A History of Israel* (Nashville: Broadman& Holman, 1998);
Eugene H. Merrill, *Kingdom of Priests: A History of Old Testament Israel* (Grand Rapids:
Baker, 1987); James Maxwell Miller, *A History of Ancient Israel and Judah* (Philadelphia:
Westminster, 1986); and Iain W. Provan, V. Philips Long, and Tremper Longman III, *A
Biblical History of Israel* (Louisville: Westminster John Knox, 2003). For a concise history
of the ancient Near East see William W. Hallo and William Kelly Simpson, *The Ancient
Near East: A History,* 2d ed. (Ft. Worth, TX: Harcourt Brace, 1998).
4. For the sake of convenience, all dates given in this chapter, unless otherwise noted, are
   those used by Merrill, *Kingdom of Priests.*

nium B.C.) and come from Mari, Babylon, Alalakh, Nuzi, Boghazkoi,
Ugarit, and Egypt. They are not a distinct ethnic group, in contrast to
the Hebrews, who appear to be the offspring of Abraham's ancestor
Eber. The description of the *Habiru* in the Amarna letters differs at
many points from the biblical account of the invading Israelites. The
letters indicate the *Habiru* were also involved in Syria and Phoenicia at
this time, but Joshua 11:8 describes the Israelites' northernmost probe
as being brief and extending only as far as Sidon. The *Habiru* also appear
in the letters as mercenaries, who were hired by local Canaanite rulers and were even assigned land. This bargaining between Canaanites
and *Habiru* does not accord with the biblical description of the Israelite
invasion. The latter aimed at the extermination of all Canaanites and
made no provision for agreements with the local population (the deal
with Rahab and the Gibeonite incident being exceptions). The letters
also picture the *Habiru* as organized in small groups, probably consisting
of fifty to one hundred men. This does not match the biblical picture
of a large unified army led by Joshua, though it could reflect an occupational stage when the Israelite tribes were operating independently
and on a smaller scale. The military tactics of the *Habiru* also differ from
those of the Israelites in two significant ways. The *Habiru* burned cities
and used chariots, whereas the Israelites did not normally burn cities
(Josh. 24:13) or employ chariots.

   In light of the preceding observations, it is best not to identify the
Habiru with the invading Israelites (Hebrews) under Joshua. However,
the situation depicted in the Amarna letters is what one would expect as a consequence of Joshua's destructive invasion and the subsequent partial, but not completely successful occupation of the land by
the Israelite tribes. Many of the most powerful kings in the land had
been defeated (Josh. 12:9–24), leaving a power vacuum and creating a
number of displaced refugees. Power struggles occurred in those places
not occupied by the Israelites. Power hungry leaders would have wel-
comed the allegiance of society's outcasts. In this context the *Habiru*,
who were not respected in the land, appear as mercenaries and ma-
rauders who took advantage of a generally anarchic situation.[5]

   For most of the fourteenth century Egypt exercised little influence

---

5. Moshe Greenberg, *The Hab/piru* (New Haven: American Oriental Society, 1955), 74–75.

over Canaan and Syria. Under Suppiluliuma (1380–1346), Mursilis (1346–1315), and Muwatallis (1315–1296), the Hittite empire, located in the central and eastern regions of modern day Turkey, expanded to the east and southeast, laying claim to territory as far south as Byblos.[6] The Hittites established treaties with various Syrian city-states. Egyptian paralysis in Canaan and Syria apparently continued until the reign of Seti I (1318–1304), who launched a military campaign into Canaan.[7] Rameses II (1304–1236) attempted to expand Egyptian influence into Syria, but was halted in 1300 by Hittite forces at Kadesh. He eventually negotiated a treaty with the Hittites and sealed the alliance through marriage. Later in the thirteenth century the Egyptian king Merneptah (1236–1223) campaigned in Palestine. In an inscription dating to his fifth year, he claims to have conquered Israel. This is the earliest extant extra-biblical reference to Israel as a socio-political entity (the personal name is attested in earlier texts).

1200–931 B.C.

Around 1200 B.C. a large group of invaders from the west, known as the Sea Peoples, conquered the Hittite empire. They also threatened Egypt, but Rameses III (1198–1166) was able to defeat the invaders.[8] Rameses mentioned several distinct ethnic or tribal groups among the Sea Peoples, including the Peleset (the biblical Philistines, who appear as a powerful force in Canaan around this time, according to the biblical record in Judges and 1–2 Samuel). Though the Egyptians were able to fight off the invaders, Egyptian influence in Palestine declined after this, as illustrated in the Report of Wen-Amon.[9] This text, which dates to around 1100, tells of an Egyptian official's trip to Byblos to secure lumber. He was treated with disrespect, suggesting that Egypt's authority was no longer recognized in Palestine.

In the mid-fourteenth century the Assyrians began to emerge as a major force in northern Mesopotamia. The Assyrians attempted, with

---

6. For the dates of these Hittite rulers, see O. R. Gurney, *The Hittites*, 2d ed. (Baltimore: Penguin Books, 1954), 216.
7. *ANET*, 253–54; *COS*, 2:27–28.
8. *ANET*, 262–63.
9. Ibid., 25–29; *COS*, 1:89–93.

little success, to seize territory from the Hittites. However, following the fall of the Hittite empire, the Assyrian king Tiglath-pileser I (1115–1077) was able to invade Syria. On several occasions he waged war with the Arameans. This is the first clear reference to Arameans in ancient Near Eastern literature.[10] Saul (1050?-1011) fought against the Aramean kings of Zobah (1 Sam. 14:47), and David (1011–971) defeated various Aramean groups (2 Sam. 8:3–8; 10:1–19). During Solomon's reign Damascus successfully revolted against Israel's authority (1 Kings 11:23–25).[11]

The Divided Monarchy (931–722 B.C.)

931–841 B.C.

Following Solomon's death, the northern Israelite tribes rejected Solomon's son Rehoboam and broke off from Judah in 931. Shishak of Egypt attacked Jerusalem in King Rehoboam's fifth year (926) and looted the temple and royal palace (1 Kings 14:25–26; 2 Chron. 12:2–9). An Egyptian inscription lists several places in Palestine conquered by Shishak.[12]

Shortly after this the Assyrians began to emerge as a powerful force in the Near East. Under Adad-nirari II (911–891) and Tukulti-ninurta II (890–884), the Assyrians started to expand westward, setting the stage for the more aggressive imperialistic efforts of their successors Ashurnasirpal II and Shalmaneser III (see below).

When war broke out between Asa of Judah and Baasha of Israel, Asa enlisted Ben-Hadad I of Damascus as an ally (1 Kings 15:16–20; 2 Chron. 16:1–4). Ben-Hadad attacked Israel and captured several towns north of the Sea of Galilee.[13]

After Omri (885–874) established a new dynasty in Israel, he conquered Moab. According to the Mesha inscription,[14] Omri "oppressed Moab for many days." King Mesha of Moab attributed Omri's success

---

10. Wayne T. Pitard, *Ancient Damascus* (Winona Lake, IN: Eisenbrauns, 1987), 82.

11. For a survey of Israelite-Aramean relations during this period, see ibid., 87–97.

12. *ANET,* 263–64.

13. Archaeological evidence supports this. See Pitard, *Ancient Damascus,* 108–9. On the problem of dating the campaign, see ibid., 109–14.

14. *ANET,* 320–21; *COS,* 2:137–38.

to the anger of the Moabite god Chemosh. Mesha claimed to throw off the oppressive rule of Omri's "son" and boasted that Israel had "completely and permanently disappeared." According to 2 Kings 3, Mesha was a subject of Omri's son Ahab (874–853). When Ahab died, Mesha successfully revolted against Ahab's son Joram (see v. 5; cf. 2 Kings 1:1). Joram (852–841) enlisted the support of Jehoshaphat of Judah (873–848). When they marched on Moab, Mesha offered his firstborn son as a sacrifice, prompting the Israelites and Judahites to withdraw.

Israel was also actively involved with the Arameans during this time. Ahab beat back Ben-Hadad's attempts to subjugate Israel (1 Kings 20). Though the Lord wanted Ahab to execute the Aramean king, Ahab instead made a treaty with him, probably to maintain a stable buffer state between Israel and Assyria. Ahab was eventually killed fighting against the Arameans at Ramoth Gilead (1 Kings 22). Second Kings 5–9 tell of an Aramean general's visit to Elisha, the supernatural blinding of an Aramean army, the Lord's miraculous deliverance of Samaria from Ben-Hadad's siege, Hazael's assassination of Ben-Hadad, and Joram's defeat at the hands of Hazael (9:14–15).[15]

Despite the tension between the Israelites and Arameans, both sides were forced at times to put aside hostilities and ally against a common enemy that threatened to destroy both nations. The Assyrian ruler Ashur-nasirpal II (883–859) aggressively campaigned in the west. He marched into Syria, reached the Mediterranean Sea, and made several coastal towns (including Tyre, Sidon and Byblos) pay tribute.[16] Ashur-nasirpal's annals testify to his bloodthirsty and sadistic nature. His soldiers used various barbaric means of torture; they skinned, impaled, burned, immured, and cut off the limbs, noses, ears, and heads of captives.[17]

His successor, Shamaneser III (858–824), launched several military campaigns in the west. In 853 he fought at Qarqar (located northwest of Hamath) against a coalition that included Hadad-ezer of Damascus and Ahab of Israel. According to Shalmaneser's Monolith inscription,[18]

---

15. Pitard, *Ancient Damascus*, 114–25, suggests that the material about the Aramean wars in 1 Kings 20–2 Kings 8 actually comes from the period of Jehu's dynasty, not from the time of the Omride dynasty.
16. *ANET*, 188.
17. Georges Roux, *Ancient Iraq* (Baltimore: Penguin Books, 1966), 263–64.
18. *ANET*, 277–81; *COS*, 2:261–64.

Hadad-ezer contributed 1,200 chariots, 1,200 horsemen and 20,000 infantry to the coalition, while Ahab contributed 2,000 chariots and 10,000 infantry. Though Shalmaneser claimed to win a great victory, a closer look at the evidence suggests otherwise.[19]

841–745 B.C.

Shalmaneser was persistent. In 841, shortly after Hazael's accession to the throne of Damascus and Jehu's coup (841), he marched westward, defeated Hazael, and forced Jehu (841–814) to pay tribute. Shalmaneser's Black Obelisk depicts Jehu bowing before the Assyrian ruler.[20]

According to 2 Kings 10:32–33, Hazael, despite his defeat at the hands of Shalmaneser, was later able to take territory from Jehu. Hazael also threatened Judah and only withdrew from Jerusalem when Joash (835–796) bought him off with riches from the temple treasuries and royal palace (2 Kings 12:17–18). Hazael and his son Ben-Hadad continued to put pressure on Israel (2 Kings 13:3, 7, 22), but when Jehu's son Jehoahaz (814–798) asked the Lord to deliver Israel, the Lord "provided a deliverer" (2 Kings 13:5–6, 23). This deliverer may have been the Assyrian king Adad-nirari III (810–783), who campaigned in the west at this time and may have diverted Aramean attention away from Israel.[21]

Following the death of Hazael, his son Ben-Hadad attempted to extend Damascus's influence northward. The Zakur inscription[22] tells how Ben-Hadad formed an alliance of seven kings and marched against Zakur, king of Hamath and Lu'ath. Ben-Hadad besieged Zakur's city Hatarikka (Hadrach), but Zakur claimed that his god Baal-shamayn answered his prayer for help and delivered him from his enemies. Ben-Hadad also experienced defeat in the south. Israel's king Jehoash (798–782), son of Jehoahaz, was able to reclaim Israelite territory from Damascus (2 Kings 13:24–25).

Under Jehoash's son Jeroboam II (793–753), Israel prospered and

---

19. See Pitard, *Ancient Damascus,* 128–29.
20. *ANEP,* 351.
21. *ANET,* 281.
22. Ibid., 501–2; *COS,* 2:155.

expanded its borders. According to 2 Kings 14:28, Jeroboam was able to make Damascus a subject state. During this period the Assyrians were also weak. The Assyrian king Shalmaneser IV (782–773) campaigned against Damascus, now ruled by Hadianu. However, after this Assyria went through a difficult time of political unrest and military defeat during which a plague broke out. It was during this general time period that Jonah (a contemporary of Jeroboam II, see 2 Kings 14:25) visited Nineveh. To the south of Israel, Judah, led by Uzziah (792–740), also experienced renewed prestige and influence.

745–722 B.C.

Following the rise of Tiglath-pileser III (745–727) to the throne of Assyria, the political situation in Israel and Judah changed abruptly. Tiglath-pileser rebuilt the Assyrian empire as he conducted a series of military campaigns.[23] In 743 he made Rezin of Damascus, Menahem of Israel (752–742), and several other western kings pay tribute (2 Kings 15:19–20).

The Assyrian threat forced Israel and Damascus to form an anti-Assyrian alliance. Pekah (752–732), who had assassinated Menahem's son Pekahiah (742–740), and Rezin tried to force Judah's King Ahaz (735–715) to join their alliance, but he refused. In 735 they attacked Judah and threatened to replace Ahaz with a local ruler (called the "son of Tabeel" in Isa. 7:6)(see 2 Kings 16:5–6; Isa. 7:1). Rather than trusting in the Lord, Ahaz enlisted the help of Tiglath-pileser and became his subject (2 Kings 16:7–10). Tiglath-pileser was heavily involved in the west during 734–732. In 732 he defeated Damascus and reduced it to a province (2 Kings 16:9). He then invaded and conquered Israel, dividing much of its territory into provinces. He set up Hoshea (732–722), who assassinated Pekah, as a puppet king over a territorially reduced and greatly weakened Israelite state (2 Kings 15:29–30).[24]

Israel's days were numbered. During the reign of Shalmaneser V (727–722), Hoshea embarked on an anti-Assyrian policy and enlisted the aid of Egypt. Shalmaneser attacked Israel, took Hoshea prisoner, besieged Samaria for three long years before eventually taking the city

23. *ANET*, 282–84, *COS*, 2:284–92.
24. *ANET*, 284; *COS*, 2:288

in 722, and deported 27,500 Israelites (according to the Assyrian records) to Assyria (2 Kings 17:3–6). Shalmaneser's successor Sargon II (722–705) claimed to be the conqueror of Samaria,[25] but this claim is in part propagandistic. Sargon was probably a general in Shalmaneser's army when the city was taken.

The Kingdom of Judah (722–586 B.C.)

722–681 B.C.

With Israel out of the picture, Judah was now a neighbor of Assyria, which had reduced Israelite territory to provinces ruled by Assyrian governors. But changes were also taking place in Assyria, where Sargon II (722–705) replaced Shalmaneser V as king. The change in rule prompted rebellions in the south and in the west, so Sargon, after solidifying his strength at home, also had to stabilize his empire. In the south a coalition of Elamites and Chaldeans, led by Merodach-Baladan (see 2 Kings 20:12), beat back the Assyrians at Der in 720. Sargon was not able to drive Merodach-Baladan out of Babylon until 710.

In the west Sargon encountered a Syro-Palestinian coalition that included rebel forces from Damascus, Samaria, and Gaza, among others. In 720 Sargon defeated the rebels at Qarqar, swept through Philistia and went as far as the Egyptian border, forcing Judah, ruled by Ahaz (735–716), to pay tribute. Sargon also brought the siege of Tyre, begun five years earlier by Shalmaneser, to a successful conclusion. After campaigning in the east for two years, Sargon was forced to put down another western rebellion in 717. In 712 he sent a force to the west again, this time to put down a rebellion by the king of Ashdod (see Isa. 20:1).

After Sargon's death in battle in 705, Sennacherib (705–681) rose to the throne of Assyria. Rebellions broke out in the empire shortly after this. In 703 Merodach-Baladan tried unsuccessfully to regain the throne of Babylon. In 701 Hezekiah of Judah (729–686), in conjunction with his religious reforms and his attempt to revive the glory of the Davidic monarchy, allied with the kings of Sidon and Ashkelon and the leaders of Ekron in an attempt to overthrow Assyrian rule.

25. *ANET*, 284–87; *COS*, 2:295–98.

Sennacherib came west to put down the rebellion. The king of Sidon fled to Cyprus, the king of Ashkelon was carried away into exile, and the rebel leaders in Ekron were impaled. That left Judah.

Sennacherib's invasion of Judah consisted of two forces. The first advanced through central Judah and established a line of approach and supply through the northern Shephelah. This force captured Azekah, Gath, and the cities of the Shephelah, including Lachish. A second force moved from Lachish up to Jerusalem, destroying several towns along the way. In his annals Sennacherib described his conquest of the land and his siege of Jerusalem.[26] He boasted that he captured forty-six walled cities, took over 200,000 captives, forced Hezekiah to pay a large amount of tribute, and trapped the Judahite king in his royal city "like a caged bird." The biblical account (see 2 Kings 18:17–19:36; Isa. 36–37) provides us with a more complete picture of what happened. Here we learn that the Lord destroyed 185,000 Assyrian soldiers, forcing Sennacherib to return to Assyria. Sennacherib did not record this disaster; this comes as no surprise, given his well-attested tendency to falsify history in his royal annals.[27] Sennacherib did not claim to have taken Jerusalem or to have deposed Hezekiah. His silence in this case speaks volumes![28]

For the remainder of his reign Sennacherib was occupied with rebellions in the south. In 700 he defeated Merodach-Baladan and his Elamite and Aramean allies. In 695–691 he campaigned against the Elamites, while in 689 he destroyed Babylon after besieging it for nine months. According to 2 Kings 19:37 (see also Isa. 37:38), two of Sennacherib's sons assassinated him while he worshiped in the temple of one of his gods. They escaped to Armenia, and Sennacherib's son Esarhaddon (681–669) took the Assyrian throne.

---

26. *ANET*, 287–88; *COS*, 2:302–3

27. Antti Laato, "Assyrian Propaganda and the Falsification of History in the Royal Inscriptions of Sennacherib," *VT* 45 (1995): 198–226.

28. Some argue that there were actually two invasions of Judah by Sennacherib, separated by fifteen years. According to this view 2 Kings 18:14–16 tells of the first, 2 Kings 18:17–19:35 of the second. For presentations, discussion, and critiques of this view see, among others, John Bright, *A History of Israel,* 3rd ed. (Philadelphia: Westminster, 1981), 284–88; J. B. Geyer, "2 Kings XVIII 14–16 and the Annals of Sennacherib," *VT* 21 (1971): 604–6; S. H. Horn, "Did Sennacherib Campaign Once or Twice Against Hezekiah?" *AUSS* 4 (1966): 1–28; K. A. Kitchen, "Late-Egyptian Chronology and the Hebrew Monarchy," *JANESCU* 5 (1973): 225–33; Merrill, *Kingdom of Priests,* 414–15n. 74; and W. H. Shea, "Sennacherib's Second Palestine Campaign," *JBL* 104 (1985): 401–18.

681–626 B.C.

Esarhaddon rebuilt Babylon, regaining the loyalty of the Babylonians and solidifying his rule in the south. In the west Esarhaddon maintained control of the Assyrian provinces and subjects, including Judah, now ruled by Hezekiah's son Manasseh (696–642), who is listed as one of Esarhaddon's subjects in one of the Assyrian king's inscriptions.[29] Esarhaddon also campaigned against the Egyptians and even forced the princes of Lower Egypt to acknowledge his sovereignty.

Esarhaddon's successor, his son Ashurbanipal (668–627), attempted to strengthen Assyrian control over Egypt. Toward the end of his father's reign, the Egyptians had rebelled against Assyrian rule. After Ashurbanipal took the throne, he marched against Egypt and defeated the rebels. However, once the main army withdrew, the Egyptians did not cooperate with Assyrian occupational troops, which had to put down the uprising.

Sometime later, probably after 648, Manasseh of Judah rebelled against Assyrian rule. He was taken to Babylon in humiliation, but eventually was allowed to return to Jerusalem (see 2 Chron. 33:11–13). Manasseh was succeeded by his son Amon (642–640), who was in turn succeeded by Josiah (640–609). During Josiah's reign major political changes occurred in the Near East, as the Assyrian empire collapsed and the Babylonians and Egyptians rushed to fill the vacuum.

626–586 B.C.

Ashurbanipal was succeeded by his son, Ashur-etil-ilani, who had to suppress two internal uprisings during his brief reign. During these internal struggles (if not before in some cases), Babylon, Palestine, Phoenicia, and Media repudiated Assyrian rule. About 623, Sin-shar-ishkun seized the throne from his brother, Ashur-etil-ilani, with the help of the Chaldean Nabopolassar, who had already rebelled against Assyria in 626. Sin-shar-ishkun then broke off relations with Nabopolassar; Assyria and Babylon remained hostile until the demise of the former a few years later. In 615 the Medes under Cyaxares invaded Assyria, capturing the city of Ashur. Cyaxares and Nabopolassar

---

29. *ANET,* 291.

formed an alliance and defeated Nineveh in 612, an event described in the Babylonian Chronicle[30] and prophesied by Nahum. Assyrian forces under Ashur-uballit, an officer of the king, regrouped in Harran.

In 609 the Egyptians, under Necho (who was trying to maintain the balance of power in the Near East), marched northward to aid the Assyrians. Josiah of Judah challenged him at Megiddo and was killed in battle (2 Kings 23:29–30). Judah now became an Egyptian subject. In 609 Jehoahaz became king of Judah. He apparently rebelled against Egyptian rule, for Necho quickly replaced him with his brother Jehoiakim (608–598)(see 2 Kings 23:31–35).

In 605 the Egyptians and Babylonians, led by Nebuchadnezzar II (605–562), clashed at Carchemish (see Jer. 46:2). The Babylonians emerged victorious and Nebuchadnezzar marched southward into Palestine, making Jehoiakim his subject. When Jehoiakim rebelled in 601 (see 2 Kings 24:1), Nebuchadnezzar sent troops to the west, reestablished control of Judah, and claimed territory all the way to the Egyptian border (2 Kings 24:2, 7). Jehoiachin (598–597) succeeded Jehoiakim to the throne of Judah. Apparently Judah rebelled at this time, for Nebuchadnezzar besieged Jerusalem, replaced Jehoiachin with Zedekiah, and deported many people, including Jehoiachin, to Babylon (see 2 Kings 24:10–17).[31] Zedekiah (597–586) remained loyal for a time, but he, like his predecessors, eventually rebelled against Babylonian rule. In 588 Nebuchadnezzar besieged Jerusalem, which eventually capitulated in 586. The Babylonians sacked the city, burned the temple, and carried most of the people away into exile (2 Kings 25). The exiles would not return to their homeland until almost fifty years later, when the Persians, led by Cyrus, conquered Babylon[32] and allowed them to go back.

The Exile and Return (586–433 B.C.)

After Cyrus's decree to allow the exiles to return to Judah (538), Sheshbazzar led a group of exiles back to the land (Ezra 1–2). Though work on the temple soon began, the project was interrupted due to

30. Ibid., 304–5.
31. Ibid., 305.
32. Ibid., 306–7; *COS*, 2:314–15.

opposition and indifference (Ezra 3–4). The temple was finally completed in 515 B.C. (Ezra 5–6). Ezra led more exiles back to Jerusalem in 458, during the reign of the Persian king Artaxerxes I (464–424)(Ezra 7–8). Ezra opposed the marriage practices that were prevalent in the postexilic community. Many men had married women from outside the Jewish community. Ezra urged them to divorce these wives and commit themselves to becoming an ethnically pure community that reflected God's covenantal ideal (Ezra 9–10).

In 445 Nehemiah came to the city and organized the rebuilding of the city wall. Though the Jews faced opposition and threats from some of the neighboring peoples, they completed the task (Neh. 1–7). Ezra read the Law of Moses to the people, who committed themselves to obey it (Neh. 8–10). Priestly service was organized, the wall dedicated, and further reforms implemented (Neh. 11–13).

Of course, not all of the exiles returned to their homeland. The book of Esther, which records events that took place during the reign of Xerxes (486–465), tells how the Lord providentially saved his people from annihilation through Mordecai and Esther, a Jewish exile who became Xerxes's favorite wife. The Jewish feast of Purim originated at this time, commemorating the deliverance of the Jews from Haman's evil genocidal plot against them.

DETERMINING WHAT THE TEXT IS: TEXTUAL CRITICISM

Introduction

Identifying the text is logically prior to translation and interpretation, but in actual practice it must be done concurrently with them, for text critical decisions cannot be made in a vacuum or solely on the basis of **external textual evidence.**

Ideally a text critic collates the various textual witnesses and from this evidence chooses or reconstructs the reading of the original text. However, in actual practice most interpreters begin with the standard Hebrew text published in *Biblia Hebraica Stuttgartensia (BHS)*. Using the textual apparatus of *BHS* and the text critical notes in the standard technical commentaries, one can identify variant readings and then choose or reconstruct a proposed original textual reading on the basis of the available evidence. Before attempting to do textual criticism, an interpreter needs to be aware of the extant textual witnesses, the development of these texts and versions, and proper text critical method. Several useful introductions to textual criticism are available, including:

Brotzman, Ellis R. *Old Testament Textual Criticism.* Grand Rapids: Baker, 1994.

McCarter, P. Kyle, Jr. *Textual Criticism.* Philadelphia: Fortress, 1986.

Tov, Emanuel. *Textual Criticism of the Hebrew Bible.* Minneapolis: Fortress, 1992.

Würthwein, Ernst. *The Text of the Old Testament.* Translated by Erroll F. Rhodes. 2d edition. Grand Rapids: Eerdmans, 1995.

Two Basic Principles

While the discipline of textual criticism demands expertise from its practitioners, it also requires a good dose of common sense. When attempting to establish the reading of the original text, text critics should follow two basic principles:[33]

One Should Not Automatically Assume That the Traditional Hebrew (Masoretic) Text Preserves the Original Text

Because the traditional Hebrew (Masoretic) text is generally superior to other textual witnesses, some automatically prefer its reading to those of other textual traditions. However, the Masoretic text does not preserve the original text in every instance. A comparison of the Qumran (Dead Sea Scrolls) evidence with the Septuagint (the ancient Greek translation of the Old Testament) indicates that the latter sometimes preserves the better reading, especially in 1–2 Samuel.[34] In several cases in 1–2 Samuel, the Masoretic text, which is the basis for most modern translations, is corrupt due to accidental scribal error.

---

33. P. Kyle McCarter Jr., *Textual Criticism* (Philadelphia: Fortress, 1986), 71–75.

34. Ralph W. Klein, *Textual Criticism of the Old Testament: The Septuagint After Qumran* (Philadelphia: Fortress, 1974), 11–26.

For example, the shorter Hebrew text of 1 Samuel 10:1 is the product of scribal error; the Septuagint (LXX) preserves the original reading (the additional material from LXX is in italics):

> **The LORD has chosen you** *to lead his people Israel! You will rule over the LORD's people and you will deliver them from the power of the enemies who surround them. This will be your sign that* **the LORD has chosen you** as leader over his inheritance.

The eye of the scribe responsible for the reading in the Hebrew text skipped from the first appearance of the boldfaced clause, "The LORD has chosen you," to the second instance of the clause (also boldfaced), resulting in the omission of the intervening material. The following context supports the longer Septuagint reading; the "sign" referred to in the longer (Greek) version is described in the verses that follow.

The same type of error is evident in the Hebrew text of 1 Samuel 14:41–42, where the Septuagint again preserves the original text. Verses 41–42 should read as follows (the additional material from LXX is in italics):

> Saul said: "O LORD God of **Israel**, *why have you not answered your servant today? If this iniquity is in me or in Jonathan my son, O LORD God of Israel, give Urim. But if this iniquity is in your people* **Israel**, give Thummim." Saul and Jonathan were taken, and the soldiers went free. (v. 41)

> Saul said: "Cast the lot between me and Jonathan my **son**! *Let him whom the LORD takes die!" And though the soldiers said, "Let it not be so" to him, Saul prevailed upon them, and they cast lots between him and Jonathan his* **son**. And Jonathan was taken. (v. 42, author's translation)

In verse 41 the eye of the scribe responsible for the Hebrew reading jumped from the first appearance of "Israel" to the third; in verse 42 his eye jumped from the first use of "son" to the second. In both cases this resulted in the omission of the intervening material.

One Should Base Text Critical Decisions Primarily on Internal Considerations

Internal considerations include semantics (word meaning) and syntax (grammatical relationships). A basic rule to follow is this: The superior (original) reading is the one that best accounts for the existence of the others. If there are two variants (A and B), then we first assume A is original and seek an explanation for the existence of B. Then we reverse the process, assuming B is original and attempting to account for the existence of A. At this point, one of the proposals should be more plausible than the other.

For example, in Judges 16:13–14 the Hebrew text reads:

> [13]Delilah then said to Samson: "Up to now, you have deceived me and told me lies. Tell me how you can be subdued!" He said to her: "If you weave the seven braids of my hair into the fabric." [14]So she fastened (it) with the pin and said to him, "The Philistines are here, Samson." He woke up from his sleep and tore away the pin of the loom and the fabric. (author's translation)

The Septuagint has a longer version of the account. The words in italics reflect the additional material appearing in the Septuagint:

> [13]Delilah said to Samson: "Up to now you have deceived me and told me lies. Tell me how you can be subdued." He said to her: "If you weave the seven braids of my hair with **the fabric** *and fasten (it) with the pin to the wall, I will become weak like any other man.*" [14]*So when he was asleep Delilah took the seven braids of his hair and wove (them) into* **the fabric.** She fastened (it) with the pin *to the wall* and said: "The Philistines are here, Samson!" He woke up from his sleep and tore away the pin of the loom from the wall. (Vaticanus version; author's translation)

If one assumes that the shorter Hebrew text is original, it is difficult to explain how the longer Greek text arose. One would have to argue that the Greek translator deliberately expanded the text to make it conform stylistically to the earlier panels. If one assumes the Septuagint preserves the original text, then the Hebrew text has been shortened by an accidental error. Note that the last word before the additional Septuagint material is הַמַּסָּכֶת, "the fabric" (placed in bold in the translation above for easy recognition). This same word appears at the end of the "plus," suggesting that a scribe's eye jumped from the first instance of the word to the second, resulting in the omission of the intervening words.[35]

Contextual factors support the longer version. In the shorter version Samson's explanation seems truncated and incomplete, especially when compared to the explanations he gives Delilah both before (vv. 7, 11) and after this (v. 17). In the shorter version Delilah's response does not correspond to Samson's directions, contrary to the pattern we see before (vv. 8, 12) and after this (v. 19). In a **paneled** narrative like this (vv. 6–9, 10–12, 13–14, 15–22), one expects structural symmetry in the panels leading up to the climax, where structural deviation is then common. The longer version provides the symmetry one expects and is contextually more compatible.

Text critics sometimes argue that one should prefer the shorter and/ or more difficult text. But this example shows that sometimes a text can be shorter and more difficult due to scribal error. If one suspects textual expansion or interpretive clarification, then the shorter and/or more difficult text is preferable, but this principle should not be applied in an inflexible, mechanical manner.

Students sometimes shy away from doing textual criticism because it seems so technical and requires expertise in Hebrew, Greek, and other ancient languages. However, as McCarter points out, the primary tool one needs in doing textual criticism is common sense.[36] If one has a working knowledge of Hebrew and Greek and access to good, critical commentaries that discuss text critical issues, one should be able to weigh the evidence for competing readings and make well-reasoned decisions.

---

35. This type of scribal mistake is well attested elsewhere. See ibid., 27–29. The omission of the phrase אֶל הַקִּיר, "to the wall," in the Hebrew text of verse 14b may also have been accidental. A scribe's eye could have skipped from the final *daleth* on the preceding word (בַּיָּתֵד, "with the pin") to the very similar *resh* on the end of הַקִּיר, "the wall," resulting in the omission of the prepositional phrase.

36. McCarter, *Textual Criticism,* 18–20.

DECIDING WHAT THE TEXT SAYS: TRANSLATION

Determining what the text says is basic to the interpretive process. Translating the text requires the interpreter to do semantic and syntactical analysis of a passage. Semantics deals with the meaning of words and phrases, while syntax pertains to the relationships between words and phrases within a sentence. Ideally one begins by producing a translation based on one's own semantic and syntactical analyses, but in actual practice the interpreter rarely operates independently. It is time consuming and unnecessary to "reinvent the wheel." Others have already worked in the text and the interpreter is wise to interact with standard translations and commentaries from the outset of the interpretive process. By interacting with others, one is able to discern more quickly what the key issues are and to devote one's attention to these matters. This does not mean that the interpreter will simply perpetuate the interpretations and views of others. On the contrary, as the interpreter interacts with the work of others, it will become apparent that there is rarely unanimity on interpretive matters. One must interact critically with translations, commentaries, and other study tools and arrive at one's decision based on the textual evidence and the arguments of others.

Semantics

Tools

When doing word studies, the interpreter needs reliable tools, including dictionaries (sometimes called lexicons), wordbooks, and concordances. The three major Hebrew–Aramaic dictionaries available are the following:

1. Brown, Francis, S. R. Driver, and Charles A. Briggs. *A Hebrew and English Lexicon of the Old Testament.* Oxford: Clarendon Press, 1907. A reprint edition of BDB, keyed to *Strong's Concordance,* is published by Hendrickson.

    BDB's greatest strength is its thorough analyses of biblical usage; it is especially valuable for studying well-attested words.

As one may suspect from the publication date, BDB is outdated in some respects, especially in its English glosses and its analyses of rare words. The definitions offered by BDB are frequently archaic and do not reflect contemporary English usage. Proposed meanings for rare words are based on the limited evidence from the cognate languages (particularly Arabic) that was available at the beginning of the twentieth century. Because of numerous twentieth-century archaeological discoveries and advances in Hebrew semantics, we are now in a better position to understand the meaning of many of these rare words.

2. Clines, David J. A., ed. *The Dictionary of Classical Hebrew.* Sheffield: Sheffield Academic Press, 1993.

This expensive, multivolume work is an especially valuable reference tool because of its sound linguistic approach. With just a few exceptions, it includes every occurrence of every Hebrew word. Listings are according to syntactical function and collocations. For example, an entry on a noun groups texts where the noun functions as subject and indicates all of the verbs with which it is collocated. Other groupings include occurrences of the noun in nominal clauses, as the object of a verb (with the various verbs listed), in the construct state before a genitival modifier, and in collocations with various prepositions and adjectives. For verbs, the dictionary lists the various subjects, objects, and prepositions with which the word is collocated as well as all the passages where the specific collocation may be found. While one can find collocations easily with a good computer search program, it is convenient to have the data assembled in one place. Its thorough lists and its focus on collocations make this dictionary an extremely helpful tool for interpreters. However, since the dictionary focuses on Hebrew usage, it is of little value in determining the meaning of rare words, where one must utilize etymological evidence from the cognate languages.

3. Koehler, Ludwig, and Walter Baumgartner. *The Hebrew and Aramaic Lexicon of the Old Testament: Study Edition.* 2 vols. Revised by Walter Baumgartner and Johann Jakob Stamm; translated and

edited by M. E. J. Richardson. Leiden: E. J. Brill, 2001 (abbreviated *HALOT*). The publisher has also made available an electronic version, as well as a more expensive five-volume print edition, which is identical in content to the study edition but has larger print.

The publisher is to be commended for making available the handy, two-volume *Study Edition,* as well as the electronic version. While not as thorough as BDB or *DCH* in its discussion of usage, *HALOT* reflects the latest research in Hebrew semantics and cognate languages. Consequently it is an indispensable tool when dealing with rare words. It will be a standard lexical tool for years to come.

Two multivolume wordbooks are especially useful to the interpreter:

1. *Theological Dictionary of the Old Testament.* Grand Rapids: Eerdmans, 1977–.
2. *New International Dictionary of Old Testament Theology and Exegesis.* Grand Rapids: Zondervan, 1997.

A concordance has always been a standard tool for word studies. The best of the traditional concordances is Abraham Even-Shoshan's *A New Concordance of the Old Testament,* 2d ed. (Grand Rapids: Baker, 1989). However, with computer search tools now readily available, the traditional concordance in hard copy is quickly becoming obsolete. Computerized tools have revolutionized the study of the Bible, for their search programs give the interpreter lightning-quick access to data. In addition to functioning as a traditional concordance, these search programs can also be used to locate collocations and to conduct grammatical searches. Programs with such capabilities include:

1. Accordance Bible Software: www.accordancebible.com
2. BibleWorks: www.bibleworks.com
3. Logos Bible Software (Libronix): www.logos.com
4. Bible Software from the Gramcord Institute: www.gramcord .org

Method and Principles

Polysemism. When determining the meaning of a word, one needs to examine the usage of the term in the Old Testament. Such an examination usually yields categories or shades of meaning. Only rarely does a word have a single meaning or referent. Most terms are **polysemantic**, displaying two or more shades of meaning. Of course, in almost all cases, only one of these meanings will apply in a given context.

When developing categories of meaning for a word, the interpreter should make distinctions between the primary (or literal) meaning or referent and extended (often metaphorical) meanings or referents. For example, the Hebrew noun אוֹר literally refers to "light," including daylight or the light that emanates from a heavenly body. But it can also be used metaphorically of life and salvation (e.g., Pss. 27:1; 56:14 [Eng. v. 13]). The noun דֶּרֶךְ literally refers to a road, but by extension it can be used of a journey or enterprise (e.g., Gen. 24:21; Num. 9:10). Metaphorically it is used of behavior or conduct (a way of life) (e.g., Deut. 32:4; Hos. 14:9). The noun בּוֹר refers primarily to a cistern, but it can also refer to the grave and the world of the dead (e.g., Ps. 28:1; Isa. 14:15).

Sometimes one can distinguish shades of meaning on the basis of **metonymy**, where the cause is substituted for the effect or vice-versa. For example, the verb II עָצַב (not to be confused with the homonym I עָצַב, "to form, shape") has the primary meaning "be injured," either physically (e.g., Eccl. 10:9) or emotionally. In the latter case it means to "grieve" over a tragic loss (e.g., 2 Sam. 19:3 [Eng. v. 2]; Isa. 54:6). But the word often describes more than mere grieving. By metonymy of cause for effect, it can mean "be embarrassed, shamed," that is, emotionally injured or grieved to the point where one is upset with oneself or with others for an inappropriate action (e.g., Gen. 45:5; 1 Sam. 20:3, 34; 1 Kings 1:6; Neh. 8:10–11). Finally the metonymic use of the verb can be extended still further. Sometimes it means "be offended, insulted," that is, emotionally injured or grieved to the point where one is offended by another's action and seeks vindication (e.g., Gen. 6:6; 34:7; Ps. 78:40; Isa. 63:10). It is in this sense that the verb is used of God's response to human sin.

The verb שָׂכַל, "be wise, successful," provides another illustration of metonymic usage.[37] The primary meaning of the verb, which is used predominantly in the *Hiphil* stem, is "to understand, comprehend, have insight." However, by metonymy of cause for effect, it can also mean "to achieve success, prosper," because insight can and often does produce success and prosperity. (Compare the English expression "he's a smart businessman," which is more than a commentary on the businessman's intelligence. The statement usually means he is successful.)

Collocations. Often one must study the use of a collocation, not just an individual word. For example, the expression נִקְרָא שֵׁם עַל, "a name is called over," indicates ownership or authority. The one whose name is "called over" the object possesses or has authority over that object (e.g., Deut. 28:10; 2 Sam. 12:28; 1 Kings 8:43; 2 Chron. 6:33; 7:14; Isa. 4:1; 63:19; Jer. 7:10–11, 14, 30; 15:16; 25:29; 32:34; 34:15; Dan. 9:18–19; Amos 9:12). However, when the idiom is קָרָא שֵׁם ("he calls a name"), קָרָא שֵׁם לְ- ("he calls a name to"), or נִקְרָא לְ- ("is called [to]") no such notion is present. These expressions simply mean that something or someone was given a name that was appropriate (e.g., Gen. 16:13; Ruth 4:17; 1 Sam. 9:9; 2 Sam. 18:18; Isa. 1:26; 32:5; 35:8; Jer. 19:6). The one giving the name does not necessarily exercise ownership or authority over the thing/one being named. Any such idea must be derived from the context (e.g., when a conqueror renames a town as in Judg. 1:17); it is not inherent in the idiom itself. This means that the man's naming the animals (Gen. 2:20) and the woman (Gen. 2:23; 3:20) did not necessarily reflect or establish his authority over them. That notion, if present, must be derived from the context, not from the mere use of a collocation for naming.[38]

Fortunately the availability of Bible software programs with sophisticated search capabilities makes it relatively easy to get the data necessary for such analysis. This is great news for the interpreter, because collocation analysis can be the key to correct interpretation. A fine example of this is Basil Rebera's study of Naomi's blessing in Ruth 2:20.[39] Naomi prays: "May he be blessed by the LORD, who has not

37. *HALOT*, 1328–29.
38. See George W. Ramsey, "Is Name-Giving an Act of Domination in Genesis 2:23 and Elsewhere?" *CBQ* 50 (1988): 24–35.
39. Basil A. Rebera, "Yahweh or Boaz? Ruth 2.20 Reconsidered," *The Bible Translator* 36 (1985): 317–27.

abandoned his kindness to the living and dead" (author's translation). It is not immediately apparent who is the referent of the relative pronoun אֲשֶׁר, "who"—is it Boaz or the Lord? One might think that the Lord is the antecedent since the pronoun immediately follows his name. However, collocation analysis reveals that the antecedent is Boaz, not the Lord. Elsewhere when אֲשֶׁר, "who," follows the blessing formula בָּרוּךְ ("blessed," Qal passive participle) + proper name/pronoun, it always introduces the reason the recipient of the blessing deserves a reward. If the pronoun refers to the Lord here, then this verse, contrary to usage elsewhere, does not give a reason for the recipient being blessed. Second Samuel 2:5 provides the closest syntactical parallel to Ruth 2:20 and validates our conclusion. It reads: "May you (plural) be blessed by the LORD, you who (אֲשֶׁר) have extended (plural) such kindness to your master Saul" (author's translation). The relative pronoun אֲשֶׁר refers back to the plural independent pronoun אַתֶּם, "you," as the second plural verb עֲשִׂיתֶם, "you have done," after אֲשֶׁר, "who," indicates. Naomi calls for the Lord to bless Boaz because Boaz demonstrated kindness to the living (the widows) and thereby to the dead (their deceased husbands).

One must do collocation analysis very carefully in order to avoid erroneous interpretations. For example, Marc Brettler argues that the angel who visited Manoah's wife impregnated her.[40] In her report to her husband she states: "A man sent from God came to me" (Judg. 13:6). Brettler points out that the idiom בּוֹא אֶל, "come to," can have sexual connotations (see Judg. 15:1; 16:1) and may be translated: "The man of God slept with me." He draws attention to the text's emphasis on the human qualities of the messenger and observes that angelic parentage would account well for Samson's superhuman abilities. He draws a parallel to Genesis 6, where, in his opinion, angels cohabit with human women. It is also odd that there is no subsequent reference in the context to Manoah's wife conceiving (contrast Gen. 21:2; 25:21; 30:23; 1 Sam. 1:20), only to her giving birth to the child (see v. 24).

What is one to make of this proposal? The idiom בּוֹא אֶל, "come to," is hardly a technical expression for sexual intercourse. It is used hundreds of times without such a connotation (e.g., Judg. 3:20; 4:21–22; 6:18;

40. Marc Zvi Brettler, *The Book of Judges* (London: Routledge, 2002), 44–49.

8:15; 9:46, 57; 11:7, 12, 34; 18:8, 10, 15; 19:22, 29; 21:8). Nevertheless
the appearance of this collocation in a context where conception is a
major theme is indeed striking. Furthermore, elsewhere when a woman
uses the idiom "come to me," it has a sexual connotation.[41] However,
a closer look at the immediate context militates against Brettler's proposal. In verse 8 Manoah prays that the Lord would allow the man of
God "to come again to us" (lit. translation). Surely the idiom "come
to" does not have a sexual connotation here! Of course one could argue
that Manoah, who shows a propensity for confusion elsewhere in the
chapter, did not fully understand the implications of his wife's statement in verse 6. However, verse 9 informs us that the angel of God, in
response to Manoah's request, "came again to the woman" (lit. translation).[42] Why would he need to have sexual relations with her again if he
had already impregnated her (cf. v. 5)? There is no sexual connotation
here and the action is viewed as repeating the earlier incident (note עוֹד,
"again"). In verse 10 she simply reports to Manoah that the man "appeared" (נִרְאָה) to her. This suggests that בּוֹא אֶל, "come to" (v. 9), merely
refers to his appearing to her and has no sexual connotation. If so, then
we can safely assume that the idiom בּוֹא אֶל, "come to," in her initial report to Manoah (v. 6) refers to the man's appearing to her (cf. וַיֵּרָא, "and
he appeared," in v. 3) and nothing more. While Brettler's view is to be
rejected, there may be a subtle dimension to the language that plays
off the use of the expression for sexual contact. The messenger did not
actually impregnate Manoah's wife, but he did make a prophetic pro-
nouncement that for all intents and purposes guaranteed that she would
conceive. He did not "come to" her in a sexual sense, but his visit did
precede her conceiving! Perhaps in the original context this ironic use
of the idiom was intended to inject some humor into the story.

Rare words. The Hebrew Bible contains a large number of rare words.

---

41. See Genesis 38:16; 39:14, 17. Joshua 2:4 is ambiguous; the verb there is plural, not singular, but then again Rahab was a prostitute.
42. Elsewhere the collocation of a masculine singular form of בּוֹא, "come," with אֶל, "to," followed by אִשָּׁה, "woman," has a sexual connotation (cf. Gen. 38:8–9; Judg. 15:1; 1 Chron.
7:23; Prov. 6:29; Ezek. 23:44), but in five cases אִשָּׁה is suffixed or modified by a genitive and
clearly refers to a man's wife. In the other example (Ezek. 23:44) it is followed by apposi-
tional זוֹנָה and refers to a prostitute. When הָאִשָּׁה, "the woman," is the object of the preposi-
tion, as in Judges 13:9, there is no sexual connotation, though in both of the other instances
the verb is masculine plural, not singular (1 Sam. 28:8; 2 Sam. 17:20).

This poses a special problem for the interpreter, who must in such cases use factors other than usage to determine meaning. When rare words are involved, the interpreter must examine the evidence from the cognate Semitic languages, other words in biblical Hebrew derived from the same root, usage in postbiblical Hebrew, and contextual clues.

A couple of examples must suffice. In 2 Samuel 22:12 the difficult form חַשְׁרַת is a construct feminine singular form of a hypothetical חַשְׁרָה, which *HALOT* defines as "wing, sieve."[43] This word is a *hapax legomenon,* meaning that it appears only once in biblical Hebrew. On what basis does *HALOT* define the term? One notices that the word is derived from a hypothetical root חשׁר, which is attested in Ugaritic in a nominal form "wing, sieve," and in postbiblical Hebrew and Aramaic in a verbal form "to sift, spread."[44] On this basis one may reasonably propose that the phrase חַשְׁרַת־מַיִם in 2 Samuel 22:12 means literally "sieve of water," which is probably a poetic reference to the rain clouds. This would make good sense in the context where God comes in the storm clouds to deliver the psalmist from death.

The verb דָּאָה occurs only four times in the Hebrew Bible (Deut. 28:49; Ps. 18:11 [Eng. v. 10]; Jer. 48:40; 49:22). Yet one can determine that its meaning is "to fly, glide"[45] on the basis of the following evidence: (1) in three of the texts it is used of an eagle, and in two of these it stands parallel to "spread its wings"; (2) in Psalm 18:11 it describes the Lord soaring on the wings of the wind, having mounted his bird-like cherub, and it stands parallel to the more well-attested verb for flying (עוּף); (3) the verb has a cognate in Ugaritic meaning "to fly."

Syntax

When determining what the text says (translation), the interpreter must also deal with issues of syntax. Syntax addresses the relationships between words and phrases within a sentence. Some of the main syntactical issues one faces when translating include analyzing the case

---

43. *HALOT,* 363.
44. For later Hebrew and Aramaic one may consult Marcus Jastrow, *A Dictionary of the Targumim, the Talmud Babli and Yerushalmi, and the Midrashic Literature,* 2 vols. (reprint, Brooklyn: P. Shalom, 1967). This particular verb is listed on page 511 with the meaning "to sift" in both Hebrew and Aramaic.
45. *HALOT,* 207.

function of nouns, identifying the antecedents of pronouns, evaluating the function of verbal stem and aspect, and determining the function of dependent clauses. It is beyond the scope of this discussion to address the specifics of Hebrew syntax. The interpreter should consult the syntactical tools that are available. These include the following:

Intermediate Grammars

Arnold, Bill T., and John H. Choi. *A Guide to Biblical Hebrew Syntax.* Cambridge: Cambridge University, 2003.
Chisholm, Robert B. *From Exegesis to Exposition,* 57–117. Grand Rapids: Baker, 1998.
van der Merwe, Christo H. J., Jackie A. Naudé, and Jan H. Kroeze. *A Biblical Hebrew Reference Grammar.* Sheffield: Sheffield Academic Press, 1999.
Williams, Ronald J. *Hebrew Syntax: An Outline.* 2d edition. Toronto: University of Toronto, 1976.

Advanced Grammars

Kautzsch, E., ed. *Gesenius' Hebrew Grammar.* 2d English ed. Revised by A. E. Cowley. Oxford: Clarendon Press, 1910.
Joüon, Paul. *A Grammar of Biblical Hebrew.* Corrected 1st edition. Translated and revised by T. Muraoka. 2 vols. Rome: Pontifical Biblical Institute, 1993.
Waltke, Bruce K. and M. O'Connor. *An Introduction to Biblical Hebrew Syntax.* Winona Lake, IN: Eisenbrauns, 1990.

READING WHAT OTHERS HAVE TO SAY: SOME BIBLIOGRAPHICAL AIDS

Introductions

Hamilton, Victor P. *Handbook on the Historical Books.* Grand Rapids: Baker, 2001. This synthetic commentary provides an overview of the historical books, focusing on introductory issues, content, and major themes.

Howard, David M., Jr. *An Introduction to the Old Testament Historical Books*. Chicago: Moody, 1993. Howard discusses introductory issues and significant interpretive problems, surveys the structure and content of the books, and summarizes their theological themes.

Long, V. Philips. *The Art of Biblical History*. Grand Rapids: Zondervan, 1994. Long discusses the nature of biblical history writing from an evangelical perspective. Using the story of Saul's rise to kingship as an example, he shows how historicity, literary art, and theology must be held in balance when interpreting the Bible's historical literature.

Mathewson, Steven D. *The Art of Preaching Old Testament Narrative*. Grand Rapids: Baker, 2002. Mathewson shows how to move from "text to concept" and then from "concept to sermon." The book also includes several samples of sermons on Old Testament narratival texts.

McConville, J. Gordon. *Grace in the End: A Study in Deuteronomic Theology*. Grand Rapids: Zondervan, 1993. This study of Deuteronomic theology includes two useful chapters for those interested in the theology of the historical books: "The Deuteronomic Idea in Joshua–Kings" and "Deuteronomic Theology."

Works on Narratival Art

Alter, Robert. *The Art of Biblical Narrative*. New York: Basic Books, 1981. Alter makes a compelling case for a literary approach to biblical narrative. He discusses and illustrates a variety of literary techniques used by the biblical authors, including type-scenes and literary convention, dialogue, repetition, and characterization.

   Since Alter's groundbreaking work, several other literary critics have written introductions advocating, describing, and illustrating a literary approach to Old Testament narrative. Many view Sternberg's study (below) as programmatic.

Amit, Yairah. *Reading Biblical Narratives*. Translated by I. Lotan. Minneapolis: Fortress, 2001.

Bar-Efrat, Shimon. *Narrative Art in the Bible*. Translated by D. Shefer-Vanson. Sheffield: Almond, 1989.

Berlin, Adele. *Poetics and Interpretation of Biblical Narrative*. Winona Lake, IN: Eisenbrauns, 1994.

Brichto, Herbert Chanan. *Toward a Grammar of Biblical Poetics: Tales of the Prophets.* New York: Oxford, 1992.

Fokkelman, Jan P. *Reading Biblical Narrative.* Translated by I. Smit. Louisville: Westminster John Knox, 1999.

Gunn, David M. and Danna Nolan Fewell. *Narrative in the Hebrew Bible.* New York: Oxford, 1993.

Sternberg, Meir. *The Poetics of Biblical Narrative.* Bloomington, IN: Indiana University, 1987.

Trible, Phyllis. *Rhetorical Criticism: Context, Method, and the Book of Jonah.* Minneapolis: Fortress, 1994.

Evangelical scholars have contributed to the discussion. Particularly helpful are the following:

Longman, Tremper, III. *Literary Approaches to Biblical Interpretation.* Grand Rapids: Zondervan, 1987.

Pratt, Richard L., Jr. *He Gave Us Stories.* Brentwood, TN: Wolgemuth & Hyatt, 1990.

Ryken, Leland. *How to Read the Bible as Literature.* Grand Rapids: Zondervan, 1984.

Individual Books

In the section to follow we list some major studies for each of the historical books, beginning in each case with commentaries. Rather than annotating each individual commentary, we will characterize the various commentary series that are represented in the bibliography.

Commentaries in the Anchor Bible (AB) and Old Testament Library (OTL) series reflect a nonevangelical stance and employ a **diachronic** method. The Berit Olam and Interpretation series are more literary and **synchronic** in their approach. The Word Biblical Commentary (WBC), New International Commentary (NICOT), and New American Commentary (NAC) series are broadly evangelical and exegetically oriented. The NAC series, while generally not as technical as the other two, provides a nice balance of exegetical and applicational insights. The NIV Application Commentary (NIVAC) series, as suggested by the title, is especially sensitive to contemporary application. Each section of the commentary is divided into three parts, titled "Original Meaning," "Bridging Contexts," and "Contemporary Significance."

Joshua

Several commentaries are available to interpreters, including:

Boling, Robert G., and George E. Wright. *Joshua*. AB. Garden City, NY: Doubleday, 1982.
Butler, Trent C. *Joshua*. WBC. Waco, TX: Word, 1983.
Hawk, L. Daniel. *Joshua*. Berit Olam. Collegeville, MN: Liturgical Press, 2000.
Hess, Richard S. *Joshua: An Introduction and Commentary*. Downers Grove, IL: InterVarsity, 1996.
Howard, David M., Jr. *Joshua*. NAC. Nashville: Broadman & Holman, 1998.
Nelson, Richard D. *Joshua: A Commentary*. OTL. Louisville: Westminster John Knox, 1997.
Woudstra, Marten H. *The Book of Joshua*. NICOT. Grand Rapids: Eerdmans, 1981.

In addition to commentaries, the following literary studies are worth consulting:

Hawk, L. Daniel. *Every Promise Fulfilled: Contesting Plots in Joshua*. Louisville: Westminster John Knox, 1991.
Mitchell, Gordon. *Together in the Land: A Reading of the Book of Joshua*. Sheffield: JSOTSup, 1993.
Polzin, Robert. *Moses and the Deuteronomist*. New York: Seabury, 1980. Polzin deals with both Joshua and Judges in this volume.

For ideas on how one might proclaim the message of Joshua, see:

Davis, Dale Ralph. *No Falling Words: Expositions of the Book of Joshua*. Grand Rapids: Baker, 1988.

Judges

Commentaries on Judges include:

Block, Daniel Isaac. *Judges and Ruth*. NAC. Nashville: Broadman & Holman, 1999.

Boling, Robert G. *Judges*. AB. Garden City, NY: Doubleday, 1975.

Matthews, Victor Harold. *Judges and Ruth*. Cambridge: Cambridge University, 2004.

McCann, J. Clinton. *Judges*. Interpretation. Louisville: John Knox, 2002.

Younger, K. Lawson. *Judges and Ruth*. NIVAC. Grand Rapids: Zondervan, 2002.

Two other helpful works on Judges are:

Davis, Dale Ralph. *Such a Great Salvation: Expositions of the Book of Judges*. Grand Rapids: Baker, 1990. This volume is valuable for those interested in proclaiming the message of Judges to a modern audience.

Webb, Barry G. *The Book of the Judges: An Integrated Reading*. Sheffield: JSOTSup, 1987. Webb's literary analysis treats the book as a unified piece of literature and is filled with valuable insights.

Ruth

In addition to the commentaries by Block and Matthews listed above (see under Judges), the interpreter will find the following to be of help:

Bush, Frederic William. *Ruth, Esther*. WBC. Waco, TX: Word, 1996. This commentary is one of the finest on any biblical book. It is a model of how exegesis should be done and is filled with valuable literary and linguistic observations.

Campbell, Edward F. *Ruth*. AB. Garden City, NY: Doubleday, 1975.

Hubbard, Robert L. *The Book of Ruth*. NICOT. Grand Rapids: Eerdmans, 1988.

Nielsen, Kirsten. *Ruth: A Commentary.* OTL. Louisville: Westminster John Knox, 1997.

1–2 Samuel

Commentaries on 1–2 Samuel include:

Anderson, A. A. *2 Samuel.* WBC. Dallas: Word, 1989.

Arnold, Bill T. *1 and 2 Samuel.* NIVAC. Grand Rapids: Zondervan, 2003.

Bergen, Robert D. *1, 2 Samuel.* NAC. Nashville: Broadman & Holman, 2002.

Gordon, Robert P. *1 and 2 Samuel: A Commentary.* Grand Rapids: Zondervan, 1988.

Klein, Ralph W. *1 Samuel.* WBC. Waco, TX: Word, 1983.

McCarter, P. Kyle. *1 and 2 Samuel.* AB. Garden City, NY: Doubleday, 1980–84.

The books of 1–2 Samuel contain intriguing stories about some of the most fascinating characters in the entire Bible. Consequently they have received a great deal of attention from literary critics. The following volumes examine literary aspects of 1–2 Samuel, including analyses of the main characters in the story:

Edelman, Diana V. *King Saul in the Historiography of Judah.* Sheffield: JSOTSup, 1991.

Fokkelman, J. P. *Narrative Art and Poetry in the Books of Samuel.* Assen: Van Gorcum, 1981.

Gunn, David M. *The Fate of King Saul: An Interpretation of a Biblical Story.* Sheffield: JSOTSup, 1980.

———. *The Story of King David: Genre and Interpretation.* Sheffield: University of Sheffield, 1978.

Long, V. Philips. *The Reign and Rejection of King Saul: A Case for Literary and Theological Coherence.* Atlanta: Scholars Press, 1989.

Polzin, Robert. *David and the Deuteronomist: 2 Samuel.* Bloomington, IN: Indiana University, 1993.

————. *Samuel and the Deuteronomist: 1 Samuel.* San Francisco: Harper & Row, 1989.

1–2 Kings

Cogan, Mordechai. *1 Kings.* AB. New York: Doubleday, 2001.
————, and Hayim Tadmor. *2 Kings.* AB. Garden City, NY: Doubleday, 1988.
Cohn, Robert L. *2 Kings.* Berit Olam. Collegeville, MN: Liturgical Press, 2000.
DeVries, Simon J. *1 Kings.* WBC. Waco, TX: Word, 1985.
Hobbs, T. R. *2 Kings.* WBC. Waco, TX: Word, 1985.
House, Paul R. *1, 2 Kings.* NAC. Nashville: Broadman & Holman, 1995.
Walsh, Jerome T. *1 Kings.* Berit Olam. Collegeville, MN: Liturgical, 1996.

1–2 Chronicles

Commentaries include:

Braun, Roddy. *1 Chronicles.* WBC. Waco, TX: Word, 1986.
Dillard, Raymond B. *2 Chronicles.* WBC. Waco, TX: Word, 1987.
Hill, Andrew E. *1 and 2 Chronicles.* NIVAC. Grand Rapids: Zondervan, 2003.
Japhet, Sara. *1 and 2 Chronicles.* OTL. Louisville: Westminster John Knox, 1993.
Knoppers, Gary N. *1 Chronicles 1–9.* AB. New York: Doubleday, 2003.
————. *1 Chronicles 10–29.* AB. New York: Doubleday, 2004.
Pratt, Richard L., Jr. *1 and 2 Chronicles.* Fearn, Ross-shire: Mentor, 1998.
Selman, Martin J. *1 Chronicles: An Introduction and Commentary.* Downers Grove, IL: InterVarsity, 1994.
————. *2 Chronicles: A Commentary.* Downers Grove, IL: InterVarsity, 1994.

Williamson, Hugh G. M. *1 and 2 Chronicles*. NICOT. Grand Rapids: Eerdmans, 1982.

The following studies examine the rhetoric and theology of the Chronicler:

Duke, Rodney K. *The Persuasive Appeal of the Chronicler: A Rhetorical Analysis*. Sheffield: Almond, 1990.

Dyck, Jonathan E. *The Theocratic Ideology of the Chronicler*. Leiden: Brill, 1998.

Graham, Matt Patrick, ed. *The Chronicler as Author: Studies in Text and Texture*. Sheffield: Sheffield Academic, 1999. This volume contains sixteen essays dealing with various literary aspects of Chronicles.

Kelly, Brian E. *Retribution and Eschatology in Chronicles*. Sheffield: Sheffield Academic, 1996.

When studying Chronicles, it is important to compare and contrast the Chronicler's account of Israel's story with the synoptic accounts in 1–2 Samuel and 1–2 Kings. Newsome's volume will facilitate such comparative work:

Newsome, James D. *A Synoptic Harmony of Samuel, Kings, and Chronicles*. Grand Rapids: Baker, 1986.

Ezra–Nehemiah

Studies of Ezra–Nehemiah include:

Blenkinsopp, Joseph. *Ezra–Nehemiah: A Commentary*. OTL. Philadelphia: Westminster Press, 1988.

Breneman, Mervin. *Ezra, Nehemiah, Esther*. NAC. Nashville: Broadman & Holman, 1993.

Eskenazi, Tamara C. *In an Age of Prose: A Literary Approach to Ezra–Nehemiah*. Atlanta: Scholars Press, 1988.

Fensham, F. Charles. *The Books of Ezra and Nehemiah*. NICOT. Grand Rapids: Eerdmans, 1982.

Williamson, Hugh G. M. *Ezra and Nehemiah*. Waco, TX: Word, 1985.

Esther

In addition to the works of Bush (see under Ruth) and Breneman (see under Ezra–Nehemiah), commentaries on Esther include:

Berlin, Adele. *Esther*. Philadelphia: Jewish Publication Society, 2001.
Jobes, Karen H. *Esther*. NIVAC. Grand Rapids: Zondervan, 1999.
Levenson, Jon D. *Esther: A Commentary*. OTL. Louisville: Westminster John Knox, 1997.

Several scholars have examined the literary aspects of the book of Esther, including:

Berg, Sandra B. *The Book of Esther: Motifs, Themes, and Structure*. Missoula, MT: Scholars Press, 1979.
Day, Linda. *Three Faces of a Queen: Characterization in the Books of Esther*. Sheffield: Sheffield Academic, 1995.
Dorothy, Charles V. *The Books of Esther: Structure, Genre, and Textual Integrity*. Sheffield: Sheffield Academic, 1995.
Fox, Michael V. *Character and Ideology in the Book of Esther*. 2d ed. Grand Rapids: Eerdmans, 2001.

4

INTERPRETING
NARRATIVE TEXTS

As NOTED IN CHAPTER 3, preparing for interpretation includes establishing and translating the text, at least ideally. With this accomplished, one is in a position to address the next logical question in the interpretive process: *What did the text mean to its **implied readers** in its literary, historical-cultural context?* This question, which is at the heart of the interpretive process, recognizes the **contextualized** nature of the text. It attempts to determine what the text meant to the implied readers for whom the text was intentionally composed in its original context.

DIACHRONIC METHODS

Most evangelicals presuppose that the text of Scripture conveys a coherent message. This message may be multiplex, displaying various facets and reflecting different perspectives, but in the final analysis it is a unified message from its divine Author. Modern biblical criticism has undermined these assumptions about the text's unity and authority. Proponents of **diachronic** methods, such as **source criticism**, **form criticism**, and **tradition history**, argue from internal evidence that the text has evolved over a long period of time as different traditions and sources have been joined.[1]

Evidence for Sources

Of course, there *is* evidence that the biblical authors sometimes used sources in composing the historical books. Within the Bible itself, reference is made to some of these sources, including the Book of Jashar (Josh. 10:13; 2 Sam. 1:18, "the Scroll of the Upright One" NET), the Book of the Wars of the Lord (Num. 21:14), and various royal annals (1 Kings 11:41; 14:19, 29).

Text critical evidence also indicates that these books are composed of various sources. For example, a Qumran fragment (4QJudg[a]) omits Judges 6:7–10, the account of a prophet's confrontation with Israel in response to Israel's cry of distress. In the past some scholars, without the aid of the Qumran evidence, were suspicious of this passage being a later addition—a theory that now seems to be validated by the evidence.[2]

An even more convincing example occurs in 1 Samuel 17–18, the story of David and Goliath. The Septuagint (Vaticanus version) contains a much shorter version of the story. It lacks thirty-nine of the eighty-eight verses in these chapters, including 17:12–31, 41, 48b, 50, 55–58; 18:1–6a, 10–11, 17–19, 21b, 29b–30. It also lacks twenty-four shorter elements ranging from one to five words and it has seventeen "pluses," ranging from individual words to complete sentences. The existence of this alternate textual tradition has been explained in one of two ways: (1) The Greek text (or the Hebrew text on which it was based) has been deliberately shortened to smooth out difficulties and

---

1. For concise summaries written by proponents of these methods, see Norman C. Habel, *Literary Criticism of the Old Testament* (Philadelphia: Fortress, 1971); Gene M. Tucker, *Form Criticism of the Old Testament* (Philadelphia: Fortress, 1971); and Walter E. Rast, *Tradition History and the Old Testament* (Philadelphia: Fortress, 1972). For a defense of the legitimacy of diachronic criticism see Jeffrey H. Tigay, ed., *Empirical Models for Biblical Criticism* (Philadelphia: University of Pennsylvania, 1985). For a critique of diachronic methods, including Tigay's approach, see Adele Berlin, *Poetics and Interpretation of Biblical Narrative* (Winona Lake, IN: Eisenbrauns, 1994), 111–34.
2. See, for example, C. F. Burney, *The Book of Judges* (reprint, New York: KTAV, 1970), xli–xlii. For discussion of the issue, see Robert H. O'Connell, *The Rhetoric of the Book of Judges* (Leiden: Brill, 1996), 467.

apparent contradictions; (2) the Greek is based on a Hebrew text that preceded the longer version of the story contained in the Hebrew text.[3] Tov argues that the first option is unlikely because the Greek text is a very literal translation, not all discrepancies have been edited out of the Greek text in the books of Samuel, and not all of the Greek omissions can be explained along such lines.[4] It seems likely that the longer version has combined at least two sources to produce a fuller version of the story.[5]

Critical Challenges to Textual Unity

A Case Study: David and Goliath

Proponents of **diachronic** methods usually hear contradictory and competing voices in the text and find no unified message there. For example, most interpreters regard the sources in 1 Samuel 17–18 as contradictory and do not treat the story as if it were a consistent, unified account. Critical objections to the text's unity include the following arguments:

1. David is introduced to Saul on two occasions: 16:17–23 and 17:55–58 (the latter is not in the Greek [LXX]).
2. Saul offers one of his daughters to David on two occasions: 18:17–19 (not in LXX) and 18:20–27.
3. The first account of Saul's attempt to kill David (18:10–11 [not in LXX]) is misplaced and is virtually repeated in 19:9–10. In the LXX (shorter) version Saul's hatred of and hostility toward David develops gradually; the outburst described in 18:10–11 is premature.
4. David and his father, Jesse, are introduced in 17:12 (not in LXX), even though chapter 16 has already identified them.

---

3. For four essays on the issue representing competing viewpoints, see Dominique Barthélemy, et al., *The Story of David and Goliath* (Fribourg, Suisse: Éditions Universitaires; Göttingen: Vandenhoeck & Ruprecht, 1986). Contributors include Barthélemy, Johan Lust, D. W. Gooding, and Emanuel Tov.
4. Emanuel E. Tov, "The David and Goliath Saga: How a Biblical Editor Combined Two Versions," *Bible Review* 11, no. 4 (Winter 1986): 34–41.
5. This longer version, as the text's final canonical form, should be the basis for interpretation and preaching.

5. David is an armor bearer and mighty warrior in 16:14–23, but appears as an unknown shepherd in 17:12–31, 55–58 (not in LXX).

6. David is twice made an officer in Saul's army: 18:5 (not in LXX) and 18:13.

7. Saul's dealings with David (as described in 18:20–27) and David's statement of his unworthiness (18:23) are inconsistent with the stated policy of 17:25.

8. Eliab's reaction to David in 17:28 seems inconsistent with 16:13, where he and his brothers witnessed the anointing of David.

9. Twice we are told that David "killed" the Philistine—once with a sling (and no sword in his hand; cf. 17:50, which is omitted in LXX) and once with the giant's own sword (17:51).

The text's own attempts to alleviate some of these difficulties (see 17:12, 15; 18:21b) are dismissed as later harmonizations.

However, just because sources are evident in 1 Samuel 17–18 does not necessarily mean they contradict or that the present **canonical form** of the text is internally inconsistent. There are reasonable responses to the arguments set out above:

1. In 17:55–58 Saul may be asking for the identity of David's father, since he did promise the father's family of Goliath's slayer tax-exempt status (17:25). (The closest syntactical parallel to Saul's question is found in Gen. 24:23–24, where the servant's primary concern is the identity of *the father* of Isaac's future bride.) Saul had heard Jesse's name before (16:18), but it is possible he had forgotten it with the passing of time. In the aftermath of the battle Saul refers to David as "(this) young man" and "this boy," suggesting he did not know his identity. But Saul's words need not imply this. Earlier he had called David a "boy" in contrast to the seasoned warrior Goliath (v. 33). His description of David after the battle continues that earlier vein of thought, emphasizing the contrast in age between the victor and his defeated foe and thereby the remarkable nature of David's deed.

2. The text itself (cf. 18:21b, "second time") harmonizes 18:17–19 and 18:20–27. There is nothing inherently improbable about Saul trying this ploy a second time.

3. Does 18:10–11 really interrupt the narrative, or does it heighten the suspense and drama? (Will such an outburst occur again?)

4. First Samuel 17:12 *formally* introduces David and his family, for it is only at this point that he becomes the focal point of the narrative. Samuel is the central character in 16:1–13, while Saul dominates 16:14–23.

5. First Samuel 17:15 provides an explanation for why David, though an armor bearer, warrior, and court musician, was not at the battle site. Saul's description of David in 17:33 does not necessarily conflict with 16:18. In comparison to Goliath, David was relatively inexperienced. The label "warrior" in 16:18 may reflect David's potential, not reality, but it is certainly justified in light of David's accomplishments as a shepherd (cf. 17:34–37 where David reasons that his ability to kill wild animals makes him capable of defeating the Philistine). First Chronicles 12:28, 38 call Zadok a נַעַר, "young man" (lit. translation; cf. 1 Sam. 17:33), and a גִּבּוֹר חַיִל, "mighty man of strength" (lit. translation; cf. 1 Sam. 16:18), and includes him among the "men of war" (lit. translation; cf. 1 Sam. 16:18).

6. First Samuel 18:5, 13 probably refer to different positions in Saul's army. In 18:5 David is promoted from armor bearer (cf. 16:21), while in 18:13 he is elevated to an even higher rank.

7. David's hesitancy (18:18, 23), though seemingly not consistent with 17:25, is certainly understandable in light of 18:10–11. Did David suspect Saul's intentions?

8. Eliab's reaction to David (17:28) may seem inconsistent with 16:13, but should we underestimate the power of human jealousy, especially among siblings (cf. 16:6–7)?

9. The alleged "double killing" of the Philistine in 17:50–51 can be explained reasonably when one takes a closer look at the Hebrew text. In verse 50 a *Hiphil* form of מות, "die" (וַיְמִיתֵהוּ, "he killed him"), is collocated with וַיָּךְ, "he struck down," while in verse 51 a *Polel* form of מות, "die" (וַיְמֹתְתֵהוּ), is used to describe how David killed the Philistine with the sword. The collocation of verbs in verse 50 has the nuance "dealt a mortal blow." The *Polel* of מות (v. 51) is used in eight other passages in the Old Testament. In three poetic texts, it appears to mean simply "kill, put to death"

(Pss. 34:22 [Eng. v. 21]; 109:16; Jer. 20:17). But in narratival texts (all in Judges–Samuel) it appears to have a specialized shade of meaning, referring to finishing off someone who is already mortally wounded (Judg. 9:54; 1 Sam. 14:13; 2 Sam. 1:9–10, 16). Abimelech's statement (Judg. 9:54) is particularly instructive—he asked the armor bearer to kill him (*Polel* of מוּת) because otherwise people would say that a woman killed him (the verb is הָרַג, "kill"). So who killed Abimelech? Two answers are possible and both are correct—the woman (she delivered a mortal blow that made death certain) and the armor bearer (he delivered the death blow in the technical sense = *Polel* of מוּת). How did David kill the Philistine? Again two answers are possible and both are correct—with a sling stone (David delivered a mortal blow with the sling that made death certain) and with the Philistine's sword, which he used to deliver the deathblow in a technical sense (= *Polel* of מוּת).[6]

Another possible explanation for the "double killing" emerges when one considers the **discourse structure** of 1 Samuel 17:49–51. Verse 49 uses six *wayyiqtol* clauses to describe how David struck down the Philistine with a sling stone. He reached into the bag, took a stone, and slung it. The stone struck the Philistine and penetrated deep into his forehead, causing him to topple to the ground. The three *wayyiqtol* clauses in verse 50a summarize David's victory: he triumphed over the Philistine with just a sling and a stone, struck him down, and killed him. However, there is more to the story than this. Verses 50b–51 provide a more detailed account of how David actually finished off the Philistine, who was probably unconscious from the blow on his head. The disjunctive clause in verse 50b takes us back to where verse 49 left off; it reminds us that David had no sword in his hand at the point when the giant fell.[7] Verse 51, using a series of *wayyiqtol* clauses, then tells us that David ran and stood over the Philistine, took the giant's sword, and finished him off by decapitating him. In this case the summary statement of verse 50a looks both backward and forward. The

6. I owe this argument to my student, Joe Arthur. See his "Giving David His Due" (Ph.D. dissertation, Dallas Theological Seminary, 2005), 83–85.

7. In the Hebrew text (contrary to NIV) the statement "without a sword in his hand" comes at the end of the verse, *after* "he struck down the Philistine and killed him."

statements "So David triumphed over the Philistine with a sling and a stone" and "he struck down the Philistine" summarize verse 49, while the statement "and killed him" is filled out in detail in verses 50b–51.

The Need for Literary and Theological Sensitivity

Often source critics are simply shortsighted in their analyses. For example, in his treatment of 1 Samuel 20:11–17, McCarter argues that "Jonathan's plea for his family is probably a secondary interpolation" that interrupts the transition from David's question in verse 10 to Jonathan's answer in verse 18.[8] He also labels verses 23, 40–42 as secondary, because they continue the theme introduced in verses 11–17. With regard to verses 40–42, he states: "It has been clear all along that if Jonathan signaled bad news, David was to flee immediately (v. 22). Indeed, if it was going to be possible for the two men to meet and talk as they do here, there would have been no need for the elaborately planned signals in the first place!"[9]

McCarter seems to miss the human dimension in the story. Jonathan believed that David would someday be king (v. 15); he also knew that Saul had become David's mortal enemy. As David looked to Jonathan for help and Jonathan promised to protect him, what better time for Jonathan to make provision for his own future and the future of his offspring! As for verses 40–42, it is true that the plan called for David to run away immediately when Jonathan gave him the signal (v. 22). It reflected extreme caution and a concern for David's safety. But having given the signal, Jonathan sent the servant away, apparently hoping David would appear to say good-bye. David, realizing the coast was clear and convinced of his disarmed friend's devotion, did indeed step forward and the two friends reaffirmed their promise. McCarter's cold, analytical approach to the text is insensitive to the raw emotion of the story. Yes, David was to flee once the signal was given, but these friends could not part without saying a final good-bye.

Another example of a shortsighted **source critical** approach is Mordecai Cogan's treatment of the partially fulfilled prophecy concerning Ahab's death. Elijah warned that dogs would lick up Ahab's

---

8. P. Kyle McCarter Jr., *1 Samuel,* AB (New York: Doubleday, 1980), 342.
9. Ibid, 343.

blood in the very spot where they had licked up Naboth's shed blood (1 Kings 21:19). According to 1 Kings 22:38, the prophecy was fulfilled when dogs licked up Ahab's blood at a pool where his blood-stained chariot was cleaned following his death in battle. The author unreservedly states that this was "according to the word of the LORD which he spoke" (lit. translation). Yet the prophecy was partially, not completely fulfilled. Dogs licked up Ahab's blood at a pool in Samaria, not in Jezreel, the site of Naboth's execution (1 Kings 21:1–14). Cogan proposes that there were two traditions about the circumstances of Ahab's death. He theorizes that 1 Kings 22:38 reflects an "alternate tradition . . . that was not harmonized with the Elijah tales."[10]

However, perhaps the prophet's words, rather than being unconditional in every detail, were more than simply **informative** in function (see our earlier discussion of **speech function**) and flexible enough to accommodate human actions. If so, then the purpose of this prophecy was not simply to inform us of details surrounding Ahab's death. The language was designed to convey God's sense of outrage at what had happened and his commitment to see that justice was accomplished in an appropriate manner. The real point of the prophecy is not so much its geography, but the truth it conveys: God would punish Ahab appropriately for his murderous deed. Ahab would die violently, just as Naboth, the victim of the king's injustice, had and he would experience the same humiliation suffered by Naboth.

But there is another factor that comes into play. To some degree God makes room for human freedom and resulting contingencies in the outworking of his plans (cf. the Westminster Confession, V, 2). God did not prevent the king's men from taking Ahab to Samaria. When they did so, they seemingly circumvented the last part of the prophecy pertaining to where the dogs would lick Ahab's blood (there is no indication that the king's men did this intentionally). But God had dogs stationed in Samaria as well and the prophecy was fulfilled in its essence. Ahab died a violent and humiliating death; the punishment fit the crime. From the biblical author's perspective, this is all that really matters. God's sovereignty and justice win out in the end, even when human actions run contrary to his moral will and he allows

---

10. Mordechai Cogan, *1 Kings,* AB (New York: Doubleday, 2001), 495.

circumstances to unfold in such a way that his purposes appear to be circumvented. But in this case, the inexact nature of the fulfillment actually highlights God's sovereignty over the affair. One cannot escape his justice. As one sees and hears the dogs of Samaria lapping up Ahab's blood, one must conclude that the prophetic word has hardly failed; it has inexorably pursued the criminal. Only the dogs of Jezreel have reason to object on grounds of a technicality!

Harmonizations: The Need for Caution

While evangelicals are predisposed to view texts as unified, this does not mean we should gloss over problems and tensions or resort to arbitrary harmonizations. As Raymond Dillard states:

> Harmonizations are too often offered almost cavalierly. Hackles are raised by what appears to be an ad hoc invoking of any set of circumstances that will reconcile passages; to those steeped in higher-critical methods, such special pleading is rejected because it lacks any particular methodological control beyond the need for a quick solution. Nor are harmonizations readily amenable to proof or disproof; they may have varying degrees of probability, some more convincing than others, and some altogether too ingenious to commend the solution they attempt.[11]

We can illustrate the truth of Dillard's observation by looking at proposed harmonizations of 2 Samuel 21:19, which, according to the Hebrew text, says that Elhanan killed Goliath the Gittite, and 1 Chronicles 20:5, which, according to the Hebrew text, claims that Elhanan killed Goliath's brother, Lahmi. The identification of Elhanan as Goliath's slayer also seems to contradict 1 Samuel 17, which tells how David killed Goliath (see also 1 Sam. 21:9; 22:10). The various texts have been harmonized in a variety of ways:

---

11. Raymond B. Dillard, "Harmonization: A Help and a Hindrance," in *Inerrancy and Hermeneutic: A Tradition, a Challenge, a Debate,* ed. Harvie M. Conn (Grand Rapids: Baker, 1988), 157.

1. Elhanan is another name for David, or "David" is a title, not a
    proper name.
        Response: This is highly unlikely. In 2 Samuel 21:15–22 the
    name David appears six times and Elhanan just once. There is no
    indication the two are interchangeable. Furthermore, 2 Samuel
    21:17 suggests that David stopped engaging in this type of com-
    bat prior to Elhanan's slaying of Goliath.

2. Goliath is a title, or there were two different Philistines that hap-
    pened to have the same name.
        Response: This is highly unlikely. In 2 Samuel 21:16, 18 the
    proper names of Philistine warriors are given (Ishbi-benob and
    Saph, respectively); it is likely that Goliath is a proper name as
    well. The description of the Philistine's spear shaft in 2 Samuel
    21:19 harks back to the description of Goliath's spear shaft in
    1 Samuel 17:7, suggesting the same warrior is in view.

3. The reading in 2 Samuel 21:19 is textually corrupt; 1 Chronicles
    20:5 preserves (for the most part) the correct reading.
        Response: This is possible, but problematic. Neither text can
    be viewed as original; both clearly have corruptions. In 2 Samuel
    21:19 the addition of אֹרְגִים after Jair's name has to be incorrect;
    it appears at the end of the verse and is omitted in 1 Chronicles
    20:5. The reading "Lahmi" (לַחְמִי) in 1 Chronicles 20:5 is almost
    certainly a corruption of an original "Bethlehemite" (בֵּית הַלַּחְמִי).
    Perhaps the original text read as follows:

    ויך אלחנן בן־יעיר בית הלחמי את אחי גלית
    "Elhanan son of Jair the Bethlehemite killed the brother of Goliath."

        The following sequence of textual corruption seems plau-
    sible: Original אֶת אֲחִי was corrupted to אֲחִי due to virtual **hap-
    lography** (the two forms are almost identical). This led to two
    different secondary corruptions in the respective traditions: (a)
    in the 2 Samuel 21:19 tradition, אֲחִי, "brother of," was misread
    as the direct object marker (אֶת), which was needed before the
    following proper name, "Goliath"; (b) in the 1 Chronicles 20:5

tradition, בֵּית was altered to אֶת and הַלַּחְמִי changed to לַחְמִי, a proper name. This was perhaps deemed necessary because elsewhere the phrase "brother of [Proper Name]" invariably follows and stands in apposition to a proper name. Herein lies the problem with this text critical solution. The reconstructed original text simply has "the brother of Goliath" as the object of the verb, with no proper name preceding it.

4. Second Samuel 21:19 preserves the truth of Goliath's death. David killed an unnamed (in the original text) Philistine giant. Later the name Goliath (who was another Philistine giant, killed by Elhanan) was erroneously attached to the giant killed by David. In this regard, one should note that the name Goliath appears only twice in 1 Samuel 17 (vv. 4, 23).

    Response: This explanation is possible. If one takes this approach, the error also crept into 1 Samuel 21:9 and 22:10. Furthermore, 1 Chronicles 20:5 would reflect an attempt by a later scribe to clear up the apparent contradiction between 1 Samuel 17 and 2 Samuel 21:19.

Of the four proposed harmonizations, the first two are the "easiest" in that they resolve the apparent contradiction in a simple manner that preserves the integrity of all of the texts involved. However, they are too convenient and are invalidated by careful contextual analysis. The third harmonization, a text critical solution, assumes the existence of accidental and intentional textual corruption in both the Samuel and Chronicles traditions. However, the reconstructed original text is inconsistent with Hebrew style, making this proposal problematic. The fourth proposal, which is probably the least attractive to most evangelicals, at least acknowledges that facts sometimes were confused in the process of the transmission of the text, inviting harmonization on the part of editors and scribes.

Sometimes the interpreter is forced to admit that no convincing harmonization is possible, at least given our present understanding. Dillard cites as an example the two accounts of Ahaziah's death. According to 2 Kings 9:27–28, Ahaziah fled from Jezreel, but Jehu's men overtook him near Ibleam and wounded him. He went to Megiddo, where he died. Second Chronicles 22:8–9 gives a different scenario. Here Ahaziah is captured while hiding in Samaria, brought to Jehu, and executed. Dillard admits that "one can concoct an amalgam of the two passages" that involves Ahaziah being captured and then escaping. But, as he says, "the uneasy feeling persists that this 'solution' is forced and contrived."[12] Furthermore, why would each author give only a partial account of what transpired that omits key details?

When faced with such tensions, what should the interpreter do? Dillard commends Edward J. Young's advice:

> It may very well be that there are some passages which, save by strained and forced attempts, we cannot harmonize. If such is the case, by all means let us be sufficiently honest and candid to admit that we cannot harmonize the particular passages in question; for to employ strained and forced methods of harmonization is not intellectually honest. . . . Far better it is to admit our inability than to produce harmonization at the expense of honesty and integrity.[13]

Beyond this, sometimes solutions can be found in literary (synchronic) readings of the text, and so we turn now to these.

SYNCHRONIC METHODS

Focus on Unity

Newer literary and rhetorical methods have challenged the higher-critical consensus to some degree. Rather than trying to reconstruct the history of how the text arrived at its present form, **synchronic critics** focus on its final, **canonical form**. While they usually acknowledge that the text did go through some sort of evolutionary process to reach its present form, they are skeptical about the ability of modern critics to reconstruct this process. **Diachronic critics** generally have a low opinion of the work of the editors responsible for the present form of

---

12. Dillard, "Harmonization," 159.
13. Ibid, 151. See Edward J. Young, *Thy Word Is Truth* (Grand Rapids: Eerdmans, 1957), 124.

the text. Synchronic critics, however, have a relatively high opinion of the editors' skills and tend to see the present form of the text as unified literarily. They prefer to view the text from a literary angle, addressing the issues surveyed in the first chapter of this book.[14] According to synchronic critics, careful literary analysis of this type often undermines the conclusions of diachronic critics by demonstrating the text's unity.

Synchronic critics refuse to allow tensions within the text to deter their effort to appreciate the text at a literary level. In the introduction to his study of 1 Samuel, Robert Polzin, after surveying the history of diachronic criticism on the book, opts for a synchronic approach. He writes:

> The present book presumes the text of 1 Samuel makes sense, however worked-over the text is scribally and hermeneutically, and however deficient it is text-critically. Perhaps this sympathetic attitude will gloss over or excuse a number of textual warts or obvious genetic defects, but such mistakes are, in my opinion, a fair price to pay for trying to redress a lamentable neglect of an ancient treasure. That-which-is is certainly as valuable as all the valuable might-have-beens upon which biblical scholars continue to focus their attention. Many who have read the Bible down through the ages have understood this.[15]

In contrast to diachronic critics, Robert Alter likewise takes a radically different approach to tensions within a text that seem to undermine its unity. He speaks of "composite artistry" and argues that the tensions may well be by authorial design. Using the "internal contradictions" of Numbers 16 as an example, he observes, "the biblical account actually seems devised to confuse the two stories and the two modes of destruction."[16] Alter recognizes that the author's purpose in doing this "is bound to remain a matter of conjecture because it runs so drastically counter to later notions of how a story should be put together." Yet

---

14. See the works cited in chapter 3 under the heading "Works on Narratival Art," pp. 157–58.

15. Robert Polzin, *Samuel and the Deuteronomist* (San Francisco: Harper & Row, 1989), 17.

16. Robert Alter, *The Art of Biblical Narrative* (New York: Basic Books, 1981), 135.

he does not think "the confusion can be facilely attributed to mere editorial sloppiness, for there is evidence of some careful aesthetic and thematic structuring of the story." Alter decides to take the pathway of humility and give the ancient author the benefit of the doubt: "All this leads one to suspect that the Hebrew writer may have known what he was doing but that we do not."[17] With regard to the story of David's introduction to Saul (1 Sam. 16–17), Alter concludes that the narrator has included both of "the seemingly contradictory versions" in order to give a full picture of David's character and complementary perspectives on his rise to prominence.[18]

Respecting the Author's Authority

While this focus on the authorial design of the text in its final **canonical form** is a welcome departure from the shopworn **diachronic** approaches that characterize so much of traditional commentary writing, the new wave of synchronic analyses does have its dark side. Some synchronic critics, heavily influenced by postmodern philosophical trends, reject the idea of an authoritative meaning rooted in history and prefer to "make meaning" of the text as they encounter it from their own perspective. Reader-response criticism of this type brings its own agenda to the text; there is no unified meaning reflecting authorial intention, but a plethora of meanings created by various readers. Radical forms of reader-response criticism display disregard for the narrator's authority. Taking a more cynical approach, some "deconstruct" the presuppositions of the text.

For example, Esther Fuchs argues that Jephthah's indictment of his daughter (Judg. 11:35), while not necessarily reflecting the author's point of view, is allowed to stand "as the only explicit evaluation of the daughter's actions."[19] The silence of the narrator and of God makes Jephthah out to be a victim. She also contends that the daughter's relatively calm and reasoned response (v. 36) endorses and justifies Jephthah's point of view.[20] In short, she argues that the narrational style

---

17. Ibid., 136.
18. Ibid., 147–54.
19. Esther Fuchs, *Sexual Politics in the Biblical Narrative: Reading the Hebrew Bible as a Woman,* JSOTSup 310 (Sheffield: Sheffield Academic, 2000), 186–87.
20. Ibid, 190.

is designed to protect both Jephthah and the Lord from criticism.[21] Fuchs is correct that the text gives no direct criticism of Jephthah, but Old Testament narrative rarely offers such overt moral commentary. The narrative seems to reflect a father's perspective, perhaps to create sympathy for Jephthah and highlight the tragic and ironic dimension of what happened. After all, he is the central character in this section of Judges. This narratival focus need not mean that the narrator blames Jephthah's daughter. Jephthah's words display a realistic quality; when people face the consequences of their foolish behavior, they often try to place the blame elsewhere. Pressler calls his response "a classic case of blaming the victim."[22] Perhaps the contrast between Jephthah's irrational accusation and his daughter's obedient demeanor highlights his folly, as well as her vulnerability. The wider context of the story must also be taken into account.[23] The book of Judges traces the changing roles of women in conjunction with a corresponding deterioration in male leadership. Against this background, Jephthah's daughter is definitely a sympathetic figure, while Jephthah's folly marks a further descent in leadership.[24]

Identifying the Implied Reader(s)

Synchronic criticism, when done properly, attempts to discover and explain how the text as a unified piece of literature would have been read and understood in its original context. This entails that the interpreter identify the **implied reader**(s) of the text. The implied reader(s) is the audience that the author(s) envisioned as hearing the text and being impacted by it. Exactly who are the implied readers of the historical books? For exilic and postexilic books (1–2 Chronicles, Ezra–Nehemiah, Esther), the audience is obviously the postexilic

---

21. Ibid, 193.
22. Carolyn Pressler, *Joshua, Judges, and Ruth,* The Westminster Bible Companion (Louisville: Westminster John Knox, 2002), 204.
23. J. Clinton McCann, *Judges,* Interpretation (Louisville: John Knox, 2002), 83–85.
24. See Robert B. Chisholm Jr., "The Role of Women in the Rhetorical Strategy of the Book of Judges," in *Integrity of Heart, Skillfulness of Hands: Biblical and Leadership Studies in Honor of Donald K. Campbell,* ed. Charles H. Dyer and Roy B. Zuck (Grand Rapids: Baker, 1994), 34–49. On the narrative's negative portrayal of Jephthah as one who lacks wisdom, see Julie Claassens, "Theme and Function in the Jephthah Narrative," *JNSL* 23, no. 2 (1997): 211.

community (early Second Temple Judaism). The book of Ruth may come from the early monarchy (cf. 4:22), but the situation with the Deuteronomistic History is more complex. The corpus clearly evolved over time, but in its final **canonical form**, when viewed as an entity, the implied readers are the exilic community (cf. 2 Kings 25:27–29).

This means that the books can be read at different levels, including and perhaps fundamentally from the standpoint of the exilic community. For example, as we noted earlier, the book of Judges has at least three major purposes:

1. It is in part an apology for the Lord, whose reputation was jeopardized by Israel's failure.
2. It warned Israel of the dangers of assimilation to their environment, which in turn jeopardized national unity.
3. It demonstrates Israel's need for competent leadership.

However, isolating these purposes does not allow us to pinpoint the date of the book or its sources. The Yahwistic apology, especially the polemical dimension, would have been relevant in the preexilic period, when the people were so tempted to worship other gods. It also would have been relevant in the exilic and postexilic periods when Israel's history had seemingly culminated in failure and many were probably wondering about the implications of this failure for Yahwistic faith. Recent events mirrored the nation's early history and were actually the inevitable consequence of its early failure. Israel's moral decline and exile were rooted in the assimilation to Canaanite culture and religion that had begun after the death of Joshua and his generation. As in the period of the judges, the Lord had once more allowed his people to experience defeat, but this did not mean he had abandoned them. Judges demonstrates that even in the darkest of times, God is always there, working out his salvific purposes for his people.

The dual theme of assimilation to paganism and loss of national unity would have been relevant throughout Israel's history. The preexilic generations perpetuated the sins of the judges' period. They failed the test of loyalty by refusing to separate from the pagan influences around them. The nation, now split in two, was moving inexorably on a path leading to the disaster of exile. From an exilic and postexilic perspective,

Judges exposed the root of the exiles' problem and the ultimate reason why they were in such dire straits. The prophets held out the hope of a restored nation, but there needed to be genuine covenant renewal to avoid the old cycle of sin and judgment being repeated in the future. The people had to take seriously their calling to be distinct from the nations around them and embrace a renewed vision of a united covenant community.

The leadership theme would have been relevant at any point in Israel's history. In the preexilic period Judges would have provided justification for the monarchy, and the Davidic dynasty in particular, but Gideon's words to the people (8:23) were a reminder that human kings must be subservient to the true King. As the epilogue makes clear, an effective king pointed people toward God's authority so that each person was not a law to him- or herself. Rather than giving kingship a blanket endorsement, the book of Judges reminded Israel of the royal ideal and served as a rebuke to the rebellious kings of the preexilic period. For the exilic and postexilic community, Judges complemented the message of the prophets. The Israel of the future needed a king—the right kind of king—to avoid the errors of the past.

Consider as well the tragic story of David, the new Caleb who turned into a new Samson. In ancient Israel David's story would have been read in different ways at different times. For example, in the united monarchy period, when many Benjaminites may have wanted to promote Saul's family as the rightful heirs to Israel's throne, David's story would have functioned as an apology for the Davidic dynasty, designed to show that David was the rightful heir and that Saul had been rejected by God. In the period of the divided monarchy, when the northern tribes rejected the house of David, the story of David served as a reminder of God's ideal and his commitment to David. But in its final canonical form, as part of the history that runs from Joshua–2 Kings, David's story should be read in an exilic context. Israel had started well, but failed. Judges 2:7, 10–11 states: "The people worshiped the LORD throughout Joshua's lifetime and as long as the elderly men who outlived him remained alive. These men had witnessed all the great things the LORD had done for Israel. . . . That entire generation passed away; a new generation grew up that had not personally experienced the LORD's presence or seen what he had done for Israel. The Israelites did evil before the LORD by worshiping the Baals." That evil led to the chaos of the judges' period from which David seemed to deliver the nation. Their greatest leader, David, started well, but then he too, like the nation, failed. Israel and the Davidic king were now prisoners in exile, but through the writing prophets God offered the exiles a new start. The story of their ancestors and of the great king David became a sober reminder that good starts do not necessarily mean good finishes. The ancient story also was a challenge to them to avoid the sins of the past, to start well and, more importantly, to finish well.

A PROPOSED EXEGETICAL-LITERARY METHOD

We propose an interpretive method that is essentially **synchronic**, but that is also sensitive to the historical and cultural background of the text and respectful of the narrator's authority. We acknowledge that the text as it stands may include various sources, but we prefer to focus on the text in the form in which we have it and to assume an editorial unity. Voices may seem to compete, but close analysis shows that they complement and qualify one another. Using literary methods, we seek to demonstrate the unified message of the text as it stands, presupposing that those responsible for its present form were literary artists who were part of a Yahwistic tradition that had a theological agenda. Yet literary analysis must not be done in a vacuum; it must take into account what we know of the historical–cultural background of the text.[25] It must also be sensitive to **macroplot** and **canonical** context. This means that a text may be read legitimately against its primary historical background, but also against the background of its larger literary context.

When attempting to determine what the text meant in its original context(s), one should address the following issues:

1. Place the text in its historical, cultural, and broader literary contexts.

---

25. See Simon B. Parker, *Stories in Scripture and Inscriptions* (New York: Oxford University, 1997), 4–5.

2. Evaluate the text from a literary point of view, observing the principles developed in chapter 1. Those principles are repeated here for the reader's convenience:

   a. Analyze the basic elements of a story (setting, characterization, plot) and determine how they contribute to its message.

   b. Identify a text's **discourse structure**, **dramatic structure**, and other structural features and explain how they contribute to the story's message and impact.

   c. Analyze the narrative's quotations and dialogues with respect to their **discourse type** and **speech function**.

   d. Avoid excesses when filling gaps, but do not be afraid to try to resolve ambiguity in a cautious manner that is sensitive to context and utilizes common sense.

   e. Respect the authority of the narrator and attempt to identify his assessment of events and characters. However, also be alert for the rhetorical use of a **limited and/or idealized point of view**.

   f. Relate individual stories to their macroplot and explain how the various genres within a book contribute to its overall message.

   g. Be sensitive to matters of **intertextuality** and how they contribute to the message of the narrative.

3. Summarize the theme(s) of the story and how they contribute to the theme(s) of the book as a whole.

4. Consider how the story should have impacted the **implied reader**(s), given their time, place, and circumstances.

The process outlined above should not be viewed as formulaic, as if following the prescribed steps in this exact order will yield "the correct interpretation" of a passage. Though interpretation has its technical aspects (especially when one is doing text critical, syntactical, and lexical analyses), it should not be reduced to a mathematical formula. The suggestions offered above are guidelines designed to help interpreters view the narratives of the Old Testament contextually, holistically, and literarily. The process of considering these issues need not be understood as linear, nor should it be viewed as mechanical. Many of the guidelines are interrelated. In actual practice they end up being concurrent. It is important to remember that interpreting the text is just as much an art as it is a technique.

At this point, we are ready to move to the next question in the interpretive process: What does the text mean to contemporary readers who are part of the community of faith (application)? This question is the concern of the next chapter.

5

PROCLAIMING
NARRATIVE TEXTS

ONCE WE HAVE CONSIDERED THE meaning of the text in its original
context, we are prepared to consider the question to which the entire
interpretive process leads: *What does the text mean to contemporary readers who are part of the community of faith?* This question recognizes that
the text is Scripture and has meaning and relevance beyond its original context. In seeking an answer to this question we move from the
sphere of exegesis proper into the related arenas of biblical theology
and homiletics. Biblical theology forms the necessary bridge from then
(what the text meant to its **implied readers**) to now (what the text
means to the community of faith). Homiletics then completes the process by proclaiming how the text applies to contemporary readers.

A PROPOSED HOMILETICAL STRATEGY

Some use the historical literature of the Old Testament simply
for illustrative purposes. Since we see the New Testament writers
sometimes doing this, we must assume that this is a valid use of the
narratives that is consistent with Paul's statement concerning the
practical relevance of Scripture (2 Tim. 3:16–17): "Every Scripture is
inspired by God and useful for teaching, for reproof, for correction,

and for training in righteousness, that the person dedicated to God may be capable and equipped for every good work." For example, James illustrates his point about the effectiveness of prayer by appealing to the example of Elijah (James 5:16–18).

However, this illustrative use of the biblical stories does not necessarily reflect the purpose(s) of their original author(s) in the context in which the texts originally appeared. For example, the author of Hebrews includes four judges (Gideon, Barak, Samson, and Jephthah) in his "Hall of Faith" (Heb. 11:32). All of them exercised faith and consequently "conquered kingdoms," "escaped the edge of the sword," and "became mighty in battle, put foreign armies to flight" (Heb. 11:33–34). The author is correct in using them as illustrations of his overriding principle—God can use mightily those who trust in him. If one were preaching a message on Hebrews 11, it would be proper and wise to refer to the stories of these judges and to show how God rewarded their faith by giving them victories over the enemies of Israel.

Yet if one were preaching or teaching through Judges as one's primary text, this theme would be secondary. A literary analysis of the stories of these four judges reveals that they were flawed leaders, whose deficient wisdom and/or faith (at least when compared to the paradigmatic leaders presented at the beginning of Judges) marred their careers and contributed to a downward spiral that eventually left a leadership void in Israel. They had a measure of faith that enabled them to fight God's battles, but they also exhibited leadership deficiencies that contributed to Israel's spiritual decline during this period.[1]

While the illustrative use of Old Testament narratives may have its place, it fails to deal with the texts as literary-theological entities that exhibit specific themes and express an overall purpose. As such, it fails to apply the text in the form in which God has given it to us. The illustrative use of an Old Testament narrative text works best when it is employed as a *supplement* to a message on another text. But if one's *primary* text is the narratival text, we need to take a different approach that does justice to the text's own agenda. This approach involves thematic analysis, theological analysis, and contemporary application.

---

1. See Robert B. Chisholm Jr., "The Role of Women in the Rhetorical Strategy of the Book of Judges," in *Integrity of Heart, Skillfulness of Hands: Biblical and Leadership Studies in Honor of Donald K. Campbell,* ed. Charles H. Dyer and Roy B. Zuck (Grand Rapids: Baker, 1994), 34–49.

We first move back into the world of the text and attempt to answer the question: What did this text mean in its ancient Israelite context? This involves a close exegetical–literary reading of the text that surfaces the thematic emphases of each major literary unit. The previous chapters of this book focus on this part of the process (see especially chap. 4).

Next we move outside the world of the text and attempt to answer the following questions: What theological principles emerge from a thematic analysis of the text? How are these principles nuanced in their larger canonical context? We discuss this more fully below, under the heading "Finding the Principle(s)."

Finally we move back into our modern world, where we take the theologically nuanced thematic emphases of the text and develop homiletical trajectories from these theological vantage points. If done with skill and savvy, the audience will be able to see how the ancient text yields the principles, how the rest of Scripture nuances the principles, and how they, the audience, both individually and corporately, should and can appropriate the principles in their own experience and in the life of the church. We discuss this more fully below, under the heading "Applying the Principle(s)."

Another way to think of the process is in terms of **contextualization**, decontextualization, and recontextualization. In exegesis we examine the contextualized meaning of the text in the world of its **implied reader**(s). Next we decontextualize that meaning to some degree by examining the theological principles that emerge from the text and transcend its historical–cultural context. The context broadens to include the Bible as a whole. Finally we take these theological principles and recontextualize them in our modern situation, asking how they are relevant to our lives. In this way the proclamation and application of the text, because they are rooted in biblical theology derived from sound exegesis, have an authoritative foundation that is not present if a reader simply brings his or her own agenda to the text and "makes meaning" of it.

FINDING THE PRINCIPLE(S)

Finding the principle(s) in a narrative does not mean we simply reduce the stories to a series of moral lessons. Such an approach tends to produce a list of proverbial style statements that may or may not relate to one another and may or may not reflect the intention of the author(s). As discussed earlier, one must look at the story as a whole before attempting to derive principles from a narrative. Only then is the interpreter in a position to evaluate how each part fits into the whole. The process is akin to watching a movie or reading a novel. One does not stop after every **scene** or **episode** and consider the lesson it may be teaching. Such an atomistic approach would lead to interpretive chaos. One can appreciate the significance of a scene or episode only when it is viewed in its larger context and evaluated in light of the work's overall theme(s).

When trying to derive theological principles from a biblical narrative it is helpful to ask the following questions, which at times are interrelated:

1. How are the themes of the story, surfaced in the interpretive process (see chap. 4), nuanced and developed in the Bible as a whole, especially the New Testament?
2. What does God reveal about himself in the story? What does the story suggest about how he relates to people? How does God's self-revelation in the story compare/contrast with his self-revelation in the Bible as a whole?
3. Does the story offer any insight into how people should respond and relate to God? How should we evaluate the human responses we see in the story in the light of principles we see in the Bible as a whole?
4. How should the story be evaluated in light of the Christological emphasis and themes of the Bible?

As we approach the stories of the Old Testament we come with at least two underlying assumptions: (1) God is unchanging and (2) ancient Israel, God's covenant community in the Old Testament period, provides a model (to emulate or reject, as the case may be) for the community of faith in the present age. Armed with these assumptions, it is tempting to treat as normative the actions of God and other characters in the story. The assumptions are correct and the stories do indeed yield timeless principles that are relevant to the community of faith in all ages. However, one must avoid the error of overgeneralization, which can result in assigning normativity to every action.

Though God is unchanging in his very essence, this does not mean that he always reveals himself in the same manner or relates to people in the same way. For example, as our earlier discussion of God's self-revelation to Abraham illustrated (see chap. 1), at times God revealed himself in the patriarchal account as if he were less than omniscient because his primary concern was to emphasize that he is fair and that humans are responsible for their actions. His self-revelation was tailored to his purpose in the world of the story. If we learn anything from the stories of the Old Testament, it is that God cannot be placed in a box where his response can always be predicted. On the contrary, he is free to act as he pleases, even though his actions may seem contradictory or inconsistent from our limited perspective.

For example, as we pointed out earlier (see chap. 2), the stories in Judges demonstrate that God cannot be manipulated like some good luck charm and that he often operates outside the expected norms. In the Gideon story he confronts his people with their sin before commissioning a deliverer; in the Jephthah story he wearies of intervening, even when the people persist in crying out to him and seemingly repent of their idolatry. But in the Samson story he decides to deliver Israel even though no one asks for his help. In each case God disciplined Israel for its sin (Judg. 6:1–6; 10:6–9; 13:1), yet his subsequent action varies from story to story. We must take into account the reality of divine freedom and avoid the temptation to overgeneralize about God from the stories in which he reveals himself. It would be inaccurate to draw a universal principle from any one of these three accounts. Such a principle might take one of the following forms: (1) God always urges his people to repent before intervening on their behalf (cf. the Gideon story), or (2) God always withdraws his favor from his sinful people (cf. the Jephthah story), or (3) God always shows mercy to his sinful people, even when they refuse to seek his favor (cf. the Samson story). It is better to synthesize the distinctives of the three accounts into a single, multifaceted principle that we may state as follows: "Sin prompts God to discipline his people, yet he subsequently deals with his sinful people in ways he deems appropriate. Sometimes he may urge them to repent or he may withdraw his favor. Yet at other times he may graciously intervene on their behalf, even when his help is not sought or appreciated."

If we must carefully evaluate God's actions in order to know what is and is not normative, then it stands to reason that we must exercise extreme caution when evaluating the actions of human characters in the biblical stories. The actions and experiences of sinful, flawed human beings are not necessarily normative or designed as models to emulate. In this regard, analysis of a story's plot type and characters is important. As noted earlier (see chap. 1), negative example and admiration stories tend to present characters as examples to shun or follow, respectively, but the characters in other plot types, especially the comic and tragic varieties, are more challenging to evaluate. Typical characters usually provide an example of one character trait that is to be rejected or emulated, while full-fledged characters are more difficult to assess. Full-fledged characters may be exemplary in some respects, but this does not mean all of their actions set a moral norm or ideal. Each action must be evaluated in light of the narrator's overall presentation of the character in the broader context of the story.

For example, consider Gideon's use of the fleece to confirm God's willingness to deliver Israel (Judg. 6:36–40). Ignoring the broader literary context, some have used Gideon's actions to justify seeking God's will in similar ways today. However, when Gideon's actions are viewed in the context of the story, one realizes this episode contributes to the author's overall assessment of him as one who is skeptical and lacks faith. His fleece test, rather than providing an example of how one should seek God's will, highlights his deficiencies at this point in the story and delays, rather than expedites, God's program. Rather than providing a norm for how we should seek God's will, the story illustrates God's patience in developing a weak individual's faith.

Similarly, some have pointed to Jephthah as a positive example of one who kept his vow to God even at tremendous personal cost. However, in the context of the story, Jephthah is a tragic figure so tainted by the paganism around him that he turned a great victory into an unmitigated tragedy. His sacrifice of his own daughter stands in contrast to Caleb's kindness to his daughter Acsah, described in the book's prologue (Judg. 1:14–15). As such, Caleb, whose behavior as a typical character is exemplary, serves as a **foil** for Jephthah, whose behavior illustrates the severe decline in the quality of Israelite leadership during the judges' period. Jephthah's willingness to fulfill his vow is hardly the point of the story, which makes it clear that his vow was unnecessary and its form inappropriate and pagan. The story illustrates the devastating, sometimes inescapable consequences of a leader's weak faith and lack of foresight.

It is especially tempting to make inspiring accounts of God's intervention normative. For example, 2 Chronicles 20 tells how the Lord miraculously defeated Jehoshaphat's enemies. Judah did not even fight in the battle; instead a company of musicians led the people to the battle site (see v. 21). One can develop the following principle from this story: "God alone is his people's source of security. He is capable of delivering his people, no matter how overwhelming the odds may appear to be." One can imagine an overzealous preacher treating the story as normative in all its details and extending the principle as follows: "Because God is our only source of security, he demands radical trust from us. We must rely on him alone to protect us from danger." At this point one small applicational step could lead to advocating a bizarre form of faith that rejects all means and instruments of divine blessing (such as medicine to heal our physical illnesses). This would be, of course, an illegitimate extension and application of the principle. This event was exceptional, not normative, in Israel's experience. Though God often intervened for Israel in war, on many occasions he commanded Israel to fight. The story does not teach us that we should never use means in carrying out God's purposes; it does remind us that God is ultimately our source of security and this should give us confidence as we face our spiritual enemies.

In developing principles from biblical stories, some interpreters err by making biblical culture normative. For example, it would be wrong to conclude that God's people have the right to engage in some form of holy war because God authorized Israel to destroy the Canaanites and energized Samson to kill Philistines (cf. Judg. 14:19; 15:14–15). God has given the church no such mandate. On the contrary, Paul tells us that we do not wage war against "flesh and blood," but against "the powers, against the world rulers of this darkness" and "the spiritual forces of evil in the heavens" (Eph. 6:12). Any principles derived from the Old

Testament cultural phenomenon of holy war must be applied in a New Testament context within the framework of spiritual warfare.

APPLYING THE PRINCIPLE(S)

Once we have discovered the theological principle(s) of the text, we can establish homiletical trajectories. For example, as noted earlier (see chap. 2), the book of Judges has three major purposes:

1. The book is in part an apology for God. Israel's defeats were due to sin, not some deficiency on God's part. Yet despite Israel's disobedience and unfaithfulness, the Lord remained faithful to them. He disciplined them, but then raised up leaders to deliver them and to restore peace and stability to the land. Though Israel was intent upon worshiping foreign gods, the Lord proved his superiority to all rivals, demonstrating that he alone was worthy of his people's devotion.
2. The book also demonstrates how Israel's assimilation to Canaanite religion and culture through syncretism and intermarriage threatened the nation's very identity. This in turn fostered a tribal mentality that threatened national unity and resulted in internal conflict and civil war.
3. The book also shows how this Canaanized culture produced deficient leaders who failed to live up to the ideal established by Joshua, Caleb, Othniel, and Ehud. Their lack of adequate faith and/or wisdom made them unable to lead Israel out of its steady descent into chaos. The epilogue highlights this leadership void by illustrating how Israel followed its own moral code during this period. By reminding us there was no king, it keeps before us the Deuteronomic kingship ideal and prepares us for the realization of that ideal in 1 Samuel.

To be faithful to the message of the book, a homiletical approach should be sensitive to each of these themes as they emerge and are developed in the book. These themes provide us with homiletical angles or vantage points from which we can consider the text's relevance for us. As one proclaims the message of Judges, one should consider what the text teaches and illustrates about (1) God's relationship to his covenant community, (2) the effects of disobedience and compromise upon God's covenant community, and (3) the need for competent leadership in the covenant community.

To illustrate the process, let's consider the story of Gideon in Judges 6–8. Once again Israel's rebellion brings a foreign invader into the land (6:1–6). God continues to show mercy to his suffering, though unrepentant, covenant people. However, the prophetic accusation that precedes the story of divine deliverance indicates there is an underlying moral issue that must be addressed sooner or later (6:7–10). Perhaps a time will come when God will not automatically respond to Israel's cry for help (cf. 10:6–16).

Israel's persistence in sin produces a leadership void. When the Lord calls, Gideon hesitates (6:11–18). Yet the Lord patiently develops faith in the heart of his chosen servant. He first convinces Gideon of his identity as Yahweh, the God of Moses who desires to help his people (6:19–24). He then requires Gideon to demonstrate his loyalty in the face of severe opposition from his own countrymen (6:25–35). When Gideon later regresses and questions the Lord's ability, the Lord patiently accommodates himself to Gideon's tests and offers him further confirmation of his promises (6:36–40). Gideon's development reaches its final stage when he is forced to place his full trust in the Lord's power. Gideon finally steps to the forefront as God's warrior and once again the Lord demonstrates that he can accomplish great things through even the most unlikely instruments (7:1–25). In fact, the darker the backdrop, the more vivid and remarkable a divine display one can expect. Against overwhelming odds, God delivers in a way that should leave no doubt about his sovereignty and right to Israel's sole worship.

Nevertheless, when God's people become entrenched in paganism, spiritual blindness can keep them from responding properly to his self-revelation. When Gideon destroys Baal's altar with no repercussions from the Canaanite god, his own countrymen are ready to kill him (6:30). When the Lord puts the enemy to flight, some are concerned only with individual honor (8:1–3), while others refuse to recognize God's hand at work (8:22). When the battle is finally over, the people attribute the victory to Gideon, not to the Lord, and quickly turn what could have been a tangible reminder of God's presence into an idol.

Even Gideon dilutes his success by giving priority to personal ven-dettas, making unwise leadership decisions, and allowing success to go to his head (8:4–27). His concern for personal vengeance sends a false message and provides a misleading example. Despite knowing the peo-ple's and his own family's penchant for idols, he makes an ephod which quickly becomes an object of worship. By marrying many wives and giving one of his sons a royal name, he acts as if he is a king. While giv-ing lip-service to the Lord's kingship, his actions contradict his words and set the stage for new depths of civil strife and chaos. By the end of Gideon's career, we can see some obvious cracks in the foundation of Israelite society. In the story to follow (Judg. 9) these cracks widen and threaten to bring the whole structure tumbling to the ground.

Keeping the theological principles of the book in mind, we can de-velop the following homiletical trajectories from the Gideon story:

1. God is the compassionate king. Even when his people continue to drift from him, he remains active in their experience and seeks to win back their allegiance. He displays their false gods for what they really are and demonstrates his ability to protect his people. He is superior to all other so-called gods and is deserving of his people's undivided loyalty and worship.

2. When the covenant community becomes assimilated to the sur-rounding pagan culture, it can develop an irrational attachment to false gods and fail to see God's hand at work. When God acts in the world, the covenant community is apt to bestow honor on God's human instruments rather than the One who is truly wor-thy of their praise. As the community becomes more pagan in its outlook, it loses its sense of unity and common purpose. Petty self-interest and pride can threaten to tear the community apart.

3. Even in less than ideal conditions God chooses to accomplish his purposes through human instruments. Potential leaders raised in a pagan environment are susceptible to cynicism and likely to possess deficient faith. Yet God is willing to work with such people and mold them into effective instruments through whom he accomplishes great things. However, such individuals may be prone to put personal honor first and to make unwise decisions that foster paganism and threaten the community's unity.

We can synthesize these ideas into a single summary statement:

Persistence in sin creates a climate of spiritual blindness and insensitivity, but during such times God continues to show compassion to his people and can accomplish great things through unlikely instruments. In such dark times the Lord can patiently develop hesitant people into heroes of faith. However, God's purposes can be compromised when his chosen instruments lose focus of their mission, make naive and unwise leadership decisions, and allow their lifestyle to contradict a theologically correct message.

In applying the principle(s) derived from the text, one must move beyond the ancient cultural context. For example, Elijah's encounter with Baal proved that the Lord was the sole source of prosperity and security for his people and, therefore, the only God worthy of Israel's worship. But people do not worship Baal in our modern world, though in many cultures they do worship such idols. In developing this theological principle for a contemporary audience, one must address the issue of what constitutes idolatry. Most of those in a modern audience, at least in the context of the Western church, will not be involved in literal idolatry. However, the New Testament, while denouncing literal idolatry, also gives the concept an ethical dimension. Paul calls greed "idolatry" (Col. 3:5). According to James 4:4, "friendship with the world" constitutes spiritual adultery (a metaphor for idolatry in the Hebrew Bible). In this context, James associates friendship with the world with greed and the pride, envy, and hostility it invariably produces (see 4:1–3, 5–6).

In this chapter we have proposed a strategy for moving from exegesis (what the text meant in its original context) to proclamation (what the text means to the contemporary community of faith). Once one has studied the text exegetically, two more basic steps are necessary prior to preaching:

1. Find the theological principles that are present in the narrative. To facilitate this one can ask the following questions:
   a. How are the themes of the story, surfaced in the interpretive

process (see chap. 4), nuanced and developed in the Bible as a whole, especially the New Testament?

   b. What does God reveal about himself in the story? What does the story suggest about how he relates to people? How does God's self-revelation in the story compare/contrast with his self-revelation in the Bible as a whole?

   c. Does the story offer any insight into how people should respond and relate to God? How should we evaluate the human responses we see in the story in the light of principles we see in the Bible as a whole?

   d. How should the story be evaluated in light of the Christological emphasis and themes of the Bible?

2. Using these principles as a foundation, establish homiletical trajectories that will be the basis for applicational principles. Since a picture is better than a thousand words, we illustrate the proposed process in the following chapter.

FROM TEXT TO APPLICATION:
TWO SAMPLES

IN THIS FINAL CHAPTER WE illustrate the method proposed in the previous chapters. The first illustration utilizes a very short excerpt from the story of Elisha in which the prophet calls a curse down upon some youths, and two bears then rip forty-two of the boys to shreds (2 Kings 2:23–25). The story raises questions about God's character and, on the surface at least, poses a formidable challenge to the would-be preacher or teacher. What possible applicational value does such a strange story have today? Our second illustrative example is Ruth 1, a longer text that yields a more readily apparent application.

BLOODBATH AT BETHEL: SOME BAD BOYS,
A BALD PROPHET, AND TWO SAVAGE SHE-BEARS
(2 KINGS 2:23–25)

What Is the Text? What Does the Text Say?

As noted in chapter 3 the interpreter, at least ideally, first determines the original text and deals with basic exegetical matters involving semantics and grammar. The reader will recall that textual criticism, though logically prior to interpretation, is best done in conjunction with exegesis, for text critical decisions must take into account semantics and grammar. In this short text the *BHS* text critical apparatus lists no textual variants. However, there are some lexical issues that deserve comment.[1]

The first concerns the meaning of the plural noun נְעָרִים, which is qualified by the attributive adjective קְטַנִּים, "small" (v. 23). The noun נַעַר, "boy, youth," covers a broad age range, including infants as well as young men. But the qualifying phrase suggests these boys were relatively young. (Note that NIV translates the entire phrase "youths.") A grammatical search reveals that the phrase occurs only five other times in the Old Testament (all of which are in the singular): 1 Samuel 20:35 (used of the "small boy" [NIV] who retrieved Jonathan's signal arrow); 1 Kings 3:7 (used by the young man Solomon to describe himself after he had become king [NIV]); 1 Kings 11:17 (used of the "boy" Hadad, the heir to the Edomite throne); 2 Kings 5:14 (used to describe Naaman's skin after he was healed; his skin was like that of a "young child"); and Isaiah 11:6 (used in the prophet's vision of a time when a "small child" will lead once-savage predators around with no danger of being harmed). Solomon's reference to himself as a "little child" might suggest the phrase can be used of young men, but the usage in this case is clearly rhetorical and hyperbolic. Solomon wanted to emphasize how relatively young a king he was, so he described himself in exaggerated terms. Usage suggests that young boys are in view in 2 Kings 2:23, perhaps in their early teens or even younger.

The Hebrew verb וַיִּתְקַלְּסוּ (from the root קָלַס), "jeered," describes the boys' taunting of the prophet. This verb occurs in only three other texts: Ezekiel 16:31 (which compares unfaithful Jerusalem to a prostitute who, oddly enough, "scorned" payment); Ezekiel 22:5 (which describes how the surrounding nations would "mock" Jerusalem); and Habakkuk 1:10 (which describes how the arrogant Babylonians "deride" other kings). Since the verb is used so little, it is helpful to examine its nominal derivatives קֶלֶס and קַלָּסָה, which occur in Jeremiah 20:8 (used of the prophet being a "reproach" to others); Ezekiel 22:4 (used to describe how Jerusalem would become a "laughingstock" to

---

1. There are several exegetical issues, all relatively minor, that one could discuss here, but because of space limitations, we confine our comments to three lexical issues that are particularly important in the interpretation of this passage.

the nations); and Psalms 44:14 (Eng. v. 13) and 79:4 (used by the lamenting people to describe themselves as a source of "derision" to the surrounding nations). This survey of usage reveals that the verb and its derivatives do not refer to mere playful kidding or childish joking, but to derisive jeering that reflects disdain.

It is also important to understand exactly how Elisha responded to this mocking. The text says that he "called down a curse on them in the name of the LORD" (v. 24, NIV). This does not refer to an insulting or profane response, such as we sometimes mean in English when we say that someone "cursed" or "swore" at someone. A curse was a formal appeal to the Lord to vindicate one's cause through an act of judgment. The precise phrase used here (*Piel* of קלל collocated with the phrase "by the name of") occurs only in this text, but a similar expression is used by Goliath, who "cursed David by his gods" (1 Sam. 17:43). The idea seems to be that Elisha appealed to the Lord to execute judgment against these boys. The logical assumption is that the Lord sent the two bears to maul the boys.

What Did the Text Mean?

The next phase of the interpretive process is more involved. We must look at this passage from a literary angle, considering the various issues we discussed in chapter 4. For the sake of convenience, we repeat that list here as we illustrate the proposed method.

Place the Text in Its Context

This incident appears to have taken place during the reign of King Joram (852–841 B.C.), a son of Ahab (2 Kings 3:1). King Ahab continued in the sins of Jeroboam I, who had set up a calf idol in Bethel (1 Kings 12–13). He also married a Phoenician queen, Jezebel, and made the worship of Baal a state religion in the northern kingdom (1 Kings 16:31–33). This was a time when the kings of Israel did not worship the Lord or respect the authority of his prophets (cf. 1 Kings 19:1–2; 2 Kings 1:1–17). During this time the Lord's prophets were persecuted. Jezebel had many of them executed, apparently with the approval and support of many of the Israelite people (1 Kings 18:4; 19:2,

10, 14; 22:27; 2 Kings 1:9–12; 6:31). In the broader context Bethel appears as a center of idolatry (1 Kings 12–13). The passage records an incident that occurred early in the career of the prophet Elisha, who is the central figure in 2 Kings 2–8. It contributes to the narrator's overall portrayal of Elisha as the Lord's chosen successor to Elijah. (See further our comments under no. 6 below.)

Evaluate the Text from a Literary Point of View

1. Analyze the basic elements of the story (setting, characterization, plot) and determine how they contribute to its message.

   As noted above, the incident occurs on the road near Bethel, which was the center of an idolatrous **cult** (1 Kings 12–13). Following the incident, Elisha first travels to Carmel, the site of Elijah's triumph over the prophets of Baal and the place where the Lord demonstrated his sovereign power and authority. He then goes to Samaria, the capital of the northern kingdom. The geographical settings of the **episode** have great symbolic significance. The prophet calls judgment down on some residents of idolatrous Bethel. As if identifying with Elijah (in this regard, see 2 Kings 2:9–10, 13), he then visits the scene of his predecessor's greatest triumph before moving to Samaria to challenge the evil king of the northern kingdom. The three sites named symbolize Elisha's ministry. He confronts idolaters in the spirit and power of Elijah and opposes the dynasty that authorizes rebellion against the Lord.

   Elisha is the central character in this and the surrounding episodes. While he is the main character in 2 Kings 2–8, he is a relatively flat figure who appears as the typical prophet called by God to confront wrongdoing and demonstrate the Lord's authority over his people. As such he represents the Lord. Consequently when the youths oppose him, their actions may be viewed as an affront against the Lord himself. The youths who oppose Elisha are **antagonists**, but since they appear only briefly in this one episode, they are best labeled **agents**. The episode has a punitive plot type: the Lord punishes the boys for their disrespect. As agents in the story they represent their parents and Israel at large.

The **plot structure** of the episode is simple. The confrontation occurs, creating tension, but this tension is swiftly resolved as Elisha's curse is realized immediately. The swiftness of the plot resolution highlights the Lord's commitment to his prophet's well-being and the serious nature of the boys' verbal attack.

2. Identify the text's **discourse structure**, **dramatic structure**, and other structural features and explain how they contribute to the story's message and impact.

One may outline the discourse structure of the text as follows.[2]

Verses	Discourse Structure	Type of Clause
23a	From there Elisha went up to Bethel.	initiatory and sequential
23b	**As he was walking along the road,**	circumstantial
23c	**some youths came out of the town**	synchronic
23d	and jeered at him.	sequential
23e	They said to him:	focusing
23f	*"Go on up, you baldhead! Go on up, you baldhead!"*	
24a	He turned around,	sequential
24b	looked at them	sequential
24c	and called down a curse on them in the name of the LORD.	sequential
24d	Then two bears came out of the woods	sequential
24e	and mauled forty-two of the youths.	sequential
25a	And he went on from there to Mount Carmel	sequential
25b	**and from there returned to Samaria.**	concluding

2. *Wayyiqtol* clauses that form the main line of the story are translated in regular font, while offline constructions are in bold. (See the earlier discussion of discourse structure in chapter 1, under the heading "Structural Features.") The lone quotation is italicized. Our proposed classification of each *wayyiqtol* and offline clause appears in the third column after the translation of the clause. Comments on the discourse structure are included after the translation, which is an adaptation of NIV.

Comments on Discourse Structure

a. The *wayyiqtol* clause in verse 23a, while continuing the on-going story, also initiates a new episode, in which Elisha proceeds to Bethel.

b. Hebrew narrative sometimes juxtaposes disjunctive clauses to indicate synchronic action, as in verse 23bc (see Judg. 15:14). The first clause, which has a participle as its predicate, indicates action that is circumstantial to the action described in the second clause, which has a perfect verbal form as its predicate. Some youths came out of the town as Elijah walked along the road.

c. The *wayyiqtol* clause in verse 23e, in combination with the attached quotation, specifies how the youths jeered at Elisha.

d. The disjunctive clause in verse 25b, by interrupting the sequence of *wayyiqtol* clauses, signals **closure** for the episode. Note also that the next episode begins with a disjunctive clause (3:1).

This incident is a short episode in the larger story that extends from 2 Kings 2–8. As such it has no dramatic structure of its own. (As for its place within the larger **macroplot**, see our comments under no. 6 below.) The episode displays an **inclusio**. At the beginning and end of the account the narrator refers to Elisha's movements; note the use of מִשָּׁם, "from there," in verses 23a and 25ab.

3. Analyze the narrative's quotations and dialogues with respect to their **discourse type** and **speech function**.

The episode contains only one brief quotation—the youths' derisive words directed against the prophet. The tone is **hortatory**, as the youths employ an imperatival form of the verb "go up." Their use of a hortatory style speaks volumes about their attitude toward the prophet. Who were they, mere children, to command the prophet to do anything! The last time unauthorized personnel used a hortatory tone of superiority to command

God's prophet, their insolence proved deadly (2 Kings 1:9–12). The same will prove to be true here (see no. 7 below). The speech function is best understood as **expressive**. Their words express outwardly the inner disdain they felt toward God's prophet and, indirectly, toward God himself.

4. Avoid excesses when filling gaps, but do not be afraid to try to resolve ambiguity in a cautious manner that is sensitive to context and utilizes common sense.

    This terse narrative has some gaps that can be filled by attention to context. The narrator stops short of saying that God sent the bears to maul the youths, but their appearance immediately after Elisha's curse leaves no doubt that they were instruments of divine judgment. The narrator does not reveal why the youths jeered the prophet, but the fact that they were from Bethel provides a clue (see no. 6 below). Finally, the significance of Elisha's movements to Carmel and then Samaria is not explained. But once again, the broader context suggests an explanation (see no. 1 above).

5. Respect the authority of the narrator and attempt to identify his assessment of events and characters. However, also be alert for the rhetorical use of a **limited and/or idealized point of view**.

    This gruesome account of the bears mauling the youths may offend our modern Western sensibilities, but we must not let our antipathy to violence cloud our interpretation of the story. Elisha is clearly presented in a positive manner in the broader literary context. This episode indicates the Lord was on his side in his conflict with idolatrous Israel. Consequently this episode must be read in light of the author's positive portrayal of the prophet, whose actions must be viewed as justified. (For more on this see no. 6 below.)

6. Relate individual stories to their macroplot and explain how the various genres within a book contribute to its overall message.

    The episode in 2 Kings 2:23–25 needs to be evaluated in light of its broader literary context. In 2:1–18 the narrator presents

Elisha as the legitimate successor to Elijah (cf. 1 Kings 19:19–
21). Elisha sees Elijah's dramatic exit (2 Kings 2:10–12) and uses
Elijah's cloak to divide the waters of the Jordan, just as Elijah had
done (vv. 13–14; cf. vv. 7–8). When the prophets are unable to
find Elijah, it is clear that the mantle has been passed to Elisha (vv.
15–18). The two brief episodes in 2:19–25 demonstrate Elisha's
authority and his God-given capacity to bring life and blessing
to those who recognize his authority, or death and judgment to
those who reject him. Chapter 2 serves as a prologue to the following chapters, where Elisha exercises his authority in a variety
of settings and proves to be the Lord's instrument for judgment
and blessing.

   Failure to read this episode in light of its larger literary context and macroplot can lead to faulty theological conclusions.
David Penchansky's interpretation of 2 Kings 2:23–25, which he
develops in a chapter titled "The Mad Prophet and the *Abusive*
God," illustrates our point.[3] In the introduction to his study he
states that he asks his classes to read biblical stories with this question in mind, "If all you knew about God you knew from this
passage, how would you describe the divine being?"[4] He then
explains that he follows this method in his book. From a prag-
matic standpoint, this is a valid question to ask when beginning
the study of a passage, for it reminds one to consider a text in its
own right and not to read into it foreign ideas. However, as one
interprets a passage and constructs a biblical theology, one cannot
interpret texts in isolation, for, as linguists have demonstrated, no
text has meaning apart from a context. To read a text in isolation
is akin to isolating a scene in a movie and trying to evaluate its
characters and message without watching the entire movie. One
can understand certain actions of God only if one views those
actions in light of the text's broader literary context.

   When the episode at Bethel is viewed in isolation, as
Penchansky does, one might conclude that God grossly over-
reacted to a little playful kidding when he sent the bears to maul

---

3. David Penchansky, *What Rough Beast? Images of God in the Hebrew Bible* (Louisville:
   Westminster John Knox, 1999), 81–89.
4. Ibid., 1.

the youths. In this case, Elisha may appear to be "mad" and God "abusive." But one should not view incidents in a moral and literary vacuum. In the macroplot of Kings, this episode is the straw that breaks the camel's back, for Bethel was the center of an idolatrous cult authorized by a royal power that opposed God and killed his prophetic spokesmen. The youths' attitude toward the prophet was a symptom of a disease that infected Israelite society and epitomized the nation's disrespect for God's authority. The attack on the children, while difficult for the Western mind to justify, makes sense when understood within the framework of ancient Israelite concepts of corporate responsibility and guilt, where divine punishment could and did sometimes target a sinner's offspring.[5]

7. Be sensitive to matters of **intertextuality** and how they contribute to the message of the narrative.

When one examines the details of the episode against the backdrop of the broader literary context, significant intertextual elements emerge. The youths' command to Elisha to "go up" may suggest more than meets the eye. On the surface they appear to be telling him to continue on his way (note וַיַּעַל, "and he went up," at the beginning of v. 23), as if they do not wish for him to stop in Bethel. This alone would be a serious enough offense, but their words also echo the narrator's description of Elijah's departure (cf. v. 11, וַיַּעַל, "and he went up"). Is it possible that the youths had heard the rumor of Elijah's ascent to heaven and were sarcastically urging Elisha to do the same?

The episode mirrors an earlier episode in which Elijah was shown disrespect. In 2 Kings 1:9–12 two of the king's officers, using the imperatival mood, order Elijah to come down from the top of a hill. Elijah calls fire down upon them and their troops. Finally a third officer shows the prophet the proper respect. Instead of using an imperatival form and demanding that the prophet obey the king, he employs a jussive and begs for his and his men's lives (vv. 13–14). The Lord spares their lives (v. 15). The

---

5. For a helpful study of this theme see Joel S. Kaminsky, *Corporate Responsibility in the Hebrew Bible*, JSOTSup 196 (Sheffield: Sheffield Academic, 1995).

incident recorded in 2:23–25 is similar to this earlier episode. Here some youths order Elisha to "go up" (an antonym of the verb "go down," used in 1:9, 11), prompting the prophet to call judgment down upon them. Through this parallel the narrator indicates that these youths share the same attitude of disrespect for God's prophet as the king's officials displayed on an earlier occasion and deserve a similarly severe form of judgment.

Within the passage itself the repetition of the phrase מִן צֵא, "go out from, come out of" appears to be significant. It has a hostile connotation in verse 23, which describes the youths coming out of the city and jeering the prophet. Following Elisha's curse two bears come out of the woods and maul the youths. Once again the phrase has a hostile connotation. The repetition draws attention to the fact that the bears' hostile attack is in response to the youths' hostile verbal attack on the prophet.

Summarize the Theme(s) of the Story and How They Contribute to the Theme(s) of the Book as a Whole

The main theme of this story may be stated as follows: The Lord's prophet deserves respect, for he represents the Lord among the covenant community. Disrespect for God's spokesmen is deadly. As noted earlier, the books of Kings tell how the northern kingdom pursued idols. In response the Lord revealed his sovereign authority and established his right to Israel's exclusive worship. The kings of the north tried to silence the Lord's prophets, but the prophets demonstrated their authority over the kings and their God-given power to both bless and destroy.

Consider How the Story Should Have Impacted the Implied Reader(s), Given Their Time, Place, and Circumstances

During the preexilic period this story, along with others in the books of Kings, should have convinced the people that the Lord was the one true God, worthy of their exclusive worship. They also should have realized that his prophets were his chosen instruments and deserved their respect. To reject a true prophet was to reject the God who sent him to preach. The exilic and postexilic communities, reading the story in the context of the Deuteronomistic History, should have been motivated to respond favorably to God's will as revealed through his prophets, who were urging and encouraging the people to become the covenant community God had intended them to be.

What Does the Text Mean to Contemporary Readers in the Community of Faith?

This is the applicational phase in which the interpreter contemporizes the message of the text for a modern audience. As noted in chapter 5, a first step in this process is to derive theological principles from the text. As we do this with 2 Kings 2:23–25, we repeat the four sets of questions we suggested asking as part of this process:

1. How are the themes of the story, surfaced in the interpretive process, nuanced and developed in the Bible as a whole, especially the New Testament?

   The consistent message of the Bible is that the God of Israel revealed in the Old Testament is the one true God who deserves the exclusive worship of all people. He has revealed himself in various ways throughout history. During the Old Testament period he spoke through his prophets, but in more recent times he has revealed himself more fully in the person of Jesus Christ, the living Word (Heb. 1:1–2; John 1:1–14). As in ancient times, God's Word deserves our respect. Those who embrace this Word find favor with God, but those who reject Him are doomed to destruction (John 3:16–21; 14:6). Those of us who have embraced the living Word in faith should live in a manner that is consistent with our profession. Followers of the living Word are God's spokespersons, responsible to proclaim the Word to the world (Rom. 10:1–15). When we are persecuted for our faith and testimony, we may take comfort in the promise that the Lord will eventually vindicate his own, just as he did the prophets of old (2 Thess. 1:5–10).

2. What does God reveal about himself in the story? What does the story suggest about how he relates to people? How does

God's self-revelation in the story compare/contrast with his self-revelation in the Bible as a whole?

God reveals himself in this story as a judge who responds decisively to the legitimate appeal of his persecuted servant Elisha. Granted, the punishment is severe, but, as C. S. Lewis reminds us in his *Chronicles of Narnia,* God is not a tame lion (or perhaps we should say "bear"!). His patience should not be tested. He has the right, as an offended king, to punish rebels when and how he sees fit. The story reminds us that God is not always nice or safe. He vindicates his loyal followers, for ultimately an attack upon them is an attack against him.

3. Does the story offer any insight into how people should respond and relate to God? How should we evaluate the human responses we see in the story in the light of principles we see in the Bible as a whole?

   Those who decide to become enemies of God and who disrespect his revealed Word will eventually die. To oppose God's messenger(s) is to oppose God himself (Matt. 25:40).

   The story depicts the prophet calling a curse down upon his enemies. Is it proper for persecuted Christians to do the same in the present age? The New Testament evidence indicates that Christians are not to respond to persecution in this manner (Matt. 5:44–45; Luke 6:28; Rom. 12:14). This does not mean that those who called curses down on their enemies were wrong in doing so. Nor does it mean that Christians should not look forward to a time of vindication (2 Thess. 1:5–10). However, in this present age, when God is temporarily suspending judgment as he proclaims a message of peace and reconciliation through the cross of Christ (Eph. 2:14–18), he desires his followers and messengers to mirror his patience and mercy toward his enemies. So, while this **episode** from Elisha's career is instructive for us, it does not give us an example of how we should respond to our enemies.

4. How should the story be evaluated in light of the Christological emphasis and themes of the Bible? (See our comments under no. 1 above.)

Having considered the story's theological principles, we are now in a position to propose an applicational idea for our passage. Actually the discussion above has revealed two related themes. If we focus on the demise of the youths, we see the following applicational principle: "Disrespect for God's Word is deadly." If we focus on how God defended his prophet, we see this principle: "God vindicates his persecuted spokespersons." We can combine the two principles into a single statement: "Disrespect for God's Word is deadly, for God vindicates his persecuted spokespersons."

A LIGHT IN THE DARKNESS: SACRIFICIAL LOVE ON DISPLAY (RUTH 1)

What Is the Text? What Does the Text Say?

Because of space limitations we cannot offer a detailed exegetical analysis of Ruth 1. The *BHS* text critical apparatus has nine text critical notes for this chapter. None of these affects significantly the interpretation of the text.[6] Perhaps the most important textual issue is in verse 21, where the Septuagint has "he humbled me," as opposed to the Hebrew "he testified against me." The problem here is one of vocalization. The Hebrew text has the *Qal* form עָנָה, while the Septuagint assumes a homonym, which in the *Piel* stem (עִנָּה) means "to humble."[7]

Of the many lexical and grammatical issues related to the translation of the text, the following questions are of particular importance:

1. What is the meaning of the Hebrew term חֶסֶד, typically defined as "lovingkindness, loyal love" (v. 8)? When collocated with the phrase עָשָׂה עִם, "do with," what is its meaning?
2. How is the comparative idiom functioning in the statement מַר־לִי מְאֹד מִכֶּם, literally, "bitter to me exceedingly from you" (v. 13)? Is Naomi suggesting that her suffering exceeds that of her daughters-in-law, or is she saying that her suffering is too much for them to have to bear?

---

6. For a helpful discussion of the textual problems of Ruth 1, see Ellis R. Brotzman, *Old Testament Textual Criticism: A Practical Introduction* (Grand Rapids: Baker, 1994), 133–42.
7. For a fuller discussion of this problem, see Robert B. Chisholm Jr., *From Exegesis to Exposition: A Practical Guide to Using Biblical Hebrew* (Grand Rapids: Baker, 1998), 36–37.

3. Is אֱלֹהֶיהָ (v. 15) a true numerical plural ("her gods") or simply a plural of degree ("her god"), perhaps referring to Chemosh, the Moabite patron deity?
4. How should the second half of Ruth's oath (v. 17b) be translated: "if anything but death separates me and you," or "if even death separates me and you"?
5. What do the names נׇעֳמִי, "Naomi," and מׇרׇא, "Mara," mean (v. 20)?
6. What is the precise shade of meaning of the verb הֵרַע (v. 21)?

What Did the Text Mean?

Here we look at the passage from a literary angle, considering the various issues we discussed in chapter 4. For the sake of convenience, we repeat that list here as we illustrate the proposed method.

Place the Text in Its Context

According to the book's heading (v. 1), this story took place during the time of the judges. This was a morally dark period in Israel's history, when most people followed their own moral and ethical codes, rather than the Lord's standards as expressed in his law (Judg. 17:6; 21:25). For the literary significance of the book's temporal setting, see our comments in point 1 under "Evaluate the Text from a Literary Point of View" below. Our passage contains the first act of the story. The story is self-contained and not part of a larger literary unit, though the book's heading does invite us to compare and contrast what happens in the story with the incidents recorded in the book of Judges.

Evaluate the Text from a Literary Point of View

1. Analyze the basic elements of the story (setting, characterization, plot) and determine how they contribute to its message.
   The temporal setting of the story (the judges' period) has great literary significance. The heading provides a dark backdrop for the inspiring story that follows. During a time when people were selfish and refused to follow the moral compass God had

provided them, this story tells of a woman (a non-Israelite at that!) who demonstrates genuine love for her mother-in-law and her deceased husband. Her actions stand in sharp contrast to the moral chaos that characterized this period.

Naomi is the central character in the story, which begins with her flight to Moab with her family (1:1–2) and ends with her holding a grandson who embodies God's blessing (4:16–17). Naomi displays a variety of human emotions, ranging from deep bitterness to great joy, and can therefore be labeled a full-fledged character.

Ruth is also a major character in the story. Her driving passion is to help Naomi and then to produce offspring for her deceased husband so that his family line may continue. She may be labeled a type of one who embodies loyalty and places the needs of others above her own well-being.

Several other characters appear in chapter 1. Naomi's husband (Elimelech) and sons (Mahlon and Kilion) are mere **agents**, whose deaths create a crisis for Naomi, leaving her a widowed alien in a foreign land. They do not speak in the story and the only actions attributed to them are moving to Moab, taking wives (in the case of the sons), and dying. Orpah, another agent in the story, fulfills an important literary function as a **foil** for Ruth. Her mere goodness (cf. 1:8) stands in contrast to and highlights Ruth's greatness. The women of the town (v. 20) serve as a sounding board for Naomi. Though they are mere agents, they have a significant role in the story. In chapter 1 they listen to Naomi's lament and accusation against God, but in chapter 4 they correct Naomi's perspective (4:14–15) as they praise God and remind her that she did not return from Moab empty-handed after all (cf. 1:21).

The story has a comic **plot structure** in that Naomi is delivered from her distress and ends up blessed. Tension is introduced into the story almost immediately, first through reference to the famine, which drives Naomi and her family from their homeland, and then through the deaths of the men, which leave Naomi seemingly alone and vulnerable in a foreign land. The lifting of the famine (1:6, 22) provides a glimmer of hope, as does devoted Ruth's dogged determination to stay with Naomi. As Ruth meets Boaz the plot moves toward resolution, though some potential twists emerge before final resolution comes in chapter 4. Chapter 1, the focus of our study, contributes to the plot by introducing and heightening the story's tension, but also by moving the story toward resolution. The chapter ends with Naomi and Ruth arriving in Bethlehem at the beginning of the barley harvest. The Lord has restored fertility and life to his people where there was once famine and death. One cannot help but ask: Will he do the same for widowed Naomi and Ruth?

2. Identify the text's **discourse structure**, **dramatic structure**, and other structural features and explain how they contribute to the story's message and impact.

One may outline the discourse structure of the text as follows.[8]

Verses	Discourse Structure	Type of Clause
1a	In the days when the judges ruled,	introductory
1b	there was a famine in the land,	introductory
1c	and a man from Bethlehem in Judah, together with his wife and two sons, went to live for a while in the country of Moab.	initiatory
2a	**The man's name was Elimelech,**	supplemental
2b	**his wife's name Naomi,**	supplemental
2c	**and the names of his two sons were Mahlon and Kilion.**	supplemental
2d	**They were Ephrathites from Bethlehem, Judah.**	supplemental
2e	They entered Moab	resumptive-sequential

8. *Wayyiqtol* clauses that form the main line of the story are translated in regular font, while offline constructions are in bold. Quotations are italicized and placed in block format. Our proposed classification of each *wayyiqtol* and offline clause appears in the third column after the translation of the clause. Comments on the discourse structure are included after the translation, which is an adaptation of NIV.

2f	and lived there.	sequential
3a	Now Elimelech, Naomi's husband, died,	sequential
3b	and she was left with her two sons.	consequential
4a	They married Moabite women,	sequential
4b	**one named Orpah**	supplemental
4c	**and the other Ruth.**	supplemental
4d	They lived there about ten years,	resumptive-sequential
5a	but then both Mahlon and Kilion also died,	sequential
5b	and Naomi was left without her two sons and her husband.	consequential
6a	Then she, along with her daughters-in-law, arose	initiatory and sequential
6b	and she returned from Moab for she had heard in Moab that the LORD had come to the aid of his people by providing food for them.	sequential
7a	She left the place where she had been living	focusing or sequential, see comment below
7b	**(her two daughters-in-law were with her)**	supplemental
7c	and set out on the road to return to the land of Judah.	resumptive-sequential
8a	Then Naomi said to her two daughters-in-law,	sequential
8b	*"Go back, each of you, to your mother's home.*	
8c	*May the LORD show kindness to you, as you have shown to your dead and to me.*	
9a	*May the LORD grant that each of you will find rest in the home of another husband."*	
9b	Then she kissed them	sequential
9c	and they wept aloud	sequential
10a	and said to her,	sequential
10b	*"We will go back with you to your people."*	

11a	But Naomi said,	sequential
11b	*"Return home, my daughters. Why would you come with me? Am I going to have any more sons, who could become your husbands?*	
12	*Return home, my daughters; I am too old to have another husband. Even if I thought there was still hope for me—even if I had a husband tonight and then gave birth to sons—*	
13	*would you wait until they grew up? Would you remain unmarried for them? No, my daughters. It is more bitter for me than for you, because the LORD's hand has gone out against me!"*	
14a	At this they wept again.	sequential
14b	Then Orpah kissed her mother-in-law good-bye,	sequential
14c	**but Ruth clung to her.**	contrastive
15a	Naomi said,	sequential
15b	*"Look, your sister-in-law is going back to her people and her gods. Go back with her."*	
16a	But Ruth replied,	sequential
16b	*"Don't urge me to leave you or to turn back from you. Where you go I will go, and where you stay I will stay. Your people will be my people and your God my God.*	
17	*Where you die I will die, and there I will be buried. May the LORD deal with me, be it ever so severely, if anything but death separates you and me."*	
18a	When Naomi realized that Ruth was determined to go with her,	sequential
18b	she stopped urging her.	sequential
19a	So the two women went on until they came to Bethlehem.	sequential
19b	When they arrived in Bethlehem,	introductory
19c	the whole town was stirred up because of them,	initiatory
19d	and the women exclaimed,	sequential

19e	*"Can this be Naomi?"*	
20a	She told them,	sequential
20b	*"Don't call me Naomi. Call me Mara, because the Almighty has made me very bitter.*	
21	*I went away full, but the LORD has brought me back empty. Why call me Naomi? The LORD has afflicted me; the Almighty has brought misfortune upon me."*	
22a	So Naomi returned from Moab	summarizing
22b	**accompanied by Ruth the Moabitess, her daughter-in-law,**	supplemental
22c	**arriving in Bethlehem as the barley harvest was beginning.**	concluding

Comments on Discourse Structure

a.   The disjunctive clause in verse 4b is asyndetic (the initial conjunction is omitted).

b.   The *wayyiqtol* clause in verse 6a, while continuing the ongoing story, initiates the action for the **episode** and this initial **scene**.

c.   The *wayyiqtol* clause in verse 6b is difficult to analyze. It could summarize the story that follows (Naomi returned; cf. v. 22). If so, then the *wayyiqtol* clause in verse 7a begins a more focused, detailed account of Naomi's return. Another option is to understand the verbal sequence (she arose . . . and she returned) as a collocation having an ingressive force, "she arose in order to return," or "she set out to return." In this case verse 7a is simply sequential.

d.   Verse 9c reads literally, "and they lifted their voice(s) and wept." There are two *wayyiqtol* clauses here, but the collocation is treated as a single clause in the outline above. (See also v. 14a.)

e.   The disjunctive clause in verse 14c contrasts Ruth's action with Orpah's good-bye kiss.

    f.   The *wayyehi* clause in verse 19b marks the beginning of a new scene, with the *wayyiqtol* in verse 19c initiating the action of this scene.

    g.   The *wayyiqtol* clause in verse 22a has a summarizing function, while the disjunctive clause in verse 22c signals **closure** for the first act of the story.

Chapter 1 is the first act in a four-act drama.[9] Within the chapter, one can detect two major literary units. Verses 1–5 are a prologue that provides background details for the story. References to Naomi's return to her homeland bracket the second literary unit (note the summarizing statements in vv. 6b and 22a), which is an episode with the disjunctive clause in verse 22c formally signaling closure. Within this literary unit, the וַיְהִי clause in verse 19b formally signals a new scene. We may outline this structure as follows:

Prologue (vv. 1–5)
Episode 1 (of the book) (vv. 6–22)
    Scene 1 (vv. 6–19a)
    Scene 2 (vv. 19b–22)

    3. Analyze the narrative's quotations and dialogues with respect to their **discourse type** and **speech function**.

       This chapter contains several quotations. In verses 8–9 Naomi urges her daughters-in-law to return to Moab and pronounces a blessing on them for the kindness they have shown her. This is **hortatory discourse**; the formal blessing is **performative** and **dynamic**. By blessing her daughters, Naomi assures them that they have been loyal and are deserving of a reward. Convinced they have fulfilled their duty, they should be willing to act in accordance with common sense and go home. The daughters' brief but powerful response in verse 10 is **predictive discourse** with an **expressive** and dynamic function. The women express their strong loyalty to Naomi and thereby hope to convince her to permit them to accompany her back to Judah.

---

9. See Frederic W. Bush, *Ruth, Esther,* WBC (Dallas: Word Books, 1996), 56.

Naomi's lengthy response in verses 11–13 is hortatory and expository. Once again she urges them to return, but this time she also mounts a compelling argument for why they should do so. The **language functions** in a **persuasive–dynamic** manner. Her argument has the intended effect on Orpah, but Ruth balks, prompting another exhortation from Naomi (v. 15). Ruth then gives a lengthy speech that is both hortatory and predictive (vv. 16–17). Her oath is performative and has a dynamic function. Earlier in the chapter, Naomi's use of performative language does not dissuade the women (cf. v. 10), but Ruth's self-imprecation has its intended effect on Naomi, who gives up and allows Ruth to accompany her (v. 18).

When Naomi arrives in town, the women ask a brief question (v. 19) that expresses their shock at her arrival on the scene after such a long absence. Naomi's lengthy response (vv. 20–21) is both hortatory (she demands that they call her by a different name) and expository (she gives a convincing case for the name change). Her words are best viewed as expressive in function—she vents her emotions, expressing her disappointment and her feeling that she is an enemy of God.

4. Avoid excesses when filling gaps, but do not be afraid to try to resolve ambiguity in a cautious manner that is sensitive to context and utilizes common sense.

Why did the men die? Some have assumed, based in part on Naomi's statements in verses 13 and 20–21, that the Lord judged Elimelech for leaving the Promised Land and punished Mahlon and Kilion for marrying foreign wives. Naomi regards the Lord as directly responsible for the deaths of her husband and sons. Is she correct? When interpreting narrative literature, one cannot assume that quotations from characters reflect the viewpoint of the narrator. The interpreter must assess quotations in light of the surrounding context and the overall theme(s) of the story or book. When one examines the book of Ruth, one notices the narrator does not attribute the deaths to God, nor does God appear in an antagonistic role. On the contrary, the narrator depicts God as Naomi's ally and as her source of blessing. In this regard it is noteworthy that the famine is not attributed to the Lord (cf. 1:1), but the Lord is identified as the one who brings relief from it (1:6). While Naomi claims that God has singled her out for punishment (1:20–21), objective observers view her as an object of divine blessing (4:14). Consequently it is best to avoid the temptation to fill this gap in the story. We cannot assume that God struck down Elimelech and his sons. The context suggests he did not.[10]

5. Respect the authority of the narrator and attempt to identify his assessment of events and characters. However, also be alert for the rhetorical use of a **limited and/or idealized point of view**.

As noted above (see no. 4), one should respect the silence of the narrator and not assume that he agrees with Naomi's assessment of her situation. The narrator actually seems to counteract Naomi; he does not attribute the famine and deaths to God, but he does picture God as one who blesses people and restores fertility and life.

6. Relate individual stories to their **macroplot** and explain how the various genres within a book contribute to its overall message.

Chapter 1, as the first act in the drama, raises more questions than it answers. By the end of the chapter, one is left asking: Is Naomi correct in casting God in the role of an adversary? Will God restore Naomi's vigor as he did for Judah? The following context answers these questions.

7. Be sensitive to matters of **intertextuality** and how they contribute to the message of the narrative.

Naomi's speech to the women is counterbalanced in chapter 4. Naomi laments that God has attacked her and left her empty-handed. The statement is ironic, given the fact that loyal Ruth is standing right there at her side, committed to Naomi's well-being. The women correct Naomi's perspective in 4:14–15 when

---

10. Furthermore, if Mahlon sinned by marrying Ruth, it is odd that this supposedly off-limits foreign woman ends up being the heroine of the story and a model of covenantal faithfulness.

they observe that God has blessed her with a kinsman-redeemer to protect her in her old age. They also affirm that Ruth, who was ignored in Naomi's earlier statement, is better than seven sons.

Naomi's blessing of Ruth (1:8–9) is realized as the story unfolds, but not as envisioned by Naomi. The Lord does indeed find Ruth a new husband and home, but in Judah, not in Moab. Ironically, Naomi's seemingly logical argument that she could not provide Ruth with another husband proves to be short-sighted, for she has overlooked the possibility of one of her kinsman-redeemers marrying Ruth.

Within chapter 1 there is an interesting interplay between speech acts. Naomi's blessing (vv. 8–9) seemingly releases Ruth from the relationship and assures her of God's blessing, but Ruth's self-imposed curse counterbalances and trumps the blessing. Ironically, Ruth's oath supports Naomi's blessing, however, for it provides proof of her loyal love and worthiness of divine favor.

Summarize the Theme(s) of the Story and How They Contribute to the Theme(s) of the Book as a Whole

The book of Ruth has three related themes:

1. Naomi's experience demonstrates that the Lord cares for needy people. When they are beaten down and victimized by the harsh realities of the fallen world, he is their ally and desires to replace their sorrow with joy.
2. Ruth's example demonstrates that God often providentially helps needy people through committed individuals who display sacrificial love.
3. The Lord rewards those who sacrificially love others, often in ways that exceed their wildest imagination and transcend their lifetime.

Within this thematic framework, chapter 1 makes an important contribution to the story. Naomi attempts to convince Ruth to leave, arguing that her suffering is too much for Ruth to shoulder and that God has made her a target of his judgment. In other words, for Ruth to stay with Naomi would mean nothing but pain and possibly even death. Yet Ruth seals her commitment with an oath, giving us a model of sacrificial love that is willing to take risks and fly in the face of seemingly impeccable logic. When Naomi subsequently laments that she has returned empty-handed, one is reminded that sacrificial love is sometimes unappreciated by its recipients.

Consider How the Story Should Have Impacted the Implied Reader(s), Given Their Time, Place, and Circumstances

The story should have reminded its ancient readers that God expects his people to love their neighbors, even when it might seem inconvenient and dangerous to do so. The book challenges its readers to reach out to the poor and vulnerable and take seriously their responsibilities within their social context. At any point in Israel's history, this message would have been timely and consistent with the essence of God's covenant.

What Does the Text Mean to Contemporary Readers in the Community of Faith?

This is the applicational phase in which the interpreter contemporizes the message of the text for a modern audience. As noted in chapter 5, a first step in this process is to derive theological principles from the text. As we do this with Ruth 1, we repeat the four sets of questions we suggested asking as part of this process:

1. How are the themes of the story, surfaced in the interpretive process, nuanced and developed in the Bible as a whole, especially the New Testament?

    Sacrificial love is at the heart of the New Testament gospel message. Jesus says the whole Law can be summed up in two commands: to love the Lord God and to love one's neighbors (Matt. 22:37–39). As he commands his disciples to love one another, he reminds them that the greatest expression of love is to lay down one's life for one's friends (John 15:12–13). The implication is that genuine love may have its risks and even demand the ultimate sacrifice.

2. What does God reveal about himself in the story? What does the story suggest about how he relates to people? How does God's self-revelation in the story compare/contrast with his self-revelation in the Bible as a whole?

   The only divine action mentioned by the narrator is a gracious one—God comes to the aid of his people and reverses the effects of the famine (1:6). Naomi views God as the one who rewards the worthy (1:8–9), yet she also depicts him as her enemy who has afflicted her by killing her husband and sons (1:13, 20–21). As noted above, the chapter leaves us wondering if she is correct. The remainder of the book resolves that problem as it depicts the Lord as a just king who helps the needy (cf. Ps. 146:7–9) and rewards those who demonstrate loyal love to others (Ps. 18:25).

3. Does the story offer any insight into how people should respond and relate to God? How should we evaluate the human responses we see in the story in the light of principles we see in the Bible as a whole?

   When we experience great personal tragedy and pain, we should not necessarily attribute such events to God, nor should we cast him in the role of an enemy. When we encounter people who feel as if they are targets of divine anger, we should reach out to them in love, allowing ourselves to be God's instruments in lifting them from the depths of despair.

4. How should the story be evaluated in light of the Christological emphasis and themes of the Bible?

   Ruth's sacrificial love foreshadows Christ's sacrificial love, which we are to emulate.

Having considered the story's theological principles, we are now in a position to propose an applicational idea for our passage. One may summarize the applicational principles of the book of Ruth as follows: First, when we experience tragedy and pain, we can take comfort in the fact that God is our ally, not our enemy, and that he cares for needy people. Second, we should sacrificially love the needy, for the Lord will meet their needs through us and richly reward us for our efforts.

Chapter 1 contributes to our understanding of both of these themes. Despite Naomi's accusation against God, he appears in the background as the one who brings relief from famine, not the one who brings the famine. As Ruth tenaciously clings to Naomi, we are also reminded that sacrificial love demands great moral courage and commitment, for it can be risky. We can now combine the two applicational principles of chapter 1 into a single statement: When people are experiencing tragedy and feel rejected by God, we must reach out to them in love, even though such love may seem risky and be unappreciated.

In this chapter we have illustrated a strategy for interpreting the historical books. To summarize, the proposed method has three basic steps that answer fundamental questions about the meaning of the text:

1. *What is the text? What does the text say?* This step involves lexical, syntactical, and text-critical analysis.
2. *What did the text mean?* In this step the interpreter examines the text literarily, isolates the themes of the narrative, and considers how the text would have impacted its **implied readers**.
3. *What does the text mean to contemporary readers in the community of faith?* This final stage of the process seeks to surface theological principles and establish homiletical trajectories that provide the foundation for contemporary application.

This method grounds contemporary application in the text's original meaning, as intended by its divine Author. When modern proclamation is properly grounded in this way, it is undergirded by the authority of Scripture and has the power to transform hearts, minds, and lives. This must be the interpreter's ultimate goal, for it is the primary reason why God has given us the Scriptures:

Every scripture is inspired by God and useful for teaching, for reproof, for correction, and for training in righteousness, that the person dedicated to God may be capable and equipped for every good work. (2 Tim. 3:16–17)

GLOSSARY

agent. A minor, flat character that has a limited role to fulfill in a story and is not normally intended as a model for behavior.

antagonist. One who opposes the central character (or protagonist) of a story.

anthropomorphic. A literary device or idiom in which God is described in human terms.

canonical form. The present or final form of the text as it appears within the canon of Scripture, as opposed to a hypothetical form the text may have had before it was placed in its present location in the canon of Scripture.

chiasmus. A symmetric literary structure in which the second half of a literary unit mirrors the first half; such a structure is labeled chiastic.

closure. The way in which a narrator concludes a literary unit or signals that the unit is concluding.

contextualization. Speaking or acting in a way that reflects the historical and cultural context of the addressee or observer and facilitates understanding and relationship.

cult. A system of formal religious worship and ritual.

diachronic criticism. Critical methods that focus on the origin, sources, and development of the text.

discourse structure. A story's formal structure, consisting of various clause types combined to form paragraphs.

discourse type. A type of speech that has a distinct purpose and formal structure.

dramatic structure. The arrangement of a story's scenes and episodes, sometimes distinguished in the story's discourse structure. See also **discourse structure**.

dynamic. See **persuasive–dynamic**.

echoing. A case in which, by the narrator's design, an episode within the larger story echoes an earlier episode, inviting the reader to note the similarity, make comparisons and/or contrasts, and draw thematic and theological correlations between the episodes.

episode. An incident or a series of incidents that forms a distinct literary subunit in a narrative or story; an episode can include two or more scenes. See also **scenes**.

eschatological. Pertaining to future events, particularly those that culminate an era of history.

evaluative (speech function). When a speaker evaluates and expresses a judgment regarding a person or situation.

external textual evidence. A phrase used by text critics to describe the textual witnesses that support various textual readings. For example, one might discover that the traditional reading of the Hebrew text (reading A) is supported by the Syriac version, while a competing reading in the Septuagint (reading B) is supported by a Qumran manuscript. In this case the external evidence for reading A includes the Hebrew text and Syriac, while the external evidence for reading B includes the Seputagint and the Qumran manuscript.

foil. A character that stands in contrast to another character, thereby highlighting one or more of the latter's characteristics or traits.

form criticism. A method that attempts to identify the literary genre(s) of a text and the situation(s) in life that gave rise to these forms.

haplography. When a repeated letter, sequence of letters, or word is accidentally written only once.

hortatory discourse. When a speaker urges, commands, or exhorts the listener(s) to perform or refrain from an action.

idealized perspective or point of view. When a narrator, for theological and/or rhetorical purposes, departs from historical reality and imposes a perspective on his account of events that promotes a theological ideal.

immanence. When used of God, a term that refers to the fact that God relates to and acts within the parameters of his creation.

implied audience/readers. The reader(s) envisioned by the original author(s) of a text.

inclusio. A literary technique in which certain words or phrases appear at both the beginning and conclusion of a literary unit to mark it out as a distinct structural unit.

informative (speech function). A simple, "just the facts" presentation designed to inform the listener(s)—like the evening weather report.

intertextuality. An instance where there exists a thematic relationship within parts of a text or between two or more texts. In the latter case the interpreter studies how later texts adapt and interpret earlier ones.

keyword. A term or phrase that is repeated in order to develop themes and highlight irony and contrasts.

language function. See **speech function**.

limited point of view. When a narrator steps down from his omniscient, all-knowing perspective and assumes for rhetorical purposes the limited perspective of a character in the narrative or of an observer.

macroplot. The overall movement and theme(s) of a narrative or story when it is viewed as a whole comprised of its many parts. It is a larger plot that encompasses but also transcends the individual literary units; for example, one may speak of the macroplot of the book of Genesis.

macrostructure. The overall structure of a narrative or story when it is viewed as a whole comprised of its many parts. It is a larger structure that encompasses but also transcends the individual literary units.

metaphorical framework. A controlling metaphor (such as judge) that dictates how God reveals himself in speech and action(s). Such metaphors are designed to facilitate understanding and often reflect God's relationship to the addressee or observer.

metonymy. The substitution of one word or phrase for another with which it is closely associated in reality. For example, in the statement "The White House said today," the phrase "White House" is a metonymy for the President of the United States who resides there. Metonymy often involves a cause-effect relationship. For example, in the statement "smoking can kill you," "smoking" is a metonymy of cause for effect (the cancer that it produces).

narrative typology. A case in which, by design of the narrator, an earlier character or event supplies the pattern for a later character or event in the story.

ontological. Pertaining to the being or essence of a person or thing.

pan-Israelite. The literary perspective of Judges that views Israel as a unified nation, rather than as merely individual tribes.

paneled sequence. A literary structural technique where repeated elements appear in successive movements, yielding a structure of ABC // ABC.

performative (speech function). A speech act in which the statement performs a non-linguistic action.

persuasive-dynamic (speech function). A speech act designed to impact and change the listener's perspective and to persuade the listener to act in a particular way.

plot structure. The structure of a story's plot, culminating in the resolution of the complication.

polysemism. When a word has more than one meaning.

predictive discourse. When a speaker describes what he anticipates will happen.

protagonist. The central character in a narrative or story.

providence. The way in which God rules the world and indirectly accomplishes his purposes in human history, often by utilizing the decisions and actions of human beings.

scene. A subunit of an episode; it records an incident that takes place in a different place and/or at a different time than the incidents that precede and follow it. See also **episode**.

soundplay. A creative use of words that sound alike, but are not necessarily derived from the same root word.

source criticism. A method that attempts to identify and distinguish a text's alleged literary sources.

speech (or language) function. A speech's deeper or underlying purpose(s), as opposed to its surface function.

synchronic criticism. Critical methods that focus on the meaning of the text in its present form.

temporal overlay. A literary technique where the narrator juxtaposes episodes or scenes that overlap chronologically, rather than presenting events in strictly chronological succession.

tradition history. A method that attempts to isolate and trace the alleged individual traditions reflected in a text.

transcendence. When used of God, a term that refers to the fact that God exists above his creation and is independent of it.